Collect Call

# Collect Call

E Lloyd Kelly

# Chapter One

## The Turners

He was out early in the morning, as usual, plowing. Mrs. Turner, though, his wife, and the matriarch of "the Turners clan" as they're known, was in the kitchen preparing breakfast. Cooking, cleaning, and banging pots and pans for them, nothing unusual. Lance was in the bathroom taking a shower, preparing to go off to school within the next hour. Reggie was not there; he had long gone off to university. Lidia was probably still asleep; she'd never been the early riser type. Out of the window, Lance could see the tractor, or more like, the tractor's headlights. It was streaking along as it passed back and forth, like always. But then something caught his attention. Once, twice, how many times did he see it before he saw it? The tractor was there, in one position, sort of. It was shaking, the headlights plastered against frozen evergreens partly covered under a patchy dusting of snow. But the tractor was not moving in the normal manner. It was, like, just there, shaking. Lance rubbed the soft side of the clenched fist of his right hand across the icy, cold pane of the glass window. While shading the corner of his eye from the glare of the interior lights with his left hand, he peered out through the dawning. Ma! he shouted, at the top of his lungs, Ma, it's Dad! Something's wrong, something's wrong with him. Moments later, he was out of the shower chamber and wrapped himself in a large bath towel he'd grabbed on the run, heading down the stairs. Out the back door behind his mother, who was already halfway across the yard, "Oh dear, Lord!" and heading towards the danger zone, yes, the place where the tractor was. With the motor still running and the gears still engaged. This was made obvious to him by the effects of the spinning wheel, and the hole being dug into the ground by the said spinning wheel motion. Lance was halfway across the yard when he realized that he wasn't wearing any shoes, to add to the improper mode of attire. To add to the partly naked rest of his body, I mean. He was wearing nothing but the bath towel that he had wrapped around himself on the way out, for modesty rather than for protection from the cold. The cold, though, wasn't wasting any time waiting to remind him what a big mistake that was. He was freezing off his buzz, and fast. But he could not turn back, "Not now," he's got to get to his father and get him help. His dad was in trouble; he knew it, big trouble. He got to the tractor and hence, to his father's side before his mother. For which, he'd made a mental note to thank the lord (or somebody else) later. That's because he didn't want to even think about what might happen if she should get there before him, with the motor still running and the gears still engaged. Lance climbed up, and that was the first thing he had to do: disengage the transmission and shut down the engine. His father was sitting there, slumped over in the driver's seat, seemingly lifeless. "Dad! Dad! Are you okay? Can you hear me?" His mother, by then, had climbed up onto the machine and was helping to bear him up into a sitting position properly, but his body was limp and heavy. She pinched his nose and slapped his cheeks, after which he managed to squeeze out a rather breathy, hmm? like this. "Let's get him inside," she said. Not a bad idea at all, since Lance was by then feeling the full effects of his folly. He was freezing solid and fast; his feet were begging to cramp up. It felt to him as if he was walking on the outer sides of his feet with his toes curved inward and popping while being pierced with a very sharp knife from underneath. Lance reached over and switched off the engine, but the headlights were still on. They managed to get him down off the tractor, foot first. Mrs. Turner held his feet while Lance's arms grabbed the crooks of his armpits as they carried him inside. They laid him flat out on the kitchen floor as Mrs. Turner got on the phone and called for the "Never on time" paramedics. Lance was shaking and shivering, but he was still busy at work; he still wanted to be of help. "Go put some clothes on," said his mother to him, as she reached across and turned the heater on and up to the full blast. Get me some warm towels and a blanket too, while you're at it, she said.

The morning was clearing out. "Soon it will be sunrise." Lidia was up too, and she (seemingly) had no idea that she'd almost awaken to a situation where she would be as of now, as of this day, even, fatherless, after having gone to bed with both parents very much alive and kicking. She had to make herself useful as soon as she was brought up to date on the matter, too. Things were going from bad to worse. First, there was one, now there are two, as seen through Mrs. Turner's eyes, she was seeing them through. Lance was, by then, feeling as if his blood was turning to icicles inside him. Even though he had, by then, gotten himself dressed in some of his warmest clothes. Or more like all of them; all of his warm clothes. From coats, scarves, and sweaters, all the way down to socks and boots, all at once and worn together. His body, though, seemed hell-bent on staying frozen. He was still very much into caring for his father, though. With his shaking, trembling, shivering lips and cracking voice, he was heard telling his mother and sister, who had (by then) joined in on the efforts to resuscitate, revive, and care for "Dad." What they needed to do (as if he were the physician there). "Dad!" While they were there waiting for the arrival of the (never-on-time) ambulance. Based on how he was feeling, or not feeling (as it was due to the numbness in his hands). His feet, too, were increasingly numbing and spreading throughout the rest of his body. He assumed that his father, who had been out there in the cold for much longer than he was, most certainly would have been too cold for his own good, too. But his mother was quick to remind him, "Your father is appropriately dressed for the outdoors as opposed to you, who had run outside practically naked." Lidia (surprisingly) didn't turn out to be half bad in her resourcefulness either. She quickly reached over to turn the stove on, but it was already on, thanks to Mom. She then reset the oven dial to 450 degrees and then popped the door open. That did help to speed up the warmth in the living room. To the relief of Lance and, if no one else, his father, he was sure. Thank goodness.

...

"What's to become of us now, of our entire life? Where did we go wrong?" Mrs. Turner lamented while rubbing her palms together on her lap and looking astray. She wasn't looking at her husband on this day, and the questions, too, were rhetorical. She (of all people) knew the deal; Leo (Daddy Turner) had done all he could. He was a good father to his son. To all his children, as a matter of fact, and barring none. She wasn't sure of herself, wasn't sure of anything anymore. Both of them were starting to question things. He came rather late in their lives; they were flirting with middle age when Lance arrived. She was thirty-nine, he was forty-one. They were married twenty years earlier. Leo had not gone to college as his older brother and sister did; he stayed home and helped his father on the farm. That was probably why his father willed it to him. Reggie would have managed to receive a good education and would have gone on to practice law. Look at him, he's doing quite well as it is. Lidia is studying medicine, but Lance just barely made it out of high school. It wasn't for the lack of potential or effort, though. He just happened to be the one on whose shoulders the bad luck had fallen.

He had to man up quickly after his father had a stroke. Reggie had just started law school, Lidia was on her way through med school, and the family's resources were already very strained. They could have managed all right if things had remained at the current levels, but when the stroke happened, that changed the whole game for the family. Lance was game, though, so he stepped up.

"You are not going to drop out of no school," he told his brother frankly, "we will manage here. I'll see to it if it kills me." He did step up to the plate and batted like a champion. He was closing in on sixteen then, and two years is a very long time in a teenage boy's life. Long enough for many things to change, and "change" they did. Not all for the worse, though. Reggie did manage to secure the scholarship he wanted and other funding for himself. As for Lidia? She got herself a husband a year later—a husband who not only loved her world without end. But one whose pocket was rather deep, and he didn't mind it one bit, in reaching down into those deep pockets to give her whatever she wanted, what she wants now (more than anything else) is a good education. So education, it is. She's getting a rather elite type of education. Lance (on the other hand) was quick to discover that he was not cut out for the farmer-type lifestyle either, or he wasn't quite ready for it, yet. He'd managed to endure it for a period of upwards of two years, but no longer than that. As soon as he was of age (legally), he skipped the scene. Of course, he could have quit at any time he liked; no one could have stopped him from doing so — "Really?" "Yes, 'really'". But his mother had concluded that, "he waited until he was of full legal age to leave because, he believed (and rightly so) that we would have done any and everything to try and prevent him from leaving, and he wanted to be on the right side of the law when that day comes," she'd said. Was she right or what? How ironic, though, oh how things have changed. That was then, but this is now.

2

# Chapter Two

After the stroke of midnight.

Lance stopped off for a while in Ohio, but he didn't tarry there. A farm boy from Jackson, Michigan, this city wasn't much to his liking. "Heck," no city was quite to his liking yet, so he moved on. Not knowing what he was looking for and being a freshman on the scene, he quickly got himself into some rather messy and unpleasant situations. But then, he bumped into Loise, which was (in itself) one of the biggest of the "Messes".

"Hey! Watch where you're going, will you?" shouted Mister Personality. I'm sorry, I'm so sorry. Sorry.

"You're going to be really sorry if you don't watch where you're going and what you're doing around here, dude." His six-pack abs bursting out from under the tight-fitted t-shirt was even scarier than the bone-crushing grip he'd plastered on the back of Lance's neck. Her boyfriend was quick to respond, quicker than Lance could even figure out how deeply in he was. Just like an attack dog (a pit bull, perhaps), he pounced as if he was about to break Lance's neck.

"Man! Is he that insecure, or is this how things are done in these parts?" Lance wondered while rubbing the back of his neck against his palm.

"It's okay, hey, it's okay, man, I'm alright. He's just a frightened kid," Loise blurted out at him. Lance staggered across a trash can, trying to balance himself against the bus stop.

"Hi!" she said, "Loise." While holding out a hand in greeting, I'm sorry about that. He is just in a bad mood today, don't hold it against him. What are you doing loitering around out here anyway? Are you okay? Can't recall seeing you before, are you from around here? A million and one questions came at him at lightning speed.

"Can we go now?" Mr. Sulky-face prompted, "Loise, Loise, can we go?"

"Here," she said, on the spinning back and forth of her gaze between those two who were there and wearing pants and cowboy boots. "If you ever need to talk," she said, "if you need help or anything, don't hesitate to call, okay?"

"Okay, thank you, Ms."

She quickly caught up with him as Lance watched them walk away, side-by-side. She was turning to look back at him periodically before they turned the corner and out of sight. That card she gave him, there, look, it's tucked between Lance's fingers under his gaze now, and reads, "Loise Arquette, counselor, and mentor, Saint Jude's Boys' School."

"Yeah! I'm sure she would like to take a jab at mentoring me," said Lance to nobody, while walking away in the opposite direction, leaving the card in the rubbish bin where he'd tossed it. It was there, though, the hungry eyes, the longing look in how she stared at him. Even while walking away, stride for stride beside Mr. Sulky-face. It was not his kind of place, though; he knew it right away, and nothing about the place had beckoned. By morning, he would have been gone to some other place, somewhere else, searching for something else.

"Whatever 'it' is that I'm going to find out here, it will have to be somewhere else down the road. This long and winding road leads out of this town, so, 'somewhere else,' here I come. Whatever 'it' is, it sure is not here, not for Lancelot Turner." Too close, perhaps, to Jackson, Michigan, and a neck injury, for his comfort.

....

A steady stream of headlights was reflecting off the slightly descending wet road surface, which was due to the effect of some earlier moisture in the air and a slight rain pitter-pattering on the road. It looked very much to him like the rich creamy flowing milk being poured from the carton container and into the bowl half-full of crispy golden-brown cornflakes, by his loving mother. His eyes and mental state had not yet adjusted and acclimatized to functioning in sync with the recent time change to daylight saving time.

Traffic on this side of the highway (the eastern side) was few and far between, as opposed to a bumper-to-bumper traffic jam on the west-bound side. Lance could discern (by way of the images in the rearview mirror) the outline of a pickup truck following him. Its headlights were occupying a permanent spot in the frame of his rearview mirror. Behind that vehicle was another one that he couldn't decide on in any way, shape, or form, other than that; it was sporting one functioning headlight.

At first, he thought it was a motorcycle, due to the single headlight and all. But the yellow hazard lights on either corner of the front area of the vehicle helped him decide the matter; yes, it was a much larger vehicle than a motorcycle. The mist had suddenly changed over to a slight drizzling rain. Lance couldn't shake the image from his mind of the cornflakes in his favorite bowl. With circles of evenly cut ripe bananas placed on top of the flakes by his loving mother, before she poured on the milk.

He reached over and picked up the phone from where it was sitting in the second cup holder on the dashboard. Humming still, the little refrain he had been singing from deep within him. He hit the menu button on the phone and then punched in a series of numbers with his thumb, tap-tap-tap, somewhat like that, to unlock the device. Then, with a few other strikes of the thumb, he dialed up his mother. "Mom," he said, "how are you?"

"Lance, where on earth are you, and what could it possibly be that you're doing that could be so important that you can't find a minute to call home?" His mother chided him.

"That's exactly what I'm doing now, Mom, haven't you noticed?"

"Don't be cute with me, boy."

"How are you doing, my sweet Mamma? Long time no see," said Lance, attempting to pacify the situation by changing the subject at once. "I've been very busy of late, Mom," he continued when she didn't respond further. "But we should be seeing each other soon."

"That's exactly what you said the last time, too, but you didn't show up, did you? Thanksgiving also came and went; you didn't show up either. Will you be here for Christmas? I hardly think so."

"I'll be there, Mom, I will be there for Christmas. I hope." He whispered this ending part rather unconvincingly. "How's dad?" he asked, after the extended pause. "Ma, how's Dad doing?"

"Your father is doing fine, Lance, he's doing just fine."

"Is he there? Can I talk to him?"

"Here," he heard her say as she handed him the phone.

"Lance?" his father grunted on his arrival on the phone-conversational scene. "How, how, how are you, I mean...?"

"I'm fine, Dad, I'm fine, and you?"

"Fine, fine. What have you been up to of late? I hope you've managed to get your life in some semblance of order by now and are thinking about settling down. You can't continue to run around like a rolling stone, you know..."

"Dad, I'm doing okay, don't worry yourself too much about those sorts of things, I've got this all covered, okay? I'm actually on the road now, though, Dad, just called to say 'hi.' I should be seeing you guys very soon. I've got a few things to take care of first, and then I'll be home. I've got to run now, I'll talk to you guys later, alright?"

"Bye, Lance."

"Bye, Dad, bye."

He had to cut short the call way before he wanted to because... It came as a surprise to him; the beep, beep, beeping sounds from the special alarm system installed on the SUV that he was driving. Not that he didn't know that it was there, no. But maybe it had something to do with that exchange between him and his folks (his parents)? Yes. It took him back for a brief moment to a calmer, gentler place, far away from the kind of life he now leads. The harshness of this new existence belied the small-town kid that his parents had raised, who, without prior warning, just up and left mere days after his 18th birthday.

They'd sought him out and found him there where he was, hanging out with a rowdy bunch of malefactors in the city seven hundred miles away. They tried hard at "talking some sense into him," trying to convince him to return home with them, but to no avail. Nothing worked for them in that regard. They would have even gone to the police in a last-ditch effort to try and force his hand, but "he's of age," the lawmen said, "he can do whatever he wants."

The beeper system on the vehicle was what sounded off the alarm. All of Manny's vehicles were equipped with special surveillance systems, the same as this one right here, that I'm now sitting in. Well, not me, but he, yes, him. It is usually disabled until it's needed for special operations, such as the one that Lance had just finished doing a day and a half ago. He'd somehow forgotten or neglected to deactivate the system on his vehicle before leaving on this "part work, part play" road trip. Lance was going on a well-earned vacation, a getaway of sorts, from the grind of the everyday hustle.

However, after learning that Lance would be crossing the border into Canada on this trip. Manny (the man) asked him (as a favor for him) to pick up some special cargo for him on the way back. Very reluctant though he was, at first, upon learning that the content of the package that he was to take back with him was currency, not "merchandise" as he'd thought. And after being further assured by Manny of a very fat payday upon his return, just for doing that, he agreed.

After all, it wasn't like Lance was a stranger to that kind of work. He would have done those sorts of assignments many times before, even with weightier kinds of stuff than currency. So, the only reason for him to be a bit hesitant at first was that this was his well-earned vacation time. His R&R break, yes, and he wasn't in the mood to mix business with pleasures, not this time.

The bonus, though, that he stands to receive on his return home with the bundle of cash for his boss, could add up to be more than enough to cover what he had budgeted for the trip. Even with enough leftovers for him to make good on his promise to his parents to be home for Christmas, and to do so in comfort. It was a win-win situation for everyone on every side, not much to complain about there.

It didn't take very long for him to begin putting two and two together to start figuring out what had caused the alarm system to sound off. Either he was being set up by someone, most likely his boss, Manny (the man). Or, it could have been a case of someone being on the run, someone who had already been marked for death and tagged. In which case (by the way), that would mean that it's a top job for somebody, like Lancelot, just for example.

He pulled over and stopped on the shoulder to study the system charts and see if he could determine from whence the signal had come. As it turned out, it was from somewhere up ahead, close to Montreal, but not quite there, in proper. Before doing anything further, Lance had an important call to make, so he did.

He'd already started to piece together (in his mind) the scheme of things as they might have been that would have caused the current situation. But he needed to report back to base for instructions on what, if anything, he needed to do and to find out what's in it to gain for him, not you. He dialed the usual numbers, hung up the phone, and waited. That's the custom in this neck of the woods. It goes something like this: Never call directly to the big man's regular phone under any circumstances.

Instead, call the special number only used for very important and urgent matters, say your phone number using a special cryptic code, hang up, and wait. One seldom needs to wait very long for the return call, and it never comes from any familiar number, never twice from any one number either. As usual, it didn't take long. The phone vibrated, signaling the incoming call.

"Delivering service in style," Lance answered the phone in his customary way. Just like he usually does for this type of call. "Man-man's pizzeria," he said.

"Have you got mushroom pizza?" asked the voice on the other end.

"Yes, but I'm a long way out of town, and my device is ringing off the hook; the calls are coming in nonstop."

"Where exactly are you? asked 'the voice.'"

"I'm on the north side of town, already over the bridge and trying to get to the addresses of all those hungry callers. Do you know anything about those calls?"

"Hell yes, I know them alright, but we'll talk about it later, go do what you've got to do, those are special orders, don't you think?"

"Ride on," said Lance before he hung up, ending the call.

...

Anastasia has been on the run, running for over a year, trying to get away from... Yes, Manny, he, with all of his world-class networking systems and technical savvy, was not able to locate and bring her back home to Norfolk, VA, to face up to the music and dance. This is all part and parcel, more testimonials to her wit and resourcefulness.

She seemed to have committed a breach of some sort or had run afoul of the big man, one way or another, and had to take off running, for her very life. No one (at least not Lance) had been able to say for sure what the issue might have been that led to these things; the current state of affairs. But for her to pick up and take off (seemingly) disappearing into thin air, without a trace, it meant that this was big, yes, "This is huge."

Most people may be inclined to go staking out the usual hot spots in these situations, you know. Like, those sheik places where the rich and famous usually go to hang out and hide, but this is Anna. She's not like "most people," she's smart.

She'd managed to get out of the dragnet, Manny's time-tested and action-proven dragnet. For her to have gotten out, and remain gone all this time, and if this is her (as Lance assumes it is). It would have taken only a chance encounter, a luck-of-the-draw buck-up of sorts. Of course, this, along with the best there is in modern technology for him to locate her without actually trying or chasing her.

Lance didn't bother to check in at the hotel he'd booked for the week in Montreal that evening. Instead, he spent the night (all night) just driving around, or sitting in the vehicle, loitering in some rather remote and isolated areas on the outskirts of town. While trying his earnest best to see if he could get another hit on his tracking device.

"Some shitty vacation," he cursed under his breath. His planned playtime had suddenly become work time, the type he hadn't signed up for at the start, "Not fair," he lamented, "not fair at all."

Anastasia is a smooth roller. She has been lying low ever since she hit the road running. This was in a bid to escape her once-ever-loving boyfriend Manny. That she had been able to elude her captors for this long seemed to suggest that her strategy had been working very well indeed. Her decision to go north into Canada, instead of going south towards the region of her native origin, must have been what did it.

This did the trick for her, seemingly. She has got enough money at her disposal to last her for years, unless... yes. Unless she should (uncharacteristically) manage to lose that huge bundle of cash she'd grab hold of on her way out. So now, she's got the money, but that is not all she has going for her. She has enough smarts to know how to stay off the radar, how to stay underground until the storm passes over, in theory. She also has the technical know-how to create, manipulate, and operate very high-tech surveillance systems such as those with which all of Manny's automobiles are equipped. One of which she'd grabbed on the way out and still has in her possession. However, she now seems to be running short on one small detail, a tiny little thing called luck. Oh sheet! Look.

# Chapter Three

A buck-up

Apart from the system mounted on the vehicle, Lance had one more card in his arsenal, his "ace of clubs" (so to speak). This is the one thing that sets him apart from all the other hitmen, at least those who would have had the dubious distinction of working for "the man."

He has an extra surveillance device at his command, his own lowly, unassuming wristwatch. The watch is rigged and programmed to interact with the central module of Manny's surveillance system, and he is the only person alive who knows about it. Well, he thinks. It's a rarely used piece of backup tool for him. Lance turned the scanner on by flicking the slide switch to the side of his watch.

He then sat back and watched as the laser-like searchlight swept across the face of the watch-turn-scanning device for any sign of a hit. Nothing happened. He just sat there, drumming on the dashboard of the truck with his fingers, while thinking and thinking yet some more, thinking these thoughts in undercover narcotics hitman language, perhaps. On this evening, though, he was coming up with nothing but blanks to show. "Oh crap!"

The difference between this (wristwatch) scanning device and the other systems installed on the vehicle he was driving was that this device is visual only. It won't be easily detected by the others, not by any of Manny's many surveillance systems, as "an unknown" device. No signal was detected from the latest scan, so Lance turned it off and sat up.

He ran his fingers through his hair and sighed. The weight of his job had been getting to him lately. It was weighing rather heavily on his shoulders. So much so that he would have assigned himself another reason for choosing to go to Montreal for a well-earned break.

Lance had read (or heard) somewhere that Montreal was fast becoming renowned the world over in those days as a World-leader in the field of plastic surgery. The place was even leading the charge in the world of sex change techniques. He, therefore, had planned on researching this further while in Montreal, but his entire plans have now been derailed, as he had come to notice; it's all work now.

...

Lester's Smoked Meat was all it was talked up to be, and much more. Lance would have heard a lot of talk about the joint. He'd heard reports of it from several of his associates and cronies. But he had forgotten all about the place when deciding on Montreal as a destination.

However, upon scrolling through the search results for "Restaurants and eateries" on his iPhone, there it was. The chance he had long waited for to sample the place and its goodies for himself. The joint was jumping, and the food was rather delicious too, more so than he'd ever expected. But the place was quickly getting a bit too crowded for his liking.

So, he took out his wallet, pulled out two payment notes, and tucked them in the leatherback folder alongside the bill. He then went into the washroom to freshen up and hastened to leave. As soon as he fired up the engine on the return to the parking lot, the alarm beeper sounded off. Quickly, very quickly. He reached over and pulled out the scanner, and voila! There it was. The object of his interest was mere minutes away, as records were to show. He backed the vehicle out of the parking lot and headed for the highway eastward towards downtown Montreal. He was quick to notice that the target was moving, which suited him just fine indeed. As long as the motor was running, he knew that it was more than likely that they would stay connected. Thus far, that's what all of the evidence has shown.

As it turned out, it was a long and interesting Montreal Street ride that evening. After a wild ride around those parts of the city, Lance finally caught up with the SUV, and just like he'd thought, it was Anna and the white Escalade. The only thing different than the norm this time, as he could see from his point of view and following behind, was the license plate. Instead of Virginia plates, it was now equipped with a Quebec registration plate.

# Chapter Four

**N**ew scene, new life

Anna was trying her darndest best to settle down into some sort of routine, trying to get back some semblance of normalcy in her life, I mean. But she found herself going back to this cozy little spot she'd found on the reservation on the other side of the river near Chateauguay. She was looking forward to, planning for, and hoping for a day when she could get her life back into some form of normal, civilized existence.

But she was not leaving things all up to mere chances; it was not in her nature to do so. So, she was putting a lot of effort into getting to know all she could about her new surroundings. To meet the people that mattered, and secure better places to go and hang out without giving too much away about who she was and what she was doing in those parts.

Manny had promised her that he would marry her, "as soon as possible," he'd said. In other words, as soon as the divorce "becomes final" between him and his current wife. They had had their fill of each other by then and were in the process of moving on. Melba wanted her fair share of the net worth, but Manny insisted that there was no money to be had: "I'm broke," he'd said.

But everybody knew full well that he was loaded. The only problem was, how were they ever going to prove that? Manny's money wasn't sourced through regular channels, so... She seemed content for a time there with the settings, Anastasia, that is. She was living all out with the man in the Malibu mansion, although most of her working hours were spent at the heart of the business hub in Norfolk, VA, far away from "home."

By all accounts and indications, Manny trusted her judgment. Much more than he could have ever trusted Melba. Like, her knowledge of all things savvy and technical surrounding the everyday operations of the business. Furthermore, Anna was never shy of getting her hands dirty, and I mean, really dirty. It's an open secret that it was Anna who had wasted Floyd and Nate in the early days, on the bay front. She's ruthless like that.

...

She has been driving more and more in rush hour traffic lately. Mostly to get used to the surroundings, which seemed to us to be working quite well for her. She doesn't go out very often at night; she doesn't want to stick out too much. She'd argued that it's easier for her to get lost in the crowd, like, in rush hour traffic. Unlike most people, she doesn't mind the "rush hour" city driving and said she can easily get lost in the crowd. But the reverse of that means that one can easily stick out like a sore thumb on the wide-open road at night. So, she opted for the brightness of daylight.

She had to go back out over the bridge that evening. There was nothing unusual about that, nothing at all. The outcome of that venture was to be drastically different, though. She had been using her friend's car more and more, of late, yes, Lenny's car. She didn't feel like driving it at that time, though; she probably should have. But as they say, hindsight is twenty — 20 vision, and now, it's too late for her to see why they had said it. The police car was parked at the base of the entrance ramp onto the Mercier Bridge. The cop was standing behind the half-open door. Why did she panic? She normally has nerves of steel, but on this day, she felt really insecure.

If she could turn around and get out of there, she would have, but there was no other place to go other than to continue straight ahead. The cop was watching her intensely. Anna flashed a fake smile in his direction as she passed by, streaming along with the crowd. But the cop was unfazed, his stone-cold eyes still watching her. She could see this even via the rearview mirror after passing him by. "I'm going to have to talk with Lenny when I get back," she said in inside talk. Is he into something that I'm not yet aware of? Did the cops spot us hanging together?

How likely is it that she would get pulled over by cops just because she was seen hanging around with the wrong dude, again? She was wondering about these things. He had just happened to be the one person she had even bothered to give the time of day since she drove into this town. Hmm, she grunted. "Did I trade a stray dog for a monkey here?" She was hanging around with him for that reason; he seemed quite the opposite of Manny or any of those who hung around with him. She didn't want to be picked out of the crowd just because of what?

...

Anna would have switched the plates on the vehicle. Her Virginia plates were hidden somewhere near the river, safely tucked away between two rocks. The Quebec plate installed on the Escalade at the time was lifted from an old Chevrolet parked under some pine trees at the back end of a property.

Lenny likes to think that he and Anna are becoming an item, but Anna is not at that place yet to write home. There are some benefits to her hanging out with him, though. She has seen enough grit in him to think that he does have some potential after all. But she has got enough of her own shit to worry about to be worrying about such things, she'd told him, "At least, not just yet." He's sitting on the front doorstep today, chain-smoking and fidgety. Rugby, the dog, is hardly any better than he is in this regard.

He's as cranky as he has ever been. He can't seem to find the sweet spot for his head on top of the fold-up hind legs. No matter which end of his bed the lot would fall upon, he kept whining and rearranging his bed. His doggy bed, that is. Lenny would have taken the risk with the car in a bid to go and find her. But again today, just like it has become the norm of late, Anna took the keys with her, or maybe she'd relocated them somewhere, even though she was driving her car and not Lenny's. Whatever the case, he can't seem to be able to lay his fingers on them.

Come to think of it, the dog hasn't been quite himself for quite some time now. Rugby has been acting up and behaving very weirdly lately. He seems to be overly alert at times, especially at night. Like, times when he would get up and trot around the house, waking people up in the process with his growling and barking, even at a mouse. Which he was not accustomed to doing before. What had changed to bring that about? Coming events casting their shadows, perhaps?

"Despite all the gloom that seemed to be bucking at us," said Lenny to the doggy pup, "we're just going to have to keep soldiering along, together. Yes, you and I." He said this while rubbing the dog's head. Smoothing out the hairy mat and manipulating the dog's eyelids in the process, yes, tearing them thin, long, and backward, like...

"Yes, I'm talking to you, Rugby," Lenny added in response to the dog's queries. This would have happened when Rugby cast a disapproving glance at him. Lenny is a bundle of nerves of late. He tends to get that way whenever he's anxious or scared. She, on the other hand, was as calm as could be, as far as he could see. Like, when she was there last evening, making herself look busy working the phone with just her pinky and ring fingers, when they last were together.

The first and middle fingers were busying themselves servicing the cigarette, you know, holding things together in place. While the thumb, now and then, would flick the tip to coax the stick obediently into its place, and at other times, to rid it of the unwanted ash reluctantly clinging onto the end. But that was then, this is now. Lenny is alone this evening; no one other than Rugby the dog is with him. He's sitting there on the front doorstep, smoking, and waiting for his girl, his new-found girl, Anastasia, to come home, but...

One could almost reach out and grab hold of the bundle of fear in his eyes. In Lenny's mind, it would seem to him like every time the "L" word starts to be brandished around him and his household, something bad would happen. I mean, like, always. As it is, old boy Lenny is now at that time and place in his life where he is smack dab in the middle of planning a wedding and preparing for his marriage to Anna. Although he hasn't yet gotten to the part where he could muster up the courage to ask her hand, it would have appeared as if that's the last thing that Anna would even want to contemplate, not at this point anyway. As of late, Anna has also been taking to the idea that she's not lucky in love at all. As soon as the love bug started buzzing around anywhere near her door, she said, tragedy was never too far behind. So, she's scared stiff at the very thought of it, especially at a time like this, like, while she's on the run.

"Oh, Anna! Where are you, Anna?" Lenny lamented. She had called to say that she was on her way home, over five hours ago. Lenny is falling apart at the seams; he has been pacing the floor nonstop. "Oh, dear God, no, this can't be good," he said, as he shook some more and shivered from deep within. Just like he has always done whenever he's brought back to that sensitive place where the only thing that's left to him is (seemingly) a prayer. So, he bowed his head and prayed.

...

Eighteen-nineteen hours earlier, she was sitting on a barstool at the counter, nursing a drink. She was not looking for trouble, or anything else for that matter. But trouble (it would seem) just seemed to have a way of searching her out and finding her, like, always.

On the barstool in a remote corner of the Natives' district in Quebec, Chateauguay, to be exact. Anna was there, just chilling, with a beer mug in hand. Her back leaned up against the wall at the farthest end of the bar counter; yes, she likes it like that. She likes to be able to see most, if not all, of her surroundings, all of the time.

At the other end, closer to the door, he was sitting... look, look at him. The stranger was there, constantly in her underhanded gaze. There were others there too, some rowdy troublemakers she didn't know. She was making sure to keep a watchful eye on them as well. But this guy, right here, look, he's the one to watch. Lenny was there, too, unbeknownst to them and you, as to their relationships, and what he does for food. Her backup man, her pit bull, Lenny, as it turned out, is getting to be quite an asset to her since her reluctant sojourn in these parts.

He likes her, she knows it, and he's trying hard to get her to take notice of him, hoping she'll become interested in something more with him. Something more than her backup, the go-to guy for hire, but? The stranger was getting bolder. Emboldened by the second and third shots of something strong that he was drinking. He walked over to the counter and stopped in front of Anna. An empty barstool is the only thing between them now. Lenny's eyes narrowed; he was quietly homing in on what was happening. The stranger said something to her, barely audible.

Anna didn't respond, not verbally anyway. She shifted her head to one side while fanning him away with a little twitching movement of the fingers. But he then ventured into doing the exact opposite. He slid his backside onto the barstool in front of her. The glass in his hand slid along the hardwood across the countertop and skittered along to get closer to where she was sitting. The right hand, meanwhile, with skillful flicking fingers, was flicking the ash off the end of her cigarette.

"You know," he said, this time louder than before, loud enough for Lenny to hear from where he was, near the door. "You know, I've been watching you, and I must confess, there is something about you that speaks to me. Can't quite put my finger on what it is, but it's there, and I like it, I think I like you too, I really like you."

"What I would like a lot is that you get out of my space and leave me the hell alone," she said. But some folks, it would seem, in all of their knowledge and the knowing of things. It would seem as if some folks don't know when to quit. So, the guy took it not one, but too many steps further. He planted a soft left hand on top of Anna's knee, and that was when Lenny planted the bottle heavily on top of his head, for me, at the exact moment Anna emptied the drinking glass of its contents, in his face.

"Hey, look out!" Someone shouted from somewhere across the floor, but it was a bit too late for Lenny. A bar stool greeted him on the head as he was turning around to look. Knocking him to the floor and coloring his face red, blood red, his blood, yes. He was going to return the favor, though. The dude was holding the stool up over his head to come down on him with the second blow when Lenny's switchblade met the calf, you know? The fat, meaty piece of beastly flesh at the back of the lower leg and slits it open. The guy came down like a ton of bricks, onto the floor, and the stool came tumbling after... on top of him.

Lenny rolled over and was on his feet really quickly. He knew that that would have been enough to calm that guy down for quite a while, as he went about thinking over what he had done (to the poor child). So, with the knife still in his right hand that was at the same time holding on to the top of his "bloody" bleeding head. He grabbed a strong-arm hold of Anna's left hand, "Let's get the hell out of here," he said, in almost a whisper. And then, they were gone, speeding away.

That night, alone again with her in his tiny apartment, Anna was to play the role of caregiver and nurse, caring for him. She cleaned up the wound, applied dressings, or some sort of concoction she had whipped up for the purpose (I'm guessing), and then bandaged it up. Whatever it was that she did, it has worked, and it's working... still working. "You're a hell of a caregiver," he said to her before asking! Are you a real caregiver, like, like a nurse, by any chance? Of course, no reply was to be forthcoming. She tucked him into bed before lighting those cigars and pulling in on a few puffs. She had not had one in ages, but on this night, "tonight," she said, "I need one. Or two."

Anna spent the night on the sofa, watching, listening, and thinking. She watched over Lenny all night while listening for the arrival of those who might be coming after them, you know. She was listening out for any such chance happenings, and she was there thinking too, thinking about some other things. Like? uh! What the... here they come again, those distant scenes tippy-toeing across my gaze.

## Chapter Five

**W**atch this wild Ride

Lance pulled up square beside the vehicle on the highway, her vehicle, when both their eyes met, the fear in her eyes said all that was to be said. It was as if she had seen a ghost, but as for Lance? To him, the reaction was quite the reverse of that; yes, it was priceless. She floored the pedal and was gone, but Lance went on calmly and coolly on his merry way.

"I've got it all in control now," he thought. He would have found his subject, identified the vehicle she was traveling in, and gotten around town. He took an intelligent guess that she wasn't about to change anything too much. Not the vehicle nor her surroundings, and certainly not the tracking system. There were no benefits, nothing to gain by doing so, he thought, all of which suited him just fine.

From that point on, Lance quickly disabled the system on the vehicle and then turned on the one on the wristwatch. In so doing, he knew he could keep a watchful eye on the subject without her noticing him. Now all he needed to do was think, lie low, bide his time, and wait for the perfect opportunity to pounce. It came just a day later, no surprise at all. Lance had been following the white SUV around town unbeknownst to Anastasia.

"Unbeknownst to her? How would you know that much?" Did you ask? Well, he knew that, because of the gradual changes in behavior on her part, yes, of Anna's. She was getting increasingly emboldened and more comfortable in her driving habits. Lance attributed that to the fact that he had disabled the system on the vehicle and was using just the one that he wears on his wristwatch, which (quite conveniently) she knew nothing about.

It was about 7:30 p.m. when he spotted her, driving along in rush-hour traffic on Auto Route 20 east toward downtown Montreal. He followed behind her, at a safe distance this time. To avoid being seen by her. Being seen wasn't the issue here, though; it was more about when he wanted to be seen. Lance was counting on being seen by her, in fact. But at the right time. He was betting that what she does after she sees him would create the perfect solution for him to get the job done and get about his business, leaving. "Let's get this all wrapped up," he said to himself, "and be gone." Then, there it was.

The traffic had begun to slow down; it would have slowed to a crawl at this point on the highway. Lance picked his timing carefully, very carefully, and then. He pulled up close behind the vehicle she was driving, and just like he'd scripted it in his mind, she spotted him in the rearview mirror and panicked. She began to "inch" her way towards the first exit on the Avenue, and then onto the service road.

The train line passes overhead just a little further ahead from the stoplight that she and all the other vehicles on the service road must negotiate through. Lance continued to the next exit, mere meters away, and used it to get off the crowded highway. He then crossed over to the other side of the highway and looped back around, and into the quiet bedroom town that squatted itself beside the railroad tracks.

Lance knew beforehand exactly how it would go down because he had been stalking her for days. She has been busy too over the past three days or so. Busily scouting out the area, tracking and mapping out the location (apparently), looking for places along the roads and highways that she frequently used, where she could quickly get off the road and hide out.

She found such a spot, right there next to the train line on a quiet street at the back end of the housing project. But just overlooking the highway. Lance found it too, in the very same area. He'd also formulated his getaway plans from there, and more.

...

He found her there that very night, sitting in the SUV, slightly slumped over and leaning sideways in the driver's seat (trying to deceive me). Apparently, in an attempt to make herself less visible. For others, this tactic might have worked, but for Lancelot Turner, it was a joke, like an effort at futility. She was like a magnet to him, and he was like steel.

He walked out from behind the apartment buildings and conspicuously aligned himself with the blind spot of the SUV driver's field of vision. As soon as he got alongside the vehicle's rear end, he reached under his coat for the gun he had been carrying in the waist of his pants, tucked away under his clothes. The gun was well-equipped with a silencer and all, with hands in gloves.

He tapped on the glass in the left rear door to get her attention before firing off three shots: a blip, a blip, and a blip. He then turned around and briskly walked back in the direction from which he had come. Wiping the gun with a dirty brown rag as he went, while detaching the silencer from the gun. He turned his head to the left side and spit, then spit again, and then... Just before turning the corner on the way leading behind the apartment buildings, he bent over and puked.

He spent the rest of the night in his vehicle, parked in an empty parking lot near an industrial estate on the far side of town. After downing a large coffee and two muffins the following morning, Lance hopped into his vehicle and moved out. Before leaving town, though, he had a few more things he needed to do. He picked up the morning paper and scanned the headlines.

He then reached over and tossed the paper onto the back seat of his vehicle. He also scanned the radio dial for the morning news and then felt the burning need to revisit the scenes of the crime (so to speak). He drove right on by that way on his way out. The way that passes right by there, by the scene where it'd all happened the other evening, and sure enough, the car was still there. The scene was cordoned off with police tape, wrapped around the entire block.

Meanwhile, traffic slowed to a crawl as curious motorists bent their necks to look, trying to see what was happening. Lance became one among them, one of those very curious motorists (apparently) just turned his head to stare at a scene of action, not knowing what was happening, as he drove on by leaving the city behind him. He has just one more detour before leaving this town for good. That is: to pick up the package for his boss, Manny "The man," and then...

Chapter Six

# A Fork in the Road

Look at this, there's a fork in the road! Yes, you can see it through the lens of this thing. Somewhere in Norfolk, VA, a drug dealer is trying to finish up a deal. "Hey! What's up, dude? It's been a while," said Waldo, who was (seemingly) surprised to run headlong into Neville, as they both turned the corner from opposite ends. But it wasn't any old chance encounter at all. Waldo was in town on business at the same time, and so was Neville. Neville was making it his business to try to get out of town as fast as he possibly could. Or maybe he was trying to get out of sight and out of Waldo's long-reaching arms before he caught up with him, in the hood. Neville came out on the losing end of the draw again. Like such things always were, one doesn't escape the long reach of Waldo's justice that easily. So now, Neville is begging for all there is to beg for, "for time," he said, I need a bit more time to get the money. I'm going downtown right now as it is, to go pick up some money and, and...

"No, you're not. Some things in this life are time-sensitive, Nevv. And this right here is one such thing; your time, in this matter, has expired, buddy. Long expired, and guess what? So are you." Those were the last words Neville heard before he was blown away by a bullet through his skull. Right there on the corner of the streets, and in front of the scampering night ladies and the other girls who were there showcasing their wares.

"And the tares too, right?"

"Maybe." Message sent. Waldo then turned around and calmly walked back towards the Chrysler 200 parked there on the sidewalk. Climbed in through the already-opened door and drove away, around the block. Two traffic lights down the way, Waldo saw the "after the party partiers" speeding by, going in the opposite direction. But why? With the entrance to the motorway being one more traffic light up ahead, he casually went along on his merry way, out of town, no big deal.

...

Meanwhile, listen, did you hear that? Manny is lamenting the loss of Anna. "I've been good to you, how could you?" he lamented. But that was while he was lying face down on his feather bed, alone, with a pillar over his head and missing her. The only problem was that Anna wasn't responding because she wasn't there. Anastasia was long gone and was majoring in making fools out of all those who were out searching for her, with a long arm, including him.

...

On the way back home. After sneaking through the border at a point where the small trail had ended up in a farmer's field. Lance was to hang out and hide out there under a wooded overgrowth. He intended to wait until it was dark, quiet, and safe enough for him to pull out under as few watching strangers' eyes as possible. Or until he gets the go-ahead from his linkman, his partner in crime. But then, while there, he heard the news on the radio. It was the type of news he dreaded and hoped would never come. But it did, and it would have caused him to spend one more night over there. Staying put right there under the canopy of the cold old evergreen trees, and then yet another five weeks (or thereabouts) on the northern side of the border, and laying low. Hanging out in low-cost motels and night spots until just a couple of days before Christmas night, when... Mom, here I come.

...

Talk about a shitty vacation! This was to be one. Things were getting shittier by the minute for him. So, Lance's left foot landed squarely on a mound of partly frozen cow droppings. It happened when he stepped down from the driver's seat and out into the darkness of the night. The darkness was made much worse by the overgrowth of the canopy of the evergreen trees. The irony was this: he was going out there to put down a heavy load of his own shitty kind of stuff when he'd happened to pick up a foot of the partly frozen type.

After hearing the news of the police operations that had clamped down on Manny's network that night, Lance returned deeper into the farther northern parts of the border, back deep into the Quebec heartlands, intent on waiting it out there. He had to go about changing some things, like the fact that he used to be an outgoing type, always on the go. This time, for the duration of his reluctant sojourn in Quebec, he would have gone on to spent most of that time indoors. Only venturing outside under the cover of darkness, but never so late at night as to risk being one of the few people in those vehicles on the streets at any given time. He knew well the virtues of getting lost in the crowds, too.

His truck, too, had to be altered somewhat to fit. He had to change some things about the truck and its appearance. He went to the scrap yard and paid them the $20 entrance fee they were asking to get on the inside. "Replacement lug-nuts," he'd said, but it was, in fact, the registration plates that he was most interested in getting. Since the lazy-bodied folks at the scrapyard didn't want to do the hands-on task of finding the exact fitting nuts and such other detailed things, it would have seemed, like, for the particular vehicular parts. That's why they would always allow the client to go inside and do their own search for such things, I think. The entrance fee was intended to be a security deposit that could go toward the purchase price later. Or in some cases, one could lose it, I suppose, well. Who knows? So, Lance was to find a plate there, which he would use to replace the one on his vehicle for the duration of the time in Quebec, I hear. His journey back from the border was under the shadows of night. His headlights and all surrounding lights would be off. He needed to steal a plate from another vehicle to replace the USA plate that he had. But he was still not comfortable with that one since it was from a vehicle that was (obviously) still in service, and parked out back in the yard. He also knew that the owner would be quick to take steps to rectify that situation. So, the hunt went on for a more permanent solution. Like, this one.

...

It was the eve of Christmas Eve, the 23rd of December, when Lance set out for home. With more cash in hand than he could ever have dreamed of, he had it all in his possession. By then, his contact person on the northern side of the border would have been among those caught up in the whole melee.

The cops would have knobbed and taken him in, with his life still intact, lucky for him. Not so much for Lance, though. Lance would have learned of the backwoods trail from Manny himself. That was the very trail that should have taken him to where he was supposed to meet with "someone," after picking up the wad of cash for him, yes, for Manny, "the man." That "someone," as it turned out, was the farmer/crony/drug dealer himself. He was tasked with giving him instructions and directions about how and when to get out and be gone. But then came those turns of events. Luckily, Lance had already gotten his hands on the money. Or was he, like, lucky? The cops would have pulled off several sting operations simultaneously in various cities across the USA and Canada that week, or a couple of days. In so doing, they would have managed to break the back of Manny's mighty drug ring. Lance (it would seem) had two things going for him. Two things that seemed to have featured prominently in the final outcome so far, for him. One, he was a lone ranger type, and second, his parents were the praying type. They were praying for him, always. That cat who is now locked up in the government's box somewhere, though. That's one more thing, or more like a person, one more person he will have to be worrying about constantly; he knew it, but they are still praying.

He was to then go on to launder all of that cash in his and his father's name, trading stocks, in the stock market, but not before...

A year has passed since Lance's return home and back to life on the farm. Among other things, of course, he seemed to have a knack for picking stocks; the right, winning types of stocks. He's now being sought after, and constantly so, by many in that small town. Many who have gotten wind of the fact that Lance is now a master at stock picking, "He's a winning stock-picking picker," I heard them say. So, he's becoming somewhat of a reluctant stock adviser nowadays. Just look at him there doing his thing, his way, killing it on the stock market. Or is it him, winning?

On New Year's Eve, a year from now. Lance is to reconnect with the girl from old times. But until then, might as well go on talking about: "The End."

## Poetry

Just a bit of spoken word poetry here for you.

Be My Muse, a Poem for Today

Little mouse, oh, you little mouse. Won't you stop running around? I've got something here that's heavy. And I want so much to write it down

Sometimes I remember it very well. But there are times when I often forget. Won't you run on over to my house, little mouse? Won't you come, be my muse?

You always seemed to remember things well, like where you'd tucked that little morsel of cheese. Or where that tiny hole was, that lets you crawl in and out again. And all with such great ease. Won't you run on over to my house, little mouse, won't you be my muse

That same tiny ledge to which you'd run. Whenever danger raises its ugly head, and helps you to beat a swift escape there in time. So as not to wind up dead. It's still there, a place of refuge to shelter you. And a place you can rest your weary head. Won't you run on over to my house, little mouse, won't you come, be my muse? Aug. 2017

# PART TWO

A Way with Wordplay
These stories, too, are (for the most part) told from a Carib-Jamericanadian perspective, in a richly blended language mix of Jamaican patois, nonsense talk, and sensational spelling, sometimes. Yes, wordplay is the order of the day around here. So.

A way with wordplay.

Who taught you that?

Just between you and me, there are a few nonsensical questions that I wanted to ask, so tell me. Who taught you to do those types of sheets? Who taught you how not to see your own unborn children in each other's eyes, but his? Who taught you to seek the other person's comfortable interest first and foremost, instead of yours?

Like, how to catch up on the sons of someone else's gods, hanging in the skies, and licking up against the waterspouts you never had? (Same as I). So much so that now you worry and cry about not wanting to die and missing the markets, selling off heaven on high, above the office. "Yes?" "Yes, with the apple pie in the sky. Now, tell me, who wants this?"

Celebrating celibacy, whilst waiting on the lords of these thieving rings of misfits to answer me, on your behalf. Who taught you that?

Who taught you not to pray and ask for what you want from the man himself at the plant? Couldn't you have gone in and stood on a stand before the king, and asked for yourself? Instead of settling for the second-hand kind of cried-out prophecy waving in the wind, on the clothesline itself?

Like what you did when you walked into the prayer room and asked them to pray for you and me; whom… For such things as: to fall upon you with the "Likkle pickney" that you've been wanting from me, and it's papa too, no?

"No."

Yes, of course, it's so, I can prove it, too. Weren't you sitting around at the time and whining, while waiting for someone to come with a hefty bag of nuts and a ripe plantain that I'm in, that can come from only him, to you? So that you could get the family fed, with what you wanted. Like milk, butter, and bread. Who taught you sheets like that, Mildred?

That wasn't the legacy I left for you when I was there, teaching and showing you how to do these things. Like, how to live and behave, sweet little thing you. Before the industrialized machines came in and started itching and melting my skin from my lungs within (there was the sinew).

All via the poison-us air I was forced to breathe in. That's when I died and went off to bed with Void, you know, but please. Here we are, you and I, together again in the tar. No, not the sky, as you'd supposed on a cache of lies from the avatar.

Although some altered skin would have happened between your times and mine since… Mine, I'm sure you already know (the signs in) couldn't stand in your walking shoe today, toe to toe with thine, Hingh. But it was at the onset of your sort of environmental things to get, on cash and carry away, that mine would have melted to the latter end of my day.

Dreams, yes, and get washed away with the summer rain down the stream. Streaming the water that you and I were left drinking after. Like, time and time again, my daughter, no? Yes, all that bleeding… remains in the showering rain, was what we were left drinking. Look, the bare bones of one of us still remain, in the dust, and it's home for both to lick up a stack against, I was thinking of…

How to stay amends, get warm, and chat. Yes, we'll soon be chatting about what would have happened to us on the way there and back.

From ashes to dust, of course, while lamenting about how best to share the contents amongst us, then chat some more via the messages we receive, and get sent in the comments. Box, yes, and boxing around yet some more. Reply if you please, then forward it along to those over there, and these. To get them to share it with the rest of the pack of thieves, sitting across from me on either side of your sleeves.

Because if we can do nothing else, we can certainly do that, like share and chat. So let's do that and see if there's any hope of a comeback for folks such as us. Yes, you and me; the whole bunch of us working things out together properly, trying to get us all to agree on how best to overcome them and their "vaguery".

Part. 2. A Call to Action

They were preparing to bury her on the family lot of land. Which wasn't really a lot to talk about, come to think of... Come on.

It was going to be somewhere down there, at the back-end corner of the family plot, I hear — "Where, on the square?"

"Yes, so I was to hear, but, look, my dear." There was nothing to indicate that there was something more on the lot of lands for them to contemplate in a discussion. The very meager piece of foreign land that they were able to secure at the hands of the thieves and the politicking man.

Well, it was really a woman who was in command at the time and acting instead of the manly kind. Those who'd long gone the ways of the blind, boozing on much too much wine, weed, and any other such thing that they were able to lay a strong arm, "Support me please," hold upon, uh, uh, yes, and breed. Thank you for reminding me of these, you're a breeze, of a hybrid."

Their family had lived there for several generations, to be fair. But now, what a strange situation! Look at me, Claire. They're beginning to notice an entire old city lying under the sandy pit, ee, mi pickney. Yes, covered up nicely, and easily good. In the library shut-pan, made of hardwood. Yes, man, it was in the recording book, over there, that they'd found the reason for this one-two punch of a fist from them to my chest, and to pass along as a gift to you, I guess. "Ready for it yet?"

"No." "Okay, dear, let's continue to go somewhere, because…"

At the time, the spotlight was just beginning to shine. It came focusing on the island home of mine, and the little ones, too. Those who were said to be the real descendants, yes, they were the offspring of the Cekko champions, not you.

"Who then, which people?" "Come, take my hand and follow me, let's go take a look at the scenery with the weevil…" You'll agree with me when you see them through this little nugget in my handling screen, ee? Yes, you devil of…

The government had decided to distribute these lots of land to the longtime little brutes of inhabitants who'd been squatting there, for much too long, my dear. Like, about one and a half thousand years, yes. Lucy would have been lucky to be counted amongst such ee. Yes, "mi pickney."

"We must gather all our forefathers' children to the original meeting place in the freed end zone." So said the master of ceremonies to those who came in and sat down. To talk satin and silk, and about who's wearing the prettiest nightgown, whilst drinking Wilks. "Geeze!"

Yes, whiskey if you please, and whispering talks of such things as those, and these. While registering the call for reparations, on the fees. Repatriation is a must, I know, it's coming with biscuits and milk from them to us, let's go. Let's go over and catch up our stomachs on potato chips and ketchup — "Oh?"

"Yes, bro, because…" "So, so, so that's how she'd managed to come into possession of the land?"

"Yes, mi bredda man, the very thing for which their forefathers would have worked off their shirt bottoms. Got busy again, you know, scaring their guts into action to get up and go. That was what got them running along, as was the command from however long. Hastening to go and submit their property claims to the governmental plan."

Otherwise, they would have shirked the work and dirtied it this time too, or three. Under the tiles that they'd borrowed from the man and me — "Because of the ancestors' kind of folks, I suppose?"

"Of course, go... go over there and wipe your nose." They weren't able to see the results of their labor in wealth before dropping off their skins on the last stitches of their clothing itself, and went missing, underground. But now, look around...

Ten thousand years have passed according to the KD's timelines in the recording books of real facts. Since the mighty Cekko people ruled the kingdom of the KDs, this, and that were as seen through the time-measuring instruments, as bottled up with the time clock, in the look-in glass box, hear this. They then passed it off and over to these, a ruthless clan of thieves who are now in command of the keys, and the entire Kingsland world is just about to feel the caring, chilling effects of their peace and passivity in their pockets.

Well, *mi gaawn yah yaadman. Mi a goh a tung goh buy sum yam lump sum fih nyam. But nung*? I'd be better off saying it this way, when saying it to you nowadays; so long, I'm off to go bulk shopping in town, for something to nyam, like, this thing that I'm eating on. Go sit down over there and eat your provisions. "Okay, *I'm gone.*"

## A way with wordplay: Story № 2.

Meanwhile, as a baby daddy wannabe, on one leg of my journey. Spent way too many wasted hours in a traffic jam ee! Yes, they were all around me, across the city, town, and country.

"Construction work" was what they said to me that day. Yes, it's what's going on out there on the motorway, even now. "Wow!"

"Yes."

We're building up the city and remaking it; shiny and new, like—"Like what, oh, little Genie?"

"Yes, because they're so in love with me, and yes, you too, Boo." Then they go off polishing my shoe with what was dropping from above my kid's knee. And you?

The greater truth behind all of this, though, my youth man pickney, is, you and I never got to see it through to the end of the quiz. We're always too busy worrying about the next cup of tea, Leigh, or when our favorite artist will be featured next on TV. Like, while doing a super gig, somewhere over there in Tell a V. Yes, cousin Vivienne, go tell that guy named Vivian; he's making mischief with me, and he needs to stop it.

So, the streets across this town remained in lockdown, with orange cones, heavy-duty machinery, and concrete blocks all around. So you were forced to turn around and go back home and stay in lockdown. Behind the doorstop, and listen to rock and roll. Rocking your nerve, yes, while rolling over the ancestors' graves to yet more craps on which to get them sold, on the sale.

Selling them on all the virtues of getting them saved, you know, like, while reminiscing about the good "ole daze." Those that other folks liked to call days, in those days.

"Well! We'll move these obstacles around and out of the way a tiny bit," they say. "Like, off to one side of the freeway; to free up your pathway for 5 working days a week, okay?" So that you may be able to squeeze your way and go through, or come in again, in June. Bringing your labor like the real wonderful blessings that they are, to us, them, and yes, him also. Not you, though, no, my friends, won't do so.

But to those who are 'our' realest of friends walking bare, (footed) towards the cowards (squared, and crooked). But as soon as you're done doing that. Be sure to go back home and sit down. We don't want to have you driving around out here in any of your beautiful automobiles. Do you hear me, O'Neil?"

"Yes, please. I guess, these…" "Well," certainly, not whilst having any of your many wonderful babies beside you, at the wheel. "Oh, dear."

"Yes, beware." Not even if you were trying to go and see the others with whom you had already made a pledge and signed the deal, no. These concrete blocks and piles of hard-boiled cushions will be piling on your boneless horse at the bottom, for us. While we stand aside and look, woo, some days it's just the smarts among us who're left gazing at you there whining, and cursing out our guts; tough luck, you'd said, but…

The poet has spoken again. Alright? As you can probably tell, I'm all cried out and running scared, as light.

A way with wordplay. Story №3

This next piece may be a bit on the sensitive side because of some of the rather delicate subject matter it addresses. However, I believe this is the right place to be, as a start, if you want to do something tangible about such issues, Mr. Smart. Here's what some critics have to say about this piece when it was first published.

*"The moment we read 'I Feel Like Crying,' we knew we wanted to be a part of sharing E Lloyd Kelly's work. Since language and storytelling is such an integral part of the piece, we felt our traditional video format wouldn't be a great fit for the poem. We wanted to ensure that our representation of Kelly's "richly blended language mix of Jamaican patois, nonsense talk, and sensational spelling" was both moving and authentic. Therefore, we're thrilled to present you with a reading from the author."* Red Noise Collective.

Now, go read it in the magazine, if you like. This story, too, is told from a Carib-Jamericanadian perspective, in a richly blended language mix of Jamaican patois, nonsense talk, and sensational spelling, sometimes. Yes, wordplay is the order of the day around here. Here for you is the piece called, I Feel Like Crying, again. And it goes like this.

These strange sightings were to come popping up against my eyes' skin, on some of our rather perplexing moral mornings. Haughty young men were seen busily dropping like flies, but the widowed women they'd married and called wives. Still, at the time, at the epicenter of the grieving nights, as seen through our eyes. Didn't seem to us to want to bother and worry too much with the wimpy, whiney cries.

Happily, went out and about celebrating their well-lived lives with the other guys. Longtime friends of the one now dead. "They've always been our good friends," yes, that's just what she'd turned to us and said, and I felt like crying.

But eye tears were drying up, and running scarce. Scarcer than these kinds of nuts on the two-tiered city bus of mine, and theirs. Look, look over yonder, and tell me, what strange sightings do you now see? Two young men looking a lot like my brothers to me, pulling guns at one, this, that, and another three. Gunplay, playing out in the public streets. Drive by, shoot, and then just walk past me, as if going towards the get-away vehicle, together. To go past my house again with the same bredda. I mean, brother, whatever.

Or drive, while their children (back a yaad,) have nothing to eat, with, or play, what could I say? "Oh lawd," was what I heard someone say, in my stead, and solicited my kindest regard. Thanks, Ned.

But Mama is the sole authority that they ever get to fall back under and see, on the bed next to me, most of the time. In and around our close proximity. Socializing with the unsocialized, those whom they must now sit comfortably beside. So, they take their cues and commands from the other man. The one who feeds them to the overfill with Philpot's pots of wrong, along with a socialistic program that he and his cronies would have planned and set in motion. Hand off a monthly check, "Check this out," he said, "isn't it enough for you and them to slow upon, mi bred?" Or down.

*Waa gwaan? Mek weh cuss nuh* man. But no, we're too settled in on our comfy zone below freezing point zero. Going nowhere fast, or slow. Makes no difference in our class, you know. He's really our mortal enemy. But we could never understand that one, two, or three steps of the theory. Because our eyes were overly needy, so, we could never seem to be able to see our fortunes slipping away speedily.

Until the rogue man came into the apartment program and came dropping in on our mama again. Then he was gone, just as soon as it was over, and he was done. In the end, here it comes, my grain, yes, like... Packets of popcorn that were mine to chew on, again. Left overnight by the same bredda man, and cold to the touch. My rewards for not talking too much, and oh, how I'd cried, over each crispy crunch that I'd bite.

Before tomorrow morning had even bothered to come, though, he was gone and done.

"No!"

"Yes." Because he cannot stay, the government will cut their pay. No, my dear Faye, not theirs only, but ours; our pay is what I meant to say,

Mr. Flowers. Which will stop the children like us from wasting away or causing them to decay. Either way, it will be the same outcome at the end of the day.

But Mama prayed and went off to church, and gave up her tithes out of our little purse. With heartfelt thanks for the check in her hands, and for the government, now headed by a good man. The one who gave her money, hand to hand, even, and got her blessings, since she must always bless him, and remember to pray for them.

This left her not guessing about him, or who next to vote for, to try and re-elect him. But chiding her children harshly, for the wickedness of dem dutty daddy, and dem faada, too. Because of what he'd caused "har"; all of the agony, agony, agony, and you. That of *dem wutliss ole puppa who naa mine him pickney dem. "Left dem pan mi a loan feh bare all a deh burden."*

*Dem right feh lock up him rasstafar-I red, green and gold cloth inna de wash pan, an chuoe weh de key. Lock up de brute Inna ji-ale, yes, with the guard man who had confiscated the sin ting dem that he should have gotten from me. And send him rasta scarf goh a prison goh geeim, feh wipe im matta yeye dem, good riddance,* and amen.

Sorry for all that mess, my friend, I tend to get carried away by the old customs of my mother tongue, but again I cried, tearing the watery river dried.


A way with wordplay. Story №4. Pt. 1
They're Wearing Us Down. Just another poem of the times, and it goes like this:
Hey, you there? When are you going to stop talking and start doing the walk, King? You know, like, getting things done, instead of just passing along information to him? Yes, that's the manly tug who is always crossing the wiring, so that he may know your plans, and set up roadblocks for you on every hand while hiring. Didn't you know? Yes. Secrets are the chiefest of his weapons business, but you never knew that one, mister man, clueless.

You never knew what was coming along to strike you hard, on the Bam-Bam (what a bam bam) Ha ha, ha, ha, um... No man, no more of those party sing-along songs, or we could be found flirting with the wrong. They're wearing us down. Yes, mi clown.

Well, not until he comes around and whacks you with his magic weapon, yes, man. Hits after chart-topping hits, coming at you, from your number one station, to hit you up against the bott... um, number two, I guess that was you. "Yes?"

No. 'Twas the same weaponed dome that he'd always depended on. But you didn't know that he had it in his right hand since you weren't paying proper attention to the one on the left side of his sham. Just there, blabbering along about what you understand (or not).

Didn't you hear what he was saying about the things he wanted to do in the act? No? Well, I know you a lot, I guess, but? They're wearing us down, yes, mi clown.

You'll never know what's on the other side of the Rainbow, Rock. Not until his plans come tumbling down on you, Mr. Never-knew-a-lot. Well, if you're allowed to survive the slaughtering, act, and get back in time to see me sneaking through the crack in the door, lock.

To see them there, making it through to "The Prosper." Only because you and I were amongst the chosen few who would have managed to slip under his weapon's bore, to survive our man, slaughter. Via the shoot and coupe, of a truth, but... They're wearing us down.

Still standing up, on top of your asker, was the same one who was there waiting for the answer, yes, Mister Monster. Whilst pressing his boots up against your throat, Caller.

But alas, you were about to find out that it wasn't this that caused it. But that. Yes, Designer Genes, my friend, sent in from Mount Haven; for your own misery and torment, oh gosh, mister. They're wearing us down.

But you're not allowed to think about anything at all, Sir. Not when you're the sort who doesn't have a clue, as a starter. Stir, stir, stir it well, man. Before you swallow the snot-ball...her. Meanwhile, I'll go over there and watch football, my star, if I'm allowed. Am I?

Yes, Siree.

Thank you, I agree. They're wearing us down, against these rhyming verses from the far side of town, where the curses are starting in our purses, my grandson.

That's why this poet would have spoken the sound... "Hey! Turn up the sound, please." Thank you for these. And now, the poet has spoken. Over to you to like, share, and comment. We sure would appreciate it if you would subscribe and follow us somewhere, too. Thank you.

## A way with wordplay. Story №4. Pt. 2

The Masqueraders. A poem of the times.

So, you thought it was for your contentment that the concrete and cement were sent. Smooth as the comforter that was meant for your walking shoe, socks, and garment, Mister, but it was not.

You went out to buy a new car, as shiny and sparkling as you were. They packaged and sold it on you for a fast talker. Look, "look how quickly it gets you from 0 to 60 knots, sir." So said the bigger boss you'd wanted to crosstalk. But, whatever you do, don't drive it fast. Or you will be made to pay the real cost, my star.

City officials sit on the bartered chairs they thought were theirs. Yes, my dear. Their very own throne with golden slippers to wear, while looking down their noses at you, my dear.

Dared you to question the things that they put on top of you to bear. In your name, they're doing it too, but what could you do? Nothing.

While the population was growing exponentially into glutenous glory. Politicians' pencils drew the top of your apartment building into the clouded territories.

But puts a large sidewalk "king-brick" to block half your street, with... Orange cones, and a massive flowerpot pit, where the streets used to "beat," around. Sit, sit, sit down, sir, and drink your cup of tea, because...

Those heavy vehicles must negotiate a path through what's left of where the streets used to be, queued. With the added risk of injury, property damage, death, and misery, my youth.

Not just the products you needed to get your table spread, with truckloads of fruits, like food to feed me, and (yes, mi Bred), bottled water and bread, get Hugh to bleed me.

Pickett signs float across your inner-city line. Do the math; it's a regular occurrence to blow off the pitiful this time. "Yeah, man, that's fine," you'd said. Since the joy of your life had already taken to the skies in flight, and fled. With far too few restful hours left to your sleepless nights. Bloodshed.

Multiplied the bleeding forces with brutal and heartless cops. The type that Mama's husband wouldn't be proud to admit he'd gotten got, because. "Ironclad buffer zone they are," he'd said, "between the masses at the bottom, and the bottomless, spineless wick head up top, mi bred."

Tossed a gaping hole across a blind man's path. Then hurled a rock from the upper flat that almost broke his hunched back, apart. Pretending as if it's his own fault, to be blamed. Such a shame, but. Just the regular everyday act in game mode, I thought.

Yet, when we turned around and looked back at them, we didn't like what came back, hitting up against our names. "Meh gaan yaah man," said another Jamaican, "because it seems as if they're about to flush us all down the drain. As if we're only as good as done, around here, my friends."

So, whose side are you on? (Tell me) Whose side will you be on when this is all over and done? Well, if. If tomorrow should even bother to come out again, from under the covers, to salute a new day's sun. Hey, what's that smell? Oh hell! That's it. The underbelly of the beast is rotten to the core already, ish. So, take a look at this and see if you won't agree with me. The Masqueraders are out again, busily walking the beats.

## A Lesson for the Teacher.

Just another poem of the times by WritingElk the poet, and it goes like this.

There was once a teacher in their corner. Anyone and everyone could have reached and tried to storm her. They did.

She taught them well; she taught them how to count on her, to read the signs, and to spell. Taught them how to learn and how to use learning to try and get things done.

Getting the tides turning in their favor, you know, and all such other sum. Adding it all up together, to weigh about one ton.

Then, one day, while waiting for the receipt for their pay, it so happened that many of them started learning, at the same time, even. They mastered the art of learning, living, and doing things. In the arts, crafts, and literature, all while reading.

But in all their learning, there were a few things that they did not learn, Hingh. Like: how to know, how to keep their secrets, in their throats. How to talk slowly, if and when they must.

So, they went out shouting their many blessings on the mountain-tops, and all other platforms that they were given to chat... on. Telling everyone about what they'd just found out.

While cursing out their guts in the public house, with no regard for how the accursed may feel about it. Or what they might do in return, to try and fix the broken bits.

Like, when they were about to fix them up good and proper. Because they knew fully well that their science was stronger than obeah. Mightier is the power in their powerhouse of blazing "gang jah."

They are known for nailing people for their rights and freedom. Will not hesitate to do so again, if they have to blaze some more fyah, pan the we-dumb. Name-call those who sit above them, with little or no regard for the sword, the scepter, or the power of the pen.

Scorned those who were in the same rocking "ole boat," with them, and sewed discord among their fellow men. Curse out their guts because they have never been anything but free men (or women), who have never been brutalized or dehumanized by others who used and abused them.

But one day, while they were waiting for the results of their pay, and for the chieftain's ascension for which the ballots were already sculpted, to hooray. In comes the stranger, against the popularist's sulks, sir.

He was gracious, uncharacteristically so. The winner wasn't who many had supposed; he would be. The winning hand came falling upon a wayward stranger like me. Winner-man started out getting our support, and his opponent's too, slowly so.

But no, the defeated wasn't going to be cheated and lay low like us; the weak head. Not for long. Started preaching his many virtues again, from the top of the "Mount-on-us" program. To the fiercest chagrin of the newly elected and growing well-acclaimed chieftain.

He wasn't accustomed to being sidelined in his own kingdom. So, guess what was next in line and waiting to come? Yes, my good son, somebody had to run. Speaking of the kingdom? There was yet one for them to overcome.

*But nung? Man, goh siddung*, because... This poet has spoken his cause. Over to you to like, share, and comment. We would appreciate it if you would subscribe and follow us somewhere, too. Thank you.

More musings of a wayward wordsmith, in a feeble attempt at poetry.

A way with wordplay. Story №6
I'm Alright, Man, just come and see. A Poem of the Time

See that one galloping along? Yes, man, he's riding away at the Dick Anse. He just loves to court the inside track on the path of low to no resistance. "Yes?" Yes, that is what will take him the distance, but he's a real winner, as you already know the sinner. So long as he can secure the key to his dinner, he'll just up and go walking the path inner, yes.

He doesn't seem to mind it one bit, no siree, doesn't care how much his loincloth is growing thinner, around me. "Don't upset the apple cart with your mouthful of talks," he'd said, over and over again, about things such as that, Mi bred.

*"Mi arright man, mi good with the likkle weh mi got inna mi an, and the bikkle inna the boiling pot ova de sin ting weh mi waan fei nyam. Yuh on da stan?"*

"Yes," I replied, "I understand you perfectly well."

So I lied and slapped my palms on my kneecaps below my thighs. Man, I almost dropped dead. With that, I would not have lied, no. Not with the laughter that I was after.

I mean, I almost lost my body parts to the frost on that disaster. But he's just about to wake up from his sweet little nap... stir, yes, my mobster. Been slumbering away for way too long in dreamlands, "I'm sure."

Very soon, he'll begin to hear the wakeup call, telling him to come over and shake the teacup over the eggs with pepper and salt. So I heard them say.

I then asked her what she was after, as if I already knew that she wanted to know more about the odd score. Yes, happened just before we went off on a binge through the back doors. This was my remark.

"Of a truth," I said, "we'll all be gone and done, in just a matter of time, my son." By then, though, I was sort of hoping that he would have shaken out of his snot cloth and begin to realize that he's already too deeply in, because...

Things aren't as bright and shiny as at first they might have seemed from behind me. I mean. The bitter medicine that we were given, like troubled water from the healing stream where we were bidden, wasn't the cure that we were hoping for. "No?"

No, my star, not at the hand of that man, and his Madam, didn't you know about her? "Yes, man, but..."

That man right there is the same one who (I swear) we thought was kidding along with us when he told us about the chorus, I mean, that his good life of living was to be coming to him off us, and at our expense, first and foremost. Was he not the same one whom the madam had slapped a pawed pause upon? Yes, my brother-man.

Happened when she'd decided to stop giving him the sin ting dem that he was so badly needing, to stay amends. Yes, my good friends. "Oh, come on! That has got to be wrong," you'd said, but. Yes, Cousin Sean, said I, in my response to your bout of scorn.

I, I, I would never lead you along, in the wrong direction. So, from that very evening on, the rest of us started noticing what he was spitting out of his thermos at us, by force, even.

"Oh shuts!" Look at that — slimy squirts of snot from behind the slit in the back of the breathing parts on his thermostat. The same small but rather dangerous spot above his stomach is what I'm talking about, Dermot.

Yes, and coming across his "teething" towards us, where we were living in a straw hut. Hopped in on us, along with those other thieving heathens who ought never even have given us anything to eat in the porridge cup. As they already knew, they must.

I beg your pardon, that's not what we should have cordoned... off, but this. Not even a farthing more than was necessary for them to keep up with the illusion that he's a fair and reasonable man. There, believe him if you want.

But know this fact, my dear Great Aunt, and yes, that one, too. The "Fact" is what I'm here pointing out and talking about, not you. You ought to know that you'll be doing so at your own peril, and the descendants down the thin line from thence too, for real... Yeah, man, a Jamaica yaad mi cum fram, sorry, I meant to say, I'm Jamaican born and bred — okay? Yes, wordplay is the order of the day around here. So over to you to like, share, and comment. We would certainly appreciate it if you would subscribe and follow us somewhere, too. Thank you.

# PART THREE

Shorter stories and poems.

### Poetic Just Ice, Cold.

Another collection of short stories and poems of the times.

When the devil, or that other fellow, is going to fix you, he (or she) will fix you right. She does it well. "Are you a Christian?" They wanted to know. Since I couldn't be a Christian, I became a writer as the next best option. A fiction writer, songwriter, and poet is what I am now at the core. Here are some of my writing arguments wrapped up in parchment, behind the door. You're sure to find something within on which to build another set of arguments, sent. So. Knock yourself out, while I hang around here and continue writing love letters to my beloved lost brothers, and yes, sisters too, if you want. Note: Wordplay is the order of the day here. Each story is told with poetic flair, and snippets of Jamaican Patois are inserted here and there throughout, as may be found fitting. Yeah man, yes, a Jamaica yaad mi cum fram. Oh, sorry, I meant to say, I'm from Jamaica, okay?

### Welcome to Montreal. An ode to the city of my chief joy.

Welcome to Montreal once again, a place where all and varied views can contend. Even though one might get turned around and sometimes get sent to the far side of the farm, to water and tend.

Yes, it's okay to get upset on some days, but be sure to make it to Montreal one more time, again.

This is my Montreal, she's the fairest, finest city of them all. World-renowned for its many festivals. Rubbing shoulders with street protesters and carnivals.

So, what if there are a few traffic delays? Or if a construction worksite causes them to turn you away, because the ramp had just been closed, which leads to the highway. This is Montreal for you; enjoy it anyway.

This is not a problem about which to complain. You just might be pleasantly surprised at what awaits you down the lane; it might just be another reason to ditch the plan, to never set foot here again. But go and add this new find to your bucket list. And make it Montreal, one more time, again.

The plan you had made to tour Centerville was disrupted by backhoes, jackhammers, and a thousand drills. Now you're finding it hard to swallow the bitter pill; it's okay, make a U-turn today. Go, see Saint Joseph's on top of the hill.

But whatever you do, wherever the road leads you from here, my friend. Be sure to make the effort, and make it Montreal one more time, again.

"Ever felt your dad's tough love firsthand? ◈ How did you react?

## Heavy-handed Jamaican Justice.

It's Saturday morning, somewhere between seven-thirty and eight o'clock. Look at that. Two young boys are on their way up the winding dirt track, not too far from home yet, in fact. Levan is quite sure that he can throw a rock from here to land on the housetop down there, their own housetop, better not, though, beware. He's strong, alright, but Dad is much stronger in might, and… "he's the one who's got the rod of correction in his hand, you hear, always." Little brother steers Levan away from the wrong; he's always saddled with Levan's correction: "Let's carry on." Said the younger of the two, to guess who?

Raleigh is 11. Two years younger than Levan. But he carries around the smarts in his right hand, and the one on the left, too, most of the time. So "carry on" is what they're doing, even now.

Twenty-two steps further along the path, yes, they're counting them off while walking the dirt patch. Now, look at this and that. Here comes the "on again, off again" friend of theirs, on the lot, in the person of O'Neil. Yes, the friendship is on again, for real. For now, at least. He quickly catches and matches up steps with the brothers and walks on in strides with them as the forks in the path draw nearer before the bend, and hence, the splitting up of the clans. Of them leaving him by himself to carry on and to go their separate ways again, across the pasture lands. Not a moment too soon for them. Well, for Raleigh mostly so, my friends, but listen on.

"Listen up, Boys!" The words came floating in across their eyes. "Don't you hear your father calling you?" Yeah, that's him. O'Neil's big mouth is now threatening to throw them out, like, to "out" brothers and their whereabouts. Bingo. Lucky O'Neil's wins go again. Father's keen and discerning ears had just swallowed up each of O'Neil's blabbering words, from all the way down there where he was. Father heard and wanted to know where the brothers were going. Since it was surely not in the general direction that they should have been going if they were intent on going where he had sent them.

Father wanted the boys to gather Guinea grass for the tiny herd of cattle he kept in a pen near the backend of the half-acre lot on which they lived and farmed the cows and pigs to our asked... favors and rattle... Levan (a smart-ass wannabee) knew of a better place than him and me, halfway up the road on the route to Jackson, where (when not tending the herd and farm) the brothers attend primary school in that town. The spot of which Big Brother spoke, and swore on a choke, the grass was much greener there. Definitely, more mature, fuller, and better there. Better than those over in the already grazed-out lot where Dad had sent them to gather and cut. So up the road headed those two, even after the intervention of blabbermouth O'Neil, their friend who... had just featured so prominently in the task of outing them and giving their whereabouts away. They didn't turn around and go back as their father had sternly instructed them in the talk. They should have, as events will come to prove later on. The winding, dusty shortcut path they are now walking on will lead them to a point joining up with the road towards Jackson. Look, brothers are landing plumb here at this point of connection and intent on continuing in Jackson's direction.

Kickikicup kickikicup kickikicup. Hear that? That can mean one thing. Mr. Charleston and the horse again. Well, maybe two. Mass Ivan also has a horse that he rides around these parts, but it's hardly likely to be him. He's more likely to be out riding in the evening, carrying the message of the lord to the many eager hearers near and far off around these parts, and feeding. But they're coming, still. Horse and man, up the hill. Of course, it was him. Raleigh was right again. He can pick out the man and his horse coming from a country mile away. The man on his mount quickly catches up with the brothers and slows it down a bit. To allow boys to keep up with man and horse as they exchange greetings in small talk and kick. They matched strides now as boys trotted along with the man on the horse, until...? Somebody is going to get lucky very quickly. It was probably due to his height from up there, where he was sitting in the saddle. The man saw a pretty shiny shilling grinning up at him from among the dust and gravel, lying there on the unpaved country road, look.

"Which one of you wants a shilling?" The man is now asking while pointing down at the prize, waiting anxiously in the dust to be picked up by the willing. What a sweet, soothing surprise, look! Ten fighting right-handed fingers now tussling for the chance to be the lucky ones owning the buck. But I have a feeling that the prize will soon be going towards a split-up. Kickikicup kickikicup kickikicup, man on his mount is speeding away again, leaving boys peering at him through mushrooming clouds of Saturday morning dust and eye-wiping. Boys walked on through the planning conversation, trying hard to decide what goodies each one's pennies will get them at the end-of-school fair, which comes next weekend.

The road continued and led them towards the weed path that branched off into Mr. Lindo's banana plantation. Then, on further through and to a somewhat secluded and (seemingly) neglected patch of the field where the most beautiful Guinea grass grew to a grown man's neck height. But as for boys, they're over their heads deep in the itchy green leafy things. "Yikes!" No, this is not for joys, nor for weeping, yet, but... The well-sharpened machete went to work chopping away at soon-to-be hay and placing grass in two bundles. One for the meek and one for the humble. Look, look, here comes Henry, the head cook and bottle washer around these parts of the property. But boys aren't overly concerned about him today. "We're just here gathering wildly grown Guinea grass as hay, to feed our father's cows and calves." So whispered Raleigh's attempts to say. Calves that were too young to be out in the pasture at last. "Yay!"

"Make sure you cut it low," said Henry on the go. "I don't want you leaving the roots sticking out like sharp stakes there to harm anybody, you hear?"

"Okay, Sir," said the boys, in a chorus of joy. He was gone, Henry on the farm.

Enough grass is now gathered to last a whole week. Boys begin to bundle it all up properly, getting ready to leave for home with it. Each boy heaves the haystack to the standing position like Joseph's holy standing sheaves. Yes, those from back over there in the promised land, dead fields. Beckoning boys to bend down and worship. Boys bend down, yes, towards the warship, but to pry each bundle up. Shoulder first, then up to the head from the neck. Picked up next was the boy's machete and headed for home, long before the time for bedding down should come.

Back on the road again, heading home. Look, the weight of their errors is now weighing them down. If they try to take another step under the heavily bundled burden. Somebody will be pulling their heads, necks, and spinal columns out of the seats of their pants down home by nightfall. Come to think of it, that might turn out to be a better option than what is already there, awaiting the seats of their pants. As well as every other part of their backside, upon their return home, at once. For having disobeyed their father's instructions to them. But first things first, boys have got to lighten this load, while we hang around here and watch you watching the node. Look, they're loosening each bundle now. After removing a portion from each stack (look at that). Boys rebound each bundle with binding strings attached, leaving the portion they had removed from the bundle right there by the side of the road, stranded and humbled, is now the new code. Boys are once again toeing the road home; vroom, vroom, vroom. What's that sound? Look, Mass Peter's pickup truck is coming on down, down, down on them.

"Oh my! A moment sooner and we would have been in luck, real luck that is."

"Well, we're in luck now as it is, no?"

"I know, I know, but...," said the other boy. It's because we're going to get a ride home with the grass. "Had it been here five minutes earlier, we would have been able to get the whole batch home, fast, easier, and sweet enough to last the whole week." Yay, so to speak. Anyway, no need to cry over spilled milk, I'd say. Let's be thankful for the ride home on wheels, instead of footing it all the way there on tired heels.

The boys are back home now with two lovely bundles, which seems good enough to appease Father's wrath somehow for them to be home good. But is it? Boys can always hope for that and this. For the rest of the day and into the night, until tomorrow morning, as a matter of fact, because... If they get through the night without the rod of correction being put to work on their backsides, then all is well, as far as Dad is concerned. He likes to serve it up hot and boiling to burn. Mom, on the other hand, is quite the opposite of that one. Such things with her are quite another story to Nyam and stir. She will store it up until it's most convenient for her, not for them. It never was. Then, she would serve up the accumulated batch of punishment over however long a while to lay it on them all-in-one. Luckily, this one's for Dad, and he only; boys think and hope. Yeah, hopefully, but nope, not really. All went well for the rest of the day and into the night on the prayers they'd prayed. But Sunday morning is coming down fast, be afraid!

"Levan, Levan, we've got company, man."

"Who's it?"

"I *don't* know, why not go see who it is for yourself?"

"You go,"

"Why do I have to do everything for you all the time? Just shut up and go."

Four eyes now peek out through a crack in the window curtain. "Oh, it's Miss Edwards, of course, it's her, from over near Jackson."

"Mrs. Edwards is the proper term here, I'm certain."

"What's she doing here so early? What does she want…?"

"How am I supposed to know, wise guy? Why don't you go ask her, smart ass?"

"You go ask, you're the clever one, no?"

"No. It's none of our business anyway, move over, go, "I'm going back to lie down and… and to sleep."

"And while you're at it, don't forget to pray, you're going to need it." Cuffed.

"Wha'aaht!" the brother reacts to the other brother heel-kicking his back.

Mrs. Edwards is a family friend who lives in Jackson, near the school, children, who's asking? "Me."

"Certainly." She's very kind to boys. Especially, our father's overly willing-handed boys. Most evenings after school, boys can expect to receive some goodies and treats, like food. Other children, as far as boys were able to say of them, weren't so lucky that way, but then. The devil was in such a mix, it would seem, from the first day on and in. When something goes wrong in such a setup situation, it becomes easy to point a finger at the familiar ones. Those who are closest to the happenings and are known by all. "Obviously," something went wrong on Saturday, sometime around the morning way. That's why Mrs. Edwards came to visit early today.

According to her story, as it was told to somebody, and then relayed to the boys cruelly by their daddy.

"Levan and Raleigh came to Jackson on Saturday morning along with one other person." Make a wild guess who that "other person" might have been, and worsen. If you'd said, O'Neil, yes, you'd have been spot-on right, or the left one on the heels, in a dress, "right?"

"Maybe."

"Most assuredly, but yes." When the devil, or that other fellow. When he's going to fix you (or she), she will fix you right. She does it well. Mrs. Edwards' story went on to say that the boys (all three of them) came to her house and home while she was out, broke in, and stole things from there. Now, what a perfect fit. Of course, no such thing had occurred. Not from the boy's perspective and standpoint, you can rest assured. All of their stated events and timelines were able to corroborate their stories when checked out. By then, though, the damage had already been done, no? "Yes." But now, back up to where we'd left off in the story, down home.

How long it was afterward, like, after Mrs. Edwards arrives in the yard, one might never know. But the boy is waking up again in the hard, cold grip of his father's cruel hand—"Oh Lord!" Yes, that's Raleigh, praying. He is the first lamb up for the slaughter, correcting rod in hand, all ready to lay it on. Father now begins to... "Began."

"Where did you go yesterday morning?"

"We went to Mr. Lindo's farm to cut grass."

"Was that where I'd sent you?" He asked.

"No, but... but Levan said that 'no more grass was over there and that he knew of another place where the grass is greener and good,' so, so we went there."

"Where else did you go yesterday?"

"Nowhere. We got the grass and then got a ride home with Mass Peter."

"You didn't go to Jackson!"

"No."

"Who else was with you yesterday?"

"Nobody, it was just Levan and me."

"Weren't you with O'Neil?"

"No... yes, yes, at first. We met up with him up there on the shortcut while we were walking through there, then we split up and parted company. He went towards Allensworth, and we continued towards Jackson, but... but we didn't go that far. We didn't go to Jackson. You can ask Mr. Charleston; he will tell you. We saw him on the road going towards Jackson, and then we ran behind the horse and him until we couldn't keep up with them anymore. He rode away and... and we then went to the banana plantation where we saw Mass Henry. He told us to cut the grass low, so as not to leave sharp stakes there that may injure someone's foot (near the toe). He left us there. We then gather the grass and leave. When we got back out on the road, we realized that it... it. The bundles were too heavy for us, so we stopped and lightened the load by taking out a portion of the grass. As soon as we left there, Mass Peter's pickup truck caught up with us, and we were lamenting over the fact that, if we had not "lightened" the load and left the rest of the grass up there, by the road, we would get it all home that easily, and with time to spare."

Meanwhile, other than for adding his inputs here and there to firm up the story (in style), look... look at him through the lens of this thing. See? Levan is just there making himself as small as he possibly can in the farthest corner of the bed, waiting for his turn at bat, you know, like, at the battering. Yeah, just waiting on them in the left-wing bullpen. As soon as Raleigh's turn is done. Father is surely going to be putting it on him, on the backbone. Even though he's (obviously) slanted toward believing his boys' story, his logic and reasoning are that: had the boys gone where he had sent them, and done what he'd told them to do, he would have chased that woman away from his door so fast that she would have mistaken him for the pit bull, and you. But with all that heat now behind them, the father's righteous bouts of punishment were not done. To seal the deal, boys had forfeited their privilege, he had said, that of going to the fair he had promised them that they could, before bed. That was then, though; this is now, no? "Yes." Boys still have a shilling in their pocket, though, waiting for the split up and sharing, and for another hometown show. Coming on down, slow.

The takeaway here is this: in my father's Jamaican household, same as things are in some other places, so I'm told. You're not there to think, you're there to follow instructions and wink. The little boy was to learn more about this point later on, even as a big grown-up man. Other stories for other days? Perhaps. Yeah, man, *a Jamaica yaad mi cum fram.* Sorry, I meant to say that I'm Jamaican-born and bred, okay?

I give you two guesses to see if you can tell me who or what this poem is about.

**Wanted. A poem of the day**

Alert! Alert! Here is the Amber Alert.

There's a prowler on the loose, and he is to be avoided and approached with extreme caution. Here now is a description of our subject, mi boss-man: He goes by the name: The Poet.

He's known to lurk around in deep, dark corners such as your mind.

He's likely to pounce with sharp, piercing objects such as the tongue.

He was last seen in a Montreal, Quebec, city, area.

But he's known to move around very frequently.

Jackson, oh Jackson! That's the place, they say, where he was born.

But his restless, rambling spirit would not be held down, so he moved on.

Creating havoc along the way with the provocative things he's known to say, but he's now wanted, by special request and popular demand.

He's known to frequent such far-flung places as Georgetown, onward to Ewarton. Linstead and on through to Homestead. Cool shade and retirement, all the way to Time-and-Patience.

He'd shifted the scene over to the islands and spent some time in Grand Cayman. But he could not stay, so he ditched the bay and parted. But he's still wanted.

In recent times, as the records were to show. He has been moving around and is busy on the go. Found and reestablished old ties in Chicago. Trek through Waterloo and on through to Toronto.

But don't you ever get it slanted, because he's still very much wanted. By special request, and very popular demand. Thank you, Mighty man.

## Am I Missing Something? A poem of the times.

Just before COVID-19 was "a thing," this was "the thing," the big thing. Meanwhile, the politicians were there busily arguing: take a look at this, and hiss, because voter perils are lurking lazily under polling fingers, so, here's to you, oh! A little thing called What am I missing? A poem of the times, and it goes like this:

Hey! Why are you all looking at me like that? Am I missing something here? Am I missing something? Anyways!

The convergence of the mighty minds and the elitest of the elite of mankind were arguing it out. This side was there, making a mocking fool out of that side's clout.

One was at a loss as to why the other's boss had gotten it all so very wrong, in class. Arguing yet more about the letter and the law, and about the real meaning, and spirit of the long-drawn draft that they drew, on the draw.

As you already know, the law is the law; no one is above it, nah. Not him, not her. But you also know that I'm really, really rich and can afford to buy her a whipping switch, said that same one at the top of the glitch. "We'll see. We'll see." Yet they argued on about this, and that. About what the framers of those very laws samer, must have thought when they were writing it down, and would have etched it in class.

From hundreds of thousands of years ago, "They're long dead though." But, "what were they thinking when those same laws were being framed and fenced in?" asked some of them over here on this siding.

All the while, though, those of high profile were there defending on one side, or amending on the other, to try and send some other "some-ones" somewhere through the turnstiles, on the border. Especially those "some-ones" who were known to have lied, stolen, and cheated, among many other awful vices that were well known and documented that she did, or was it he, him?"

"Well, same thing." Increasing foul play along the way. From the very first day of stepping in... their first right feet, so it would have seemed. Or even the wrong one to eat, seasoned with beans.

"Or was... wasn't it the head instead? Could've been that you know, no?"

"Yes — Ned, yes, but..." Still lying on the bed was the one who was known to have bragged around somewhere in town. Talking about such deeds long done, or even those that could yet be done in times to come, without anyone stopping his gun. So he spoke openly in the streets.

Never even bothered to think a stink thought to tone it down in parts, even when the thermostat was getting turned up really hot, to get heated, yet the more at that spot. Yes, on the headship of his kindred up top.

The council of councilors was known to have begged him when they said it to her clients, via the hearing aids, yes, as said, they would have begged him to refrain from the speaking game.

Said it to him just before praying them off to bed again. "You're unwell," they said, "and you can't help yourself. So, go on up to sleep on the topmost bunk bed, and don't forget to cover your feet with the spread." This they pleaded and begged, but...

Eloquent was the one who stood on a stand in front of a frenzied, admiring clan. Yes, man. The cheering fans were there, prodding him along, as he lied straight, long ties — sorry, I meant to say, face. Lied straight-faced, to no one's distaste, oh, what a disgrace.

But, "just in case they should stick a microphoned camera in your face tomorrow. Say nothing more than this to her; we did nothing wrong; we did nothing wrong."

Yet they argued on about this, and that. Them and their highly placed able-bodied men up top, "we did the same thing as you and yours would have done. They would have wronged them too, nothing more than that one or two... times the sum. Nothing wrong with that, nor with you, my son. So, tell me, how come?

Why has no one from that clan been called in for any form of reprimand? No accountability was to be found coming at hand, Dan. Not such as you're now calling for, from these our highly-placed men of war. Therefore, this is a hoax, this is a farce, fake news, and the rest of the arts on which to muse.

But, as for us, we are instructing everyone under our immediate command not to be found cooperating with anyone. Not you, nor them, not with the sleuth of your demands (count ten).

Should the cooperators cooperate? Then, we'll have to open up the floodgates and call them out straight. Those from over there on your side of the plate, who (just like us) did nothing wrong on the bus. They, too, did nothing wrong.

Not even that which they would have done when they did it in a like manner as our very own, no. They did nothing wrong when they did those things. Nothing that they would want to hide from anyone, it would have seemed. Same as how we didn't do it over here on our side of the pew stand, near the podium beam.

But come they must, just like us. They must also come and testify about all the right things that they (just like us) did do. Or even the wrong ones that both of us, on either side of the bus stand near the commons, did not do. "Neither them, nor us, true?"

"True."

This one over here, though, has got overwhelming evidence to show. He was heard saying so, and then go... yes. Gone running off to the picture show, saying that he was going to use it all to prove that; what he'd said that that one had abused and did, is true. "She is culpable, like you, and you ought to have her removed."

Although I would really appreciate it if you were to show me some more of those facts and things. "Yes?" "Yes, those fat facts that you've got lots of over there under locks, and hiding." But that one would not. Because, "These facts," he said, "are all that we've got here, *mi bred*, and it's all that we'll ever need to put ourselves in the clear."

These facts are here to prove that we are aware of your hiccups and the pact you'd signed from way back, and of course, we did nothing wrong. We're not like you and your "such man" friends, who (on the other hand) can't ever seem to be able to get anything right, come on, come on.

Not even the other side of your left-handed bills that you write. Nor the articles you would have wronged when you'd set out to right out our wrongs," so went on those educated ones. Well, nothing wrong with that part, yardman, nothing at all. Except for the buttoning up of the bottom lines that were hanging off his hip joint above the bottomless pit point, at the time. That which he was just about to fall into quick... "Ointe!"

"Yeah, man, headlong he went, to the fall in it." So said the top-most third of the Tiers of the wisest of the wise men here. The same also came from among the elites over there. None was able, though, to bridge the gap or shorten the divide that exists and persists up until this, between the two, too many sides.

But this one over here has got the perfect solution clear, the answer is holed up in his sweaty hands bare, which came down to just one, as I was to hear. Which turned out (as it must) to be just this one on the bus.

"Let's leave it up to the voters," so he said to the camera, turning up in his gaze about hers, and hence, was readying the telling team to get him in on the news, then out again to be on the front page of The Post, wrapping up the views. While being seen out there posing in the media spheres in a couple of days, all enclosed in, just over there, "do you hear?"

"Yes, my dear."

Well, of course, "let's leave it up to 'the voters,' to decide there-in." To quote ours. So he said and lied again, in my hearing. And I was like, "What did I just miss? What did I miss? What do we make of that and this? What did I miss?" Again, I would have asked and hissed, because...

In a situation such as this, I couldn't help but hiss at the Abyss and wonder out loud from the backside of my speech. "What did I miss? What did I miss?"

"We've got to trust the voters," they say, "to make the right decision on this one-sided, busted right-left punch of a left-handed play, right?"

"Right."

"And why is that?" Someone was heard asking A-mocked. Mocking the answer that was quick in coming back from the elitest of the educated pack.

"It's because..." came the answer rolling into their asked questions, fast. "Just like a paying customer in business class does and do? The voter in politics, too, is always right, isn't that right?"

"Right."

Well, of course, he's right, he has certainly got the right, as well as the left foot of the shoe ma-hite, and the power too. It's all there in his right hand, wearing the wrong shoe by the shower, that's who, and in the one left of their best of new, on the hour.

The power to make the right call, and the proper decision test after all, yeah! Of all the others with — or even those without a vested interest in it, it is he, the voter, we. It's always the "we" sorts who have got the correct answer, as we must, Hart.

We've got the power to get them and the rest of us out of this hellhole of a thinly divided one-sided messy mess brawl that I did, Paul. The one that those over there, with purely non-politically motivated interests, Claire, clearly, didn't have. Wink-wink, and nod, because... Best of all, from the very onset, even before that call, "fair?"

"Fear, I guess."

"I know," but no, it wasn't so, it wasn't "them" and their companions who had gotten us to digress and divert from serving the people's best interest then, no Bert. Which, as you already know (the little witch) was the only reason the voters had gotten interested in this messy mess business in the first...er, yes, that place right there, Buster.

Anyhow, let's move along now to the best place of the firstest. Because the people (as said before) are the ones who know what's best, for sure. So, "Let's put them to the test once more," said the one decked out in a vest, I'm sure. "The test that we would have gotten ourselves together from the past, and institute on the voter's list fast. Whatever they say is the correct answer right away. That decision shall be binding for the next four years on, and winding."

Yes, winding up to stay, and pointing us toward the next generations' spheres, too. So that, if we should (somehow) manage to last that long, under these same conditions. While the other "Them" get richer and fatter, and mightier is proper, and get to secure for themselves, an elevated place for the future, in his story too, not mine, as in the story, Hugh (mine is cuter).

While "we," the voting people, like he, who's mute and feeble (like me). We get poorer, and weaker, and fewer and meeker, whilst wasting away even yet the more, her. And become so blinded by the glistening lights shining, out of the stencil, trashy wrapping papers bright and binding.

So that they, we, us, and not them, but "Us." Those of us who can't ever seem to be able to see a thing but our own guts, and a few busted up buttons and bolts to screw us and our smoked-out cigarette butt, but... But out the doors, fuss, and foremost.

Well, of course. Perhaps there'll remain a bit of hearing left in the hearing aids for these sorts of "Us souls," to hear the piles of dressed-up nonsense they tell them there, when comes the next election year. So that we may go out again and vote for them. Not me, nor us, but them, and much more of the same: The most outrageous pile of ducklings' lame but... "But, but, but who is to be blamed? Really?"

"Surely, not me nor us, but them, Neily. Those who will be able to do the most "nothing" for most of them. Well, nothing other than to do them in, again."

"Amen."

You probably get the leader that you deserve with her, so I heard it said of them, as it occurred. Would have happened when you went out to play, and swallowed the broth they had served up and tossed... away. Now, look, these are they, those. The boss's boss and Rose. Those you get with the polling fingers from polls, yes, there they are.

From the highly sophisticated down to the lowest bum dressing up the business class, in the house of the gated near the bar on the skid, the showroom windows, and the wasted. Among all the other things that are well-known and documented, they did. "You do know what I mean, kid, don't you?"

"Yes, it's true."

"I know, but no, it wasn't so." We're not talking about those at the center of the scheme of things; we are talking about those two extremes, like, where voters in elections lie somewhere in between. Yeah, I mean, in them is where all our solutions lie, naked and bare but, but — "But, why?"

"What the heck do I care, my guy?" So said that man over there, on high. Beware! Voters, you sure had better beware.

After driving a group out of town for a football game in another town west of the city of Montreal (Rigaud, to be exact) some time ago. I found the temperature there a bit too cold for my liking. I went back to my vehicle and sat, where I could stay warm and wait it out. Looking around from the driver's seat, I became so captivated by the sights and scenery round and about me, in the region that I began shooting some shots with my phone camera. While going through those pictures later on, I couldn't resist the poetry that came jumping out at me and the brother man. Here's the result of that: a breath of fresh air for you and me, in the form of a poem called:

**Beautiful Sunset**.
Sitting here in awe, I'm a-watching. The hot yellow sun, slowly a-setting.
Tumbling down bit by bit, carrying the light of the day with it.
Watching shadows a-growing tall. As the dark grew braver into nightfall.
And geese flying south to yonder rest. To feed their young and cover the nest.
But I just sat here in the same old spot, as I blinked my eyes in awe and watched.
The golden sun's long, spiky rays. Besides the stained-glass windows in a tall "Frame-A."
In front of a church, where the speckled bird perched.

While I still sit there in awe and stare. At the sinking sun behind the trees, there. Where it went down, and out.

And now, the poet has spoken it out. Over to you to like, share, and shout. Comment. We would appreciate it if you would subscribe and follow us somewhere, too. Thank you.

### The Message | Messages Are Coming from Everyone Else, but…

These are some messages as seen through one man's eyes, on the roads traveled in one lifetime.

He could remember it well, as a young boy in grade school, and hating the bell; always ringing them "back to class" as a tool, you know, as you can tell.

While messing around with a bunch of other rowdy boys one day, and shunning the girls who wanted to play. You know them, don't you? Yes, those who always wanted to join in on the boys' games of the day, but then again. "No way."

He'd noticed a conversation going on between the headmistress and her, yes, the head tomboy, as it occurs. That's her there, in a blue uniform dress. Beware! One of the girls vying hardest to participate in boys' games, I guess. The conversation was to continue on the inside of the classroom, too, when classes resumed minutes later than he and you. Because the headmistress wanted to use the little incident as a teaching tool. The young girl had gone in and made a complaint to her about something that she said one of the boys had said to other fools; she was sure of it. Somehow, I couldn't shake the feeling that that boy of whom she spoke was none other than yours truly; sweet and kindly, Sonny old me, going up in smoke. The boy had said something which, in her view, was a forbidden thing that should not be said by anyone, such as him or you, ever. Certainly not by boys their age and the clever ones. Luckily for him and us, and for all concerned, yes, go on and cuss, mi bredda-man. But, first and foremost, listen up and learn, don't bother with the cursing part because, as it is, Kern, he's smart. Miss wasn't too far away from the happening. She was close enough to hear everything the boy had said to him and them, out in the open, in his head to go around and spin.

"On rims?"

"No, not so, but..." Although it might have sounded quite like that thing as was heard, popping into an inquisitive girl's earshot, Ed, and in sync with her version of things, she had said about the nerds. It wasn't what the girl thought she heard. Teachable moments like these weren't going to go unused with Miss, mi bred. So, Miss, as soon as she got the rowdy bunch settled down in class, like this, she went into the act of telling the boys what she'd called a wartime story of sorts. Real or imagined, though? One is not sure, to this Day's Inn glory... oh. Did she make it up just like that, for the desired purposes? Possibly so.

"The battle was raging," she said, in boys' hearing while gazing at the chalkboard from where it was read, for their learning, right there in primary Ed. The captain needed help to forge ahead. He called for a young corporal, then sent him off to go and pass along a message to the marshals (or the base) as was usual. "Tell them," He said, "Tell them to send reinforcement, we're going to advance." However, by the time the message got to the Marshalls at the base, it said something quite different from that, to their taste. "Send three and four-pence," it said, "we're going to a dance." Needless to say, they would have lost that battle at once on the bay. Or sometime later on, that very day. Be sure to first get the message right, and then deliver it the way you got it, the right way. This is the takeaway here, my dear Faye.

My next lesson for you, from somewhere in the messaging world and lessened anew, was to come about not long afterward. Growing up in the '60s, '70s, or '80s in small-town Jamaica, you see, without the use of the telephone for most folks, and me. Messages travel on legs above the knee, mostly on the legs of fast, young runner boys like us, and yes, she, Ms. Angus, sometimes. Via mail too, sometimes, or by way of the telegrams, on the bus, Ted lines. But mostly on air, like this: Cleveland, Errol, Aston, B... you, pickney Bwoy, come yah to mi, mi dear. Or, come here this minute. *Run goh dung a Mass Chopin*, tell him...

This is the norm of getting a child's attention, and getting her (or him) into action, and useful service, according to Dad and Mom. Whenever and wherever, there are so many children in the home that there is never enough for them to "nyam," whenever they sit around the table that they used to eat their meals on. Or so that the parents can't always remember who-is-who, and that was almost every home, every time for you. They'll just say. Pickney, or hey, you Bwoy, cum yah. Or, at other times, come here, as it would be better said in the queen's most beautiful language school over there. Or go there, and boys go off running bare, (footed). Bearing important messages for them and humming, as such a pickney did. Most of which Pickney doesn't even understand most of the time, man, kid. To the boys and us, they were like codes that grown-ups and grown-ups alone could decipher, I'd supposed. But it gets the job done for the grown-ups every time on the nose, that's for sure.

...

My next such lesson was to come about when a dear old family friend died. Imagine it with me for a while. He and his family lived two township districts away from yours, on the other hillside, just a gaze, a shout, and a half-loud earshot away from the blabbermouth of the day, of course. The valley between those two is yet another town or village where one may stay to figure things out for oneself. Always in a position to be able to eavesdrop on other people's conversations, or to volunteer to share some of theirs in either direction. Quite conveniently situated they were, to be able to be a party to it, or to be meddling in everything there and, therefore... "Oh sheet!" Which may or may not be as friendly a thing, only depending on one unsettled matter, one unresolved family quarrel or two, or three maybe. Not proper for my papa, and she, that baby? Too tangled a web for the minds of the young, such as us, like you and me, Ms. Angus, to understand those times. Anyway, let's move along to better days on roots wines (or worse). It so happened that the family friend died that night. As was the norm in those places, times, and fields of corn. As soon as the breath leaves the body, warm and lying, there. (Or when the in-house announcement is made ready for the flying, clear.) Somebody was sent to go fetch somebody else, one who always knows these things and nothing else, and who has got to have and give the last word off their tongue to them and you. To get it into the hearing aid of the family home to view. Whether or not she's a physician... she never was one. The next move from there is to go and announce it abroad, oh Lord. This is where the message gets to traveling on the airtight head chord. The announcer, usually the loudest of the loudmouthers in the village square, or anywhere else in the township over there. She's who gets to go spread the news far and wide, on the wings of the windy tide, to go out and get used. Send abroad now the news.

"*Mark Cole dead, oh*!" That was what we heard floating in on the windy show. Then came the loll, low-tone chatter, and the whispers. The somber moment to pick up again all those dropped jaws of theirs, mister, and to try to digest what was heard, and of course, some reflection too, on how the man had lived with them and you. Before the tick-up buzz, which is to be the follow-through, to most of them, and guess who? Yes, Aunt Sue.

Now, on over to his house went all walking shoes. This may last throughout the night and on through until way after daylight. After the burial, weeks later, even.

As soon as the buzzing was to get started, though. Little Billy Joe was heard chiming in soft and slow, like a late echoing partridge from the windy message of moments old cartridge ago, falling off the original call of his. "*Mass Cole dead, oh*," he said. Echoing what he'd heard or thought that he had heard coming in upon the windy chords to hit a note strumming upon their hearing aids, hard. Grandfather was quick with the rebuking rebuttal, rebutting him on that one, pal; Oh-Lord, no, don't say that you hear me! A sign of respect for the dead buddy, you know, and family. And high regard towards the man who was his dear friend, not me. But then, mere moments later, the grandfather himself couldn't resist the temptation, Sir. So it would have seemed, couldn't suppress the urge, not in your dream. He was heard saying almost in a whisper, but mimicking his grandson's timely mock minister; he who was mimicking the first-come call, yeah, that call, coming in through the wall.

"*Ass hole dead, oh,*" whispered Grandpa in the hall.

In times like these, a laugh can be the greatest of remedies, and that's what that was meant to be. Did lighten up the moment somewhat, more or less like a hot fart coming in, from somewhere sitting nearby a dumb nut with a hot, heavily meat-laden fork with him. The point here is this: the message was out and riding on the wind. By tomorrow at this time, no matter where in the world the family and friends of Mark Cole may happen to be staying, to shine the lights on... him. They would have known the story. The news would have reached home to them already, with all the gory... and you wonder how? Telegram would be how, perhaps, one of the more sophisticated means for doing so at the time, my pops. On top of word of mouth, yes, no lying about, of course. The telegram man, too, the one who was to come bringing it all home to you? He was a "who's who" around those parts, no doubt, but.

...

Then came the day when Sonny boy's dear grandfather, too, decided to take a walk out in those types of shoes, the last traveling shoes, kind of... He was an old man and had lived a full and good lifespan, as measuring instruments of the place and time were to suggest. Yes, that one was the best. About a week earlier, he was admitted to the hospital in Port Maria, somewhere down by the Bay area. About five miles away from their home base, I'd say, that was where they used to stay "back-a-yaad," someone else might be heard saying it that way when they're called to pray. "Oh-Lord!" Saturday morning is Sonny boy's turn to go visit Grandpa at his new hospital home. Walking was the main mode of transportation down, as you already know, that one; run. So, walk on, soldier, or even March, or run, which was the first and quickest to come to the start of the new year, April soon comes... Sonny Boy did them all; he got there (to the grim announcement) that Grandpa was dead. "He died last night sometime after midnight," that same announcer person had said. Now, blowing the bugle from here won't do; that won't cut it this time for you. Not with all those mountains, valleys, and high uphill climbs, and Sonny Boy himself had not developed that kind of calling voice as yet, as mine. Never did, as a matter of fact, to the skid. So, as you'd guessed, the foot runners' role is now in effect. Only, no running this time for him, and you, and me, no need to sweat. A casual walking pace will do when everything you want is coming at you, and later on down the way, too.

Uncle, his son, was working for a bus company, Mac-Caughley's bus company, yes, that one at the time. Plying a route from Kingston through Spanish Town, Linstead, uphill climbs to Guys Hill, passing you by in your state of Woodpark, somewhere near Gayle, through Dressekie. Over more mountains, and down towards the northern sea coastlines, through Oracabessa, Galina, and on through to Port Maria, yuh sei mi? Yeah, the Bay Area is mine, of course. It's about a two-to two-and-a-half-mile journey from the hospital to the market house in Port Maria Bay, where the bus route terminates and stays the whole day. Until the return trip back the other way. The bus terminus is situated there. Sonny Boy is now footing it where? Yeah, there also. To go meet up with an uncle who's already on the go to come to meet up with Sonny boy and me there, and you, slowly, so. Not too far into the journey, Sonny Boy ran headlong into someone's buddy, from the hometown, one who was heading back the way home. Sonny Boy told him what had happened and asked him to deliver the message to the family for him. Not that Sonny Boy had to; what for? He would have told them anyway, Aunt Sue. It's just the way things are, and you? They parted ways. This was as important a mission as a country boy would ever get to partake in, in those days. So, there was a pep in Sonny Boy's steps, stepping to a tune both ways. Got to the terminus before the bus, and him, but not by much, sweating. How surprised Sonny Boy was to become by hearing from his uncle that he'd heard the news already. From Dressekie, as a matter of fact, rock on, baby rock on, steady. Until this very day, although Sonny Boy has grown away, seen and heard a lot of things to say... like, to say the least. He is now an old man himself, too, older than them and you. He's still having trouble a lot understanding that, one or two. How on earth did the message get around so fast, in those times and conditions, to the start? It did, though. Nowadays, everybody has a calling device in the palm, nearer to the ear, or there, than the arm. Yes, and everywhere else to stare, look in the ham, I mean, um... But ask them for the important information you want. Few can find it, a place to plant. They're talking, though, and calling around, messaging everyone about everything. Or nothing at all, as such things are known. I mean, I've got one too, but I'm very slow in calling for you. For a darn good reason, and it's true. You already know that everybody else is calling, already, or will be, soon. So why bother? You're only likely to get in others' way and clog up systems anyway, my brother. Do yourself and us all a favor, give the darned thing a break, to savor, it isn't that important, mate. Well, what — ev — ver. Yes, man. Wordplay is the order of the day around here.

*Go take a look at the tree and see if you can handle me. Anyway, that's it for today.* Thank you.

Now, what can one say about this that has not already been said? Mom, this one's for you.
My Mother's Day Wish.
Happy Mother's Day to mothers everywhere.
It was September, do you remember, mother, oh mother dear? If you don't remember it, Mother, well, that's the reason why I'm here

You gave birth to a son, a goodly son. "You're all grown up now," they said, "you are a woman." But you were not quite yet done

As the years and months came and went. So they came as if sent. Many sons and daughters, too. They were more than just a few

Dad was there, a willing hand. A helpmate, a friend, and your husband. He's gone on now, too soon, we say. We should have told him, but he went away

Oh no, not again, we won't let you go before we tell you. Even though we know that you know this truth, we love you. Mother dear. We love you so

Happy Mother's Day, oh mother dear. And that would be every day of every year. To prove that fact, you'd mark a dot in several places on the almanac

As if to remind someone that it's not just one day that is to be celebrated as Mother's Day. Because it's Mother's Day, every single day of every year. Happy Mother's Day to mothers everywhere.

## Man in the Media (Part 1)

"You are not here to think, or to speak the truth," he'd said. "Just go over there and walk those boots, mi bred." So, because I think that this is really good, and I always want to share good things with my folks, as I should. Because I know that some of us don't read very much (well, so it was said in my hearing and such). That's why I had to read it for them, and you, in a somewhat familiar voice, vernacular terms, and tongue, too, which is the reading voice of a people. The very few of us who liked anything to do with reading, in the vehicle. They are my people, though, and yes, yours too, but who are you? Wait, don't shoot just yet, not before you hear this.

I'm talking about the man in the media; he's getting you to change your ways. Waste you, and your fore-parents' goodness; things that have served you since ancient days. To show that you're mine, though. Go walk the lines, in-toe.

He puts out his messages before your gaze, anchoring it there in the palm of your hand. Settled it in to thrive, and to rest comfortably upon your thighs.

He tells you beautiful lies like no one else can. Lies such as these, and just like he knew you wanted to hear 'em. "Oh, please"! Look, look at them there, those big eyes, "so very clear, no?"

"Yes, and you, what did you do?"

You swallowed them off his charm, as he tells you, yet the more beautiful nonsense, as is the norm.

Like, what he wants you to do, to become, or to be. Guess what, you became like me? Come on over now, take a look, see? Well, look at this and that.

He's got his carefully set out plans; you've got none. One of you is lazily dragging the walking feet along, like a numbed... While singing the beloved old swan song. Now, make a wild guess and tell me, which one?

But whichever of the two the lot should come falling upon. Answer the other nonsensical question. How long will those draggy feet be able to stand, oh, you perception-less woe-management plans? Just asking a rhetorical question. To show that you're mine, though. Go, walk those lines, in-toe.

Somebody is wrong, but it isn't you or me. No, Mister Man, not at all, Booboo; bumblebee. But as for him.

"You mean, Paul Mingh?"

"Yes, he ain't nothing at all, either. "Or is it because of the way they want to kill her?"

"Yes, killing them (dead), laughing to please her with those things that are shining and glistening. Yes, the "cool and deadly kinds of 'something' things."

"'Debt,' they are called sometimes. Like, whenever they're called into the mines." That same thing that is there, reeling you in, some of the time, or something.

Still calling, though, and some are tripping over themselves to go answering that same debt call thing, Bro.

What's your name again, Paul Mingh? "No." I know, although everybody is bawling. Bawling for love, and all other manicured fingers, wrapped up in gloves. Anyway, now, my little turtle dove; come, look at my love. See what they have gone and done to you, and yes, me too?

Got us to believe that the prize to win is a girly thing. Smooth nonsense talks and wedding the rings. Nothing else is worth our efforts working with him, until you're forced to face the divorce litigation. Then forced further upon other such things in the worst directions, courting the court system. Hauling off all those things from the hind side of the curtain.

Departing and abandoning everything you've ever known, often, and which you once owned for certain, and have called in.

You would have called them all your belongings and blessings. Well, I'm just guessing this one, Mingh.

But the madam is standing upon the podium spheres and rocking the "Hail" out of those speaker systems there, again. Trying to get you to think that there's nothing wrong with them. Not at all, Mister Manly, friend.

Surely, nothing for you to plan, nor to plan for. Just like she'd already done to her. Yes, her very own beautiful daughter, the best. The other after the darkness half to which you sometimes run fast. But alas, look at that! That one is in Content Town now. Done with worrying about the frown, wow!

Gone are the lines from below her crown, and the causes are? Well, look at her; the horse will soon come through those gated doors of sorts, Sir. With the bright Knight of the night to do her a riding vice or, to run off with her, again. Comes that time when you know (the name) and then do it to her again.

Until then, though, just go down to Churchill Falls to fall in and dump it. Yes, the worrying scald sis, nearer my god to the under armpits. Yeah, man, that's it.

Go hang it all there, anchored onto an altar call chair, and go on a-calling still. Then wait upon him to come riding, bringing all the weary, wonderful things in with the glad tidings.

So, is it any wonder that the Mister Man der. Yeah, man, look at him right there. I'm talking about me, him, and them; all of those steers, and Mingh, yes, my dear friend. Those of us who do nothing other than any and every other kind of sin Ting. Anything that wears an apron string. Will even do his dear, sweet mama in, if they let him. Just so that he can say that we can win. Always whining about wanting to win the woe man fling, you know.

"No, don't do that to him. One should never do that to them, so stop, and go again, okay?"

"Okay." So, let's go back to the old-time saying, saying it that way, Hingh. "The Wonder Woman Prize, to go off window dressing." Then to the other one with the blessing. Until he's tired of this and that one, or both of them, mister man. Both of them are there on the lot... Tory scam.

Then he heads out and over to Lilliput, to go off, putting another spin on the Lilly puss. Yeah, man, look, this little one right here. (Naughty little kitten you) I swear.

"Where?"

"There, my dear," nearer my god to the barber chair and covered up nicely under the shaving skin there. Look. In wastebaskets near the dust-bin, where all those wasted barbershop droppings, like cast-out, leftover hairy clippings, off those worthless good-for-nothings, are to be found hanging out and hiding. Whilst listening to the quartet's latest hyping.

But man. What a man, thing! Look, that's him right there, playing his hand (so unfair). Now he hops from limb to limb, trying to win other fine things to fill out his cravings. He would have gone and taken the Rev up, upon the lack of offering in the collection cup. But not before there was to come her crosses, and now, look what's up, the Rev is... Standing up for those rights of his, again. Standing firm for another term upon the offered ring stands, too, is the other person who is liked by, guess who? "Yes, true". Like only she can be, not you, nor me... He would have gone in and argued with her over the lack of offering in the collection purse. Then hitched an anchor onto an altar called... "Worse". Now she's waiting in vain for him to come, Paul, bringing along something good to haul.

But in vain she waits for love from him, and for them to bring something else in his glove, in the evening. Like, something pure, good, nice, and loving. "Ugh, I'm leaving..."

Now, go, get her the things that she wants so much, like things she likes and wants a lot of. "Do you know what?" "Yes, Cracker Jack, no?" "Yes, that, bro." With daily bread and food for the pot, no? "Yes." Other steamy things too, for the home on the lot, yeah man, pressed down and packed. Like, that brood of chicks that she lacks from the chicken coup. I mean, a whole lot of them from the hatch, that's who.

Coming to her at the hand of the man, preferably, a good, godly one like Mick. Firing off the shots fast and quick... Quite unlike how it used to be with that Dickson, dick... Go on, Dick, give her Matt Hammatick, just the way you already know she likes it. A good one, though, more or less like Joe. Or that selfsame Manley bro to fit it firmly upon his toe.

But don't go off sweating too much over it, no. No Siree. She has never that worrisome road, toes the sticks to see. Yeah, man! I would have heard it when she said so to me.

"There are a few things that I'm perfectly sure of," said that same broad hip-shotted gal from over there at Glen Goff. "I will fix him up fast with skills I never get in my grasp."

"Nor did it come to you falling off the learning tree crops, I'm perfectly sure of that."

"Yeah, me too, but, but... Oh, wait a minute, who... who are you? O — Kay...! Now I see what you're talking about, Faye. But..." To show that you're mine, though, go walk the line again, in toe. Go on. Just go and walk those boots. So long, my youth, no? Yes, I hope you were made better by even one thing that was said here, in truth, my brother. Thank you.

**Jenny Was: A poem of the times.**

This is one of those sadder, darker pieces; originally published in my first book of poetry called "Waters of Silver Spring." But few ever got to see it; perhaps you'll read it here and get to love it as much as he did.

It started as a song until I finally figured out that I couldn't sing. I later discovered that a poem could be just as good a vehicle for conveying the message to them, and him. So, my song is a poem now, "since I really can't sing a blow-wow." It's here among the new collection of short stories and poems of the times. This piece is based on a true story. I did change the name and a few other small details to protect the innocent and the gory... "Details?"

"Oh hell!" Sad enough for you? Here for you is Jenny Was: a poem to reflect on.

Jenny was a very pretty little girl. Until somebody took her out of this world. Small-town cops didn't ask for help. They tried to solve the case all by themselves. They never did, and I wish Jenny had lived, oh, but she never did

So I tried hard to make some sense of it. But somehow, all the pieces did not fit. She was somebody's Queen of Hearts, who dreamt of marriage and a family to start. She never did, and I wish Jenny had lived, but she never did

That afternoon, it wasn't too late. She went for a stroll out by the lake. She wanted to soak up some fresh air before her walk back to the house out there, where Jenny lived. And I wish Jenny had lived, but she never did

Heaven only knows and can say why. Some people live, while others may die. Why then can't I stop these tears from falling? I can't help but cry. For Jenny, sweet girl Jenny. Oh, I wish Jenny had lived

...

She had big dreams and set her sights on someday seeing her name in lights. With the contest won, she was all set to go. To the big city to start the show. She never did, and I wish Jenny had lived, but she never did

To solve the case, those lawmen fail. They fouled up big on the small details. It still hurts to see the real sloppy job those lawmen did with all the leads they had. They never did, and I wish Jenny had lived, oh, but she never did

Now forty years have come, and forty years gone. Still, the killer has never been found. Those town folks want to put it all to rest, and so far, it's been without success. They never did, and I wish Jenny had lived, but she never did. Jenny never lived.

Here for you is another piece of spoken word poetry. Just what the doctor orders at this point, for me.

## My Father's Hand

A poem for my father on Father's Day, and yours too, perhaps, I'd say.

I see the years logged in colors, and rich Calypso paints in dynamic shades, which mark the timeline there on those building blocks, of how houses were then made.

With the hammer in his right hand. Bring out the shovel and bring out the spade. Where my father worked to build his own house, and farmed the delta lands out on the glade.

He gathered and brought the money home. Never gave his to the bank, then went back asking for a loan. 'Twas my father's hand that had laid the foundation. He even hewed these cornerstones.

Father was mighty with the hammer when cutting the wood and plowing the ground. A marvel of a man was my own father. The greenness of youth yet set in his bones.

Our mother made babies then, and the family prospered and grew. Year after year, they came along, so my father added yet another row. Rows of blocks, that is, they mount up high just like stairs. He bought them as the money became available and stored them in the backyard out there.

He added the rooms as we would have had the need for them. A room for Marty, one for Jack, and another for Ben. One more room is added as each child appears. One for each of them, and then for those children of theirs.

In the sixth generation, the ceiling was set. My father was still here; he had not moved on yet. Fifty years later, the picket fence is finally up. Father downs the morning with a satisfied sup. Satisfied in knowing he'd gotten it all wrapped up. As he drinks the hot coffee out of his favorite cup.

Screaming whispers are so very loud now that one can scarcely begin to see. The way these things are turning out now, from the way they used to be. Marty's home, which he has just bought in town, is yet to cover up his weary sleep. Makes my old father want so much to holler, and makes him surely want to weep.

It's hardly any bigger than one of these rooms, my father was heard to lament. At the little mushrooms on which his own son had, so much good money spent. But Marty is content, says small is the way now to go. And since the Dinosaurs are already gone, big is certainly not cool anymore.

My father lamented this, too, and shook his weary head. It's their world now; he consoles himself. "My time is over, I'm almost dead." But what ways are these for any man to live? I'd much rather get up and go than to live and work all throughout my life just to pay back debts that I owe.

I must go and lie down now; I've got to go and take my rest. I've had some great living in my time, and I've done for them my very best. But if I had it all again to do, which of these lives would I even choose? I'd build my own house all over again, and I'd just as gladly grow my own food.

That was translated from the first; a piece dedicated to the memory of my grandfather, and it goes like this.

### Grandfather's Hand. An ode to my ancestors. Your dads, too, and moms.

I see the years logged in colors, rich Calypso paint in dynamic shades, which mark the timeline there on the building blocks of how houses were then made.

With the hammer in his right hand, bring out the shovel, bring out the spade. Where Grandpa worked to build his own house and farmed the delta-land out on the glade.

He gathered and brought the money home, never gave it to the bank, and then went back asking for a loan.

'Twas grandfather's hand that had laid the foundation; he even hewed the cornerstone.

Grandfather was mighty with the hammer, cutting the wood and plowing the ground. A marvel of a man was my grandfather, the greenness of youth yet set in his bones.

Grandma made babies then, and the family prospered and grew. Year after year, they came along, so Grandpa added yet another row. Rows of blocks, that is, they mount up high just like stairs. He would buy them as the money becomes available, and store them in the backyard out there.

He added the rooms as we would have the need for them, a room for Marty, one for Jack, and another for Ben. One more room is added as each child appears, one for each of them, and then for those children of theirs.

In the sixth generation, the ceiling was set; Grandpa was still here; he had not moved on yet. Fifty years later, the picket fence; finally up. Grandpa downs the morning with a satisfied sup. Satisfied in knowing he'd gotten it all wrapped up, as he drank the hot coffee out of his favorite cup.

Screaming whispers are so loud now that one can scarcely begin to see. The way these things are turning out, from the way how they used to be. Marty's home, which he had just bought in town, was yet to cover up his weary sleep. Makes my grandfather want to holler, and surely makes him want to weep.

"It's hardly any bigger than one of these rooms," Grandpa was heard to lament, at the little mushroom on which his own son had, so much good money spent. But Marty is content, says "small" is now the way to go, and since the dinosaurs are already gone, "big" is certainly not cool anymore.

Grandpa lamented this too and shook his weary head. It's their world now, he consoled himself. "My time is over, I'm almost dead." But what ways are these for any man to live? I'd much rather get up and go, than live and work all my life just to pay back the debts I owe.

I must go and lie down now; I've got to go and take my rest. I've had some great living in my time, I've done for them my very best. But if I had it all again to do, which of these lives would I even choose? I'd build my own house all over again, and I'd just as gladly grow my own food.

The poet has spoken it properly and good.

## Yet There Are Girls, Girls, Everywhere.
(Man in the media, Part 2.)

Man, that thing really did some harm to my chances. Now, tell me. Why did that thieving no-good gal of his, and her twin dunces have to take my belongings for a spin on a rough road and bounces? Never even having the common courtesy to have asked it of me, firstly?

But then again, as it now pertains to those four-letter words that should never be uttered, or even be heard in the age of overpopulation nerds. You know them, those high-flying speckled birds that can't even be censored. But as for me, why? Why must I not be heard? Well.

"Wise men," they say, "set up catchment dams in strategic areas and varied locations." Such as are to be seen in shopping malls and restaurants. Designed to capture the flow of some women's resources, and their men's hard-earned dough, Ray. Not me, though.

But that of those men who (for whatever reason) would have happened to wind up with them, and you. You know, like, those happy-go-lucky high-heeled sneakers who are hitching a ride on those woe men, weaker, sex on the go, to meet with her, way down low.

Yes, those downhill siders who are sliding in wider. Going to get bed down beside her, with those other "woe" to men dames, on the glide-in. To go and fight for the rights of the name and the writings. Yeah, man, that's the right thing.

But the man is not there tonight, no. Just his woman and her girlfriends are bright… "So?"

Yes, his wife was there too, and oh so many of them chit-chatting, laughing, and advising you. Dishing out all that life-long gained insight when here comes them. Sitting in their regular front seats, again. Right by you and the rest of them, yes. Been coming in there ever since. Talking, of course, because their words are valued over yours, often, yes, their husbands, who's asking?

"Me."

"Yeah, man, got to be."

Although none of them sitting there with her, and him, on the hanging line chair, chatting. Yes, the chair over there in the corner square is what I mean, and telling the hell out of what she needs to do in there. Yes, in her own home sphere (one shoe in) and in her family. (The other.) To her husband (the brother). He is mostly the one who's usually out, well, especially so, nope?

None of them sitting with her there has a husband of their... no, none of such as their own to wear. Definitely, not this sort of good one to keep and care about. Well, a few of them did. They have at least one, at some point in the year, on the hid... Or another, and kids.

"Without a father?"

"Yes, that too, and kept it hidden from view." But as for you? Not anymore, my brother, no kidding as before, no blunder. Not sure what's the matter with the order. What's the reason for this? I wonder.

Another few have many children. But by "other women's many men" and borrowed husbands. Their brothers, too, are over there in the clubhouse yonder by you. Their favorite places to meet for prayer, Sunday morning propaganda, why you?

All they ever get to hear over there is: how they must wait, and don't. Like, don't date. They won't Fate. Don't do this, they're told, and don't do that, ever. But never what to do to win the pass over supper, my brother. Even while they're waiting in a queue and sitting on a pew, anticipating you coming through.

"No, that's not true."

"Yes, it is, I know you, I guess, with ease." But there's no need to do anything to be a bit more prepared for that thing, when it comes running into them, in the evening (warship). Yeah, man, that's it; the very thing for which they are there waiting. There's no need to. "And why?" you'd asked my nephew-guy, and my bigger boss?

Because they were born like that: Well-equipped and ready to attack. Already knowing all the sheets that they will ever need to spread the bed, then go fluffing the pillow up under his head. It's all done (got good) and patted down. All that is to be known, along with high-heeled sneakers and hot combs, yes, mi clowns.

Got their men to believe in them, and that the prize to win is a girly thing. Smooth nonsense talks and wedding the rings. Filing for the willing to come riding in, while filling up the curves, and dressing back the crush of wedding gowns with something sexy, nice, and round on the girls' cotton picking plum plum thing and ting but? Cut.

To show that you are mine, though. Go, walk the line, in toe. No? I hope you were made better by even one word that was said here in truth, thank you.

### Women Dressed in Black.

As the struggle continues in the arena of gender issues, and a woman's right to have control over her own body (or the misuse) versus the rights of the unborn child that she won't give you. Some women took to the streets in Poland and elsewhere some time ago to protest an attempt by lawmakers to ban abortion. This was to lead to a ditching of those efforts by said lawmakers. It was against this backdrop that this poem was written while keeping an eye on the wider spectrum and personalities involved. Now listen, because here is the poem called:
Women Dressed in Black.
One hundred thousand women dressed in black. Joined protest rallies across many city blocks. Demonstrating against plans to further tighten up an already restrictive abortion policy setup.
Meanwhile, tomorrow's children are left back to yesterday. For now, women no longer have to pay. One may recall when Henry Morgentaler said: I have no regrets, I've fulfilled the hopes and dreams of my Ma and Pa today."
"Have these people (somehow) forgotten that women used to die from self-induced and abortion quack...? And that, unwanted children were often given away to institutions where they suffered trauma that

took the joys of life away, making them become anxious, depressed individuals with grudges against society.

Have they forgotten that an unwanted pregnancy is the biggest health hazard to young women's fertility? And could result in long-term illness, death, and injury?"

That a grave injustice had been done to them was what he said drove him, when asked in the end.

And now, one hundred thousand women all dressed in black are joining protest rallies across many city blocks. To ensure that pressure is swiftly brought to bear, and to pacify the brunt of their collective wrath this year. Thank you, my dear.

### Torn to Feces.

A Piece of Creative Nonfiction wrapped in poetry.

I had to think this one through, long and hard. Should I share this with my friends, or keep it in the yard? Well, some "finds" were not meant for the keepings, as you can see (these things). Look at me, hard.

Psst, hey, you there, yes you, lean in a bit closer, I've got a little scoop for you, but first this. Promise that you'll keep it close to your knee, "will you?" "Okay, I agree to do, do..." Here goes. I'm telling you this only because we're family and I trust you, right?

"Right."

But remember, ma-hite. Don't tell a soul, it's that sensitive a slit in the night. I've got to tell you because you might be there wondering about me, and this is the cause, as you can see. I'm laid up in bed now, even while writing this, but with a fat smirk on my face, wow! You know me, I never knew anything to begin with, so no need to say it again. "Oh sheet!"

"Amen." I don't know what exactly to do about this situation, my friend. Other than to ask someone who knows how to stop these pains, like you, perhaps. Or sit still on my... No, wait a minute, my boss, wipe that word off your slate, because... It's not the best option for my current state and condition. Can't be found sitting around on this thing until eight, and this one...

So, tell me, do you know anybody in your circle with a key, like, someone who is versed in the treatment and care of such an issue as this is? Perhaps you can get a fast-healing word out of her and pass it along to my health care Sister Wiz. You know, with all those other things happening on the medical floor these days, one shouldn't be too eager to run in through those doorways of his gate. Nor go hopping onto the squares, in those hallowed spheres of theirs.

So one must think about homing it to the cure sometimes, and this may be the chiefest of those types of "sometimes," I think. But what do I know? "Nothing." Certainly not enough to have been able to keep my trap sound and still sounding good like, like... while sounding off one of those preferred sounds of his near the woods where I'm seated, good and... Like, the sound of silence (perhaps that's a good argument.) But then again?

I was lying around on my side in excruciating pain. This came about because I was torn to Feces, again. Since I must say it clearly so that uncertainty may disappear, Leigh. I tore the place where the sun doesn't shine. Happened while I was trying to relieve my constipated self of the rain that time.

Yeah, laugh as much as you like, Ma-hite, your day is coming, and it's going to be bright (or not), just wait, you'll see. Seriously, though, no, I hope not. Not for my worst enemy, which, I don't have that many on the lot, Torie, Pat, ish, really. Preparation H was suggested to me, "For your greatest good and fast relief," they'd said.

So I guess I should go out and get prepared to relieve myself of the fees down there. By releasing some shots fast, on the leaves, I hear. "Like these?" "Yes, please," While striking a few birdies away from the ladies. Or I might as well go and put a few holes on the golfing green over by you, maybe down there where I sometimes go to shoot golf each day, with my buddies, the colorectal surgeon, and you, needless to say. Do you know what I mean, Jay? "Yay."

"Okay." Anyway, here's the takeaway. Be very careful whenever you go out to do the go-things. Or you, too, might be left nursing a crack too close to the hole where you sometimes go to rock and roll down at the watering hole, for your own comfort and greatest good. With me being that type of friend, of yours, and you being who you are to me, of course. I wouldn't want to have you leaning sideways when sitting on the stool, on a side days and playing pee on hoe like a fool, while hurting in the darkest corner of the lot tory pot pool. "Oh, Kay?" Anyway, that's it for today, my friend. Keep it to yourself near the shut-in, as said. This is just between you and me, alright, mi bred? Nice. Now, the poet has spoken it twice. Be sure to like, share, and comment. We sure would appreciate it if you would subscribe and follow us somewhere, too. Thank you.

Here is a 5-7-5 haiku poem.
When doves Bill and coo.
I can think of only two.
Because I love you.
Just a saying of mine to occupy your time.
Don't go spending good money and hard-earned cash on that dead-head stash. Save it to decorate the sunny cage around your rash, after you're done, buried, and dead. "Oh gosh!" Slumbering sweetly in your grave. Go now, wash your face, and go to bed, and sleep sweet. Meat for the teeth. Speaking of teeth, here's a bite for you to eat.

Here for you is a little thing called:

Bitten, because…
Got Bitten by a Twitching Hitch. Just another poem of the times, about the little um! ...itch, like this.
Some savage beasts from a wilderness theme bite the brother hard in the crust of his bloodstream. Oh, how he cried out, oh how the brother

screamed, but no one was found worthy to reach out and save him. Or so to him, it would have seemed.

He had to holler out some more, had to curse. To stop himself from popping open, blowing up, or worse, like, bursting. Could he find you doing the wrong thing, though, like, when upon his imminent return, if he should find you and me drifting, drifting away?

Like you've been seen doing, every day. Even while you were supposed to be there doing all those other things, in the play. Like, when you were there, a-lean, lean, leaning? Leaning on the wrong side of everything.

Of course, not you, just the other Hugh, I mean, he, the other E, him, as in the Elk, I mean, not me, but him. As it is in this case, in your face, too, and the washbasin. He's the only one who could be found guilty of such wasting, Jason. But choh man, shut up yuh mouth nuh, yuh chat too much already. But then again, hit the post button and send. Steady.

An extract from the "Backsliding book, of mine and my friends'...

## Cockspurs in the Cockpits, A Poem of the Times.

In solidarity with the Jamaican Cockpit Maroons in their land claim fight with the Government, it goes like this.

Yes, mi fren. Cock spur Makkah gwine juck some of dem, right here in these Cockpit Mountains. Yes. Getting ready, they were, getting ready to knock fists, with her, knocking them downhole in the cockpits, my star.

They thought that this was going to be easy. "Just go get it done, and come back quickly." But it was for the first time ever that night that they were going there to see such a thing as the cockfight. They were wandering around and wondering in the car, "Hey, what are those bowls really good for?"

But they were going to find this out really soon, when she fell in hardened upon the old witches' boom. Yes, my friendly goon; zooming in on the wrong end of the enemy's broom, yes. This sort was not what they were whoring for, to spoon; they wanted to hit upon a really big score, yes, Mister Mistar.

"Go in and run those locals over," he said, and more. "Just like we would have done to them, often times before." But they were just about to learn the new score. Can't do us like you did those other ones, on the floor.

We'd asked you to clearly define our borderlines. You came back bringing us a protected area sign. Which fell (quite inconveniently) within the well-known and established square yards of mine. Thinking that we wouldn't hear you before the sign. Like that, before signing off on those mining lots.

Then send in the machines to get it all done fast, and clear us out of your ask, favor. Yes, mi bredda. They wanted to clear us out of their guts' bus stout and rife. But beware of them, your ears are tough, alright. So, you couldn't hear us, so it would have seemed, good night, fair enough, my queen?

"Fear, I guess, I'm in..."

Well, we'll give you that square in a dream. So, go right on in and catch up on your sleep-in. But, as for those other men with him? Look at them, sneaking in. Those pimps were newbies, new to this sort of showbiz. They did not know these things, Kids. They didn't know what went on in the cockpits.

Not to worry, though, somebody was about to know. Look, the game is now on, the roosters are in game mode as planned. All holes are corked and plugged up, the money pot scrubbed fast, and the bugs zapped.

Let's go, Jack, as is, mount keys, and clowns. Cockpit cock mouth is just about to kill a cockpit stout, and round. In a round of John Crow batty rum, man, *goh siddung*. Yes, manly good son. Go take a seat on the ground, because, Cockpit cockspur makkah stick, gwine lick somebody's cockatrice, way up there in those rear-end mountainous lattices. So, bring it on in, bring your best legs to come bust out dancing.

We've got something cooking up right here for you; the bell-a-gut pot is now simmering the stew. Your mada woman knows just what to do, to keep the family fed, then sent to bed down in a place called Content Town, as said. Now, sleep tight, "go to bed, man, and have a good night." But she was about to cross-swipe the smile and turn to sell yet more unrefined snake oil.

Falling hardened upon the already batched-up plan, and the schemes did spoil. Happened when they'd hatched another plan, and fiddled away at filing those files, off and on. As was seen when they were bringing in these things, yes. This was only the entry mile in...

They were about to wipe the white teeth off somebody's grin, yes, mi bredren, because... our troops were ready and raring to go. Just as troops had done, often times before. About things such as that, they didn't know squat. So, "Come right on in," said he to them.

"Come join us and dig into this steaming skin sin Ting that we've got here cooking."

"What's on the menu?" He'd ask Mass, "Face-screw." "Not too much to do," he replied, "bless you. Just a little chicken stew to take to task," but he lied, next to...

"...Well-seasoned and simmering, you're asked..." Guess who? With a dash of dried cockspur Makkah dust, alongside a pinch of guinea hen weed, to trust.

Here comes Mass Son with a head-cup of rum. Dried petal blossoms from the floral cock comb mixed in there, and yet more garden egg sprinkled with nutmeg, and stirring, I hear. Three duppy pumpkins and nine cornmeal dumplings.

Thirteen sliced eggplants to eat, then beat the sheet out of the Kette drum around the boiling pot and chant defeat. Freetown isn't that free for none of..., so that everyone can come and see. Then go slicing off a portion of meat to go down with a cup of gang Jah, tea.

Comical stooges wanted to drill strange holes throughout these conical hills. Yes. The very hills through which fools were trying to pursue prey, which they couldn't quite see through, still, in those days, and got themselves killed in our doorways in paradise, in one glorious night on the top of the hill. Nice place, eh, yeah, man, but still. Look at this, if you will.

Those liars were lying back down on the Brier ground, dying. Eyes wide open as if looking at chirping, chattering black-billed Amazon parrots, not flying. But one of them was seen sitting on the chieftain's head top, eying them. Those who were looking at me but couldn't quite see, the feathered fish head who was watching them pointedly.

Looking through the bushes as fools walked into a trap laid outsmart on the ancestors' back pass, with the black cats we sometimes called pusses. As in, they came towards the attack. Now, know this fact, because we won't sit passively by while you plunder and spoil the sacred endemic species. No, not those things the hands of my forefathers gave me on these hills, thriving sweetly.

Your big missteps would have happened near Quickstep, where you'd supposed you'd come to find your gold basket. Yes, of lost treasures, in the land of "Look behind you," never. The troop you were to rally and send into Cave Valley made the worst mistakes on the "Booby-trap" near our gate. Flying the trap on the spot, and testing our faith, yes. Stop, look, and listen to this fast. Hear that? "Yes."

That's the sound of the men marching into the blades' ends. Only to come bucking into a buck, and screaming out their guts. Happened when they'd lost the five barley loaves. The lovely lunch the mother-woman gave them near Martha-tick Cove, nearer to the cave than the nose, and the rest is history, as his story goes. But that was not to be told; it's still a mystery left lying listlessly at Minocal's glory hole. Our glory is in that holy hole, not yours.

Turning now to see, these things looking back at me: You take our children away, and go off putting them out on display. Then get into your old habits of boasting away, about all the wonderful things that you have done, and are still doing today. But, answer me this single question, right away: what were our children doing before you came by this way?

Well, not one, here's another for you to pander and consider the withdrawal on. What will they be doing after you are already done and gone, as may be found written in your log on...? Aah, but sir... Yes! I hear you, but sir... If you should open this door, our land won't be the same as before. A precedent would have been set for the claimants to get the claim, yes, and to score some more. To spoil the land, the people's good name, and much more than before.

While dumping your "poison-us" something-sin ting on our door, in the water main, and everything more, again. Now, tell me this, what will then become of these children whom you are here loving so very much, (hiss,) and hastening to come plunder, and spend, like dust? (Table-fist.) Now, take your dirty hands off our children's Pinckney dem, and gweh, I mean, go away, Sir, please. And get thee lost, Pleaser. Thank you for these, Sir. Yes, wordplay is the order of the day around here, I guess.

Poetry in Commotion. A poem of the times.

With the current concerns about the condition of Mother Earth, and what little may be left of her worth, this is poetry in commotion. We're showing off our devotion to her man, about how to go out and block her from the damn earth thing, feeling, like, mad about nothing. Look at how we have been treating our only habitat, called Mother Earth, and home, ha, wha... what is that, Hingh? Oh, isn't that something? "Yes."

One would have seen it in social media forums, coming to us in recent times as altered decor Rums. Imaginary imagery of other types of supposedly well-placed arguments under teleprompter letterings, captioned to say to me, "The blacks are the stupidest people in the planetary system today."

"Ugh! That's the most outrageous thing to say!" Yay, or nay? Anyway, instead of anger and outrage, someone else and I were heard shouting to have them say the phrase "Yeah." Yeah, man, on our earring page. Because that was our first reaction to the said comments coming off them at once, and that's the cause. Even to a fraction of the erring pause.

Although I, he, and they, yes, we're oblivious to the obvious reason, that he and I are these types of manly guys; we would never become so quietened that we would not be able to stand and say: We're happy in our skin today. Surprise-surprise, yay. "But why?" Someone else was heard asking him, and I?

"It's because," the answer came shooting back at the boss. One has ways of knowing the truth when it is spoken. Even if and when such a "one" never knew it before, then, and this is one such truth that has been poking hard at you and me in a recent time span. You and I can't be denied that one. But then again. Even if those reports were fake news of sorts, or falsely came those reports back to us in worthless talks. There must have been some truth to it for it to have grown winged legs and taken to the sky and to fly. Wouldn't that be a possible reason why?

I have some things to say on these and other such issues. How did we as a people get to such a place as the tissue? To have nothing but mud, smoke, and dirt hurled at us from them, with the misuse? I would have lived and seen nations born out of next to nothing, which happened in my lifetime, even. As a matter of fact, teething, I'm older than that thieving...? Yeah, at least one of those little brats they're breeding. But they would have risen out of the dust to be contending and commanding a place in the seats of powerful wielding, at us in fact. At world power, too, at last.

Even dominance, too soon, in our lives and times, in abundance, to our dads and mums. But there are a kind of people somewhere on the earth's end, a vessel... Not very sure what they are worth and less than lessened, or from whence they had come, but they are nonetheless, here. For a while yet, a moment to spare.

These people have done nothing with what they were given to get... Like, the chosen piece of earth-land, even the best. The same little piece that a few other men's beasts came over to feast and test their teeth at. Or take too big a bite out of, when they went over there to possess the lot, like this one, and that. A little bit here and there from under our feet, they took it square. Yes, and then went into making something great, out of it, and ate the fish, there, sit, sit. Yeah, man, go back and sit down on it (if you want). Then all of a sudden, those other people by the scores or a dozen would have seen it again. Saw what happened when the newcomers came and unpacked, and what they did with what they took from them, and got fat. With tiny bits of paper and the writing of the pen, look at that. Still taking and wasting what was left of us and them. "Now they want it back, but, but, 'To go and do what?'" One was heard asking things such as that, in somewhat of a mocking shock.

"To to… to go and add to the much that they still have done got? Oh my Gosh, like, like still got lit, and lighting up yet more lampposts to go lighten up a lot more of it? You don't say!" She was heard raving when she said it to me and spat, Okay! "While the rest of us are still sitting here doing nothing with our own crown?" She continued raving on, all around town. "You don't say," said that same one, that way.

Meanwhile, the other man is doing many things, yet. Observing you and building fabulous military wings like… "Like, like, jet?" "Yes." While studying and discovering some more. "You bet." Many are their "Building kinds of things," even down to the tiniest molecular beings, of genes, and the differences between… This one and that, trying to find out what makes one person (or thing) different from the other, and how to manipulate things to make them out to serve him better, better him than you, the go-getter; that's who, mi bredda. Oh yes, my dear beloved brother. But best of all, the weather, look on a bit further. He would have managed to convince those people over there on the over-laden vehicle with the chair that their ways are old and outdated, not good anymore, and underrated. So, those people would have given up on the ways and customs of their forefathers' generations. Go on, cuss them, if you want, yes, those accursed things, near the plant.

They would have taken on the things of the other men's wealth, as if it were coming to them and their children for help, yes, in the sinks, perhaps. Because they love others' ways and customs, all their fabulous must-come things too. Much more than they'd ever loved, the foolishness of their forefathers' messing with you. So now, I'm guessing this to be true, yes, it's the other men who feed them, with altered and manipulated feeding. Some kind of "Gee's-us" approved and proven food, they call it or something. After they're done praying over the cornmeal dumplings.

Hand-outs of great gifts, such as washed-up water to drink it... and wash them clean in the sinks — "Oh, sheets." "Yes, eat." Which quenches their thirst for a short season, and for a while, yes, that's the only reason, my child. But they will surely cleanse the earth of you and them in the long run of the Nile, west. Like, when you didn't even know what was his crushing style, I guess. Which was happening, until it would have happened to you, my child. "Bless."

Yet, trust and obey that man is what you do, all the while, too, go fix it, boo. Now, smile, and take a look at who? Yes, you, because... He clothes them, and you. Educate you too, give laws to govern meant to rudely awaken you, and medicine to yield you after the Seasonal Flew. After they would have gone in and sic the big bad dog on you, sorry, I meant to say, whenever you are ill-figured, go figure it out or go away, Boo.

Gave you religion about who? Yes, true; a religiously godly bout of doubt, old or new. Dwindle dumb norms abnormally stout, too, to go out and perform them on you, and your... How about those Normans' norms, remember them? "Come on..." Well, maybe. Strangely, those customs, coming in lately, money to spend to buy them some, like, sweet sugar plumb plum, mi Pinckney. Some other nothingness, nonsense from them, yes; the just-comes, and get poorer for so doing, more so are those in spirit, even. Even waste you and prepare you to die, and go off to heaven. "But, but, but why?"

"Oh my!" Look this way, don't cry. Now that the time has come for their actual dying and wasting, starting from their children's lickerish tongues tasting. Or more like, not having children as the basic chase thing, because those are bad for the Square of them. Sorry, I meant to say, beware of them. For the environment of the day, the earth's equilibrium, ecosystems, and species preservation. Such are the other ordered things of those other men, best when shunned.

"As for us and our way of life, those must be observed," said those other or theirs of the knights. "No one is going to deprive us of our ways of life, nor cause us to stop the wares and tares." "That's right." In other words, causes them to change their ways as if making it out to become ours. Because it's a given from the creator of all things, Eve, I mean, even.

That "us" here means "they," they must have the best and the most, "Yay!" All that there is to have of this earth, I suppose, of course. "Don't say."

"No, I won't, Faye." Well, okay, and at the expense and extinction of others, such as us, and the brothers too, on the bus. So why bother with us? It's not for them, though, the other men foe. It's not about them alone that we're here picking at these bones, no. It's about all of us, at home. The Neanderthals, wink-wink. That will be all.

Now, let's think about this, and that, all other such things, and the facts. All the many wonders of wonderful things about this beautiful rock band called Earth, I mean, Eden. Hey! Good evening, Bert, again, for all that you're worth, my friend. Or morning, if it's earlier over there on the dirt we're all in.

Which we want to preserve for whoever will come after us, not to be leaving after the fall-in — "Shuts". It's not about us and them, though; we are all in this together, my friend. "So?" If we've all been bad, then we shall go out back badly, together. Because together we have been bad stewards of this earth thing feeling… and the weather.

Now we must pack together towards her healing, to bring her back to her former… whether we like it or not, we must be kneeling to disarm her from that. To bring her back to her former glory, so said her, yes, she, not me. "All of us together must do this glory on us kind of weather because we are in it together."

All are equally responsible for what has happened to her in the pasture. Even now, at last, sir. Therefore, we will be rewarded equally for the ultimate outcome which we would have fabricated with our own hands — "On our knees?"

"Well, of course. Excuse me, please!"

…And out of the collective imagination airy systems of ours. "See?"

"Yeah, man, like this, ee."

"Ride on." Hey, you there, black? I mean, that man, go on, lie to me. Tell me you are worth saving again, amen.

Waters of Silver Spring. An ode to the place of my childhood.

This next poem is one of my favorites, taken from my first book of poetry, a book by the same name. Enjoy it for me.

Sweet waters of Silver Spring, oh, what soft soothing pleasures you bring. To my eyes, my ears, my thirsty lips, my tongue so longed to taste your flowing delight.

While skin touches your smooth cascades beneath the soft shadows of night, your slender arms hug the neck of Athlone, way over on the left. Whilst Georgetown's high hills caress your breast.

Yet your cool, clear waters bubble, and constantly, your waters flow. "Where do you come from?" they asked, and where do you hasten to go? No one has ever answered; nobody seemed to know.

Young ladies fair, washing their hair, bending beneath your crystal flow. Shadowed curtains around them were drawn, be it at nightfall or early dawn.

Chattering women washing their load, on the rock's smooth surfaces, by the side of the road. Valiant young men await their turn, sitting on the culvert's edge, as they discover and as they learn.

Just one short leg away from hip to toe, you burst up from the ground and hurried along to go. By lush green trees while bending low, they salute and bow in a reverent show.

Sumptuous, refreshing, savory, sweet, waters of my unassuming silver spring. You whined your way over rocks and river moss, all "Live long day." Until you pour out of your glad waters, into the anxious jaws of the Rio Sambre.

## Hey! Liars. Is Lying Wrong?

What if lying was a thing, like, a golden strategy for them and him, for instance, or a tool? Could liars use it to their benefit, against truthing fools?

We're living in an age when lies, half-truths, fake news, and miss-speaking have become the order of the day. Is lying still wrong? Is it wrong to call a liar out that way? Like, a liar? So, what if that lying liar there wants you to believe him, and everything that he and his friends tell you this year or last evening? What if liars are like that, always want-ing you to believe that truth is the right way to go, when they know full well that lying is a better show? Or, in reality, it is the only way for winners to go. But they want you to believe the opposite is true, that there's a virtue in truth. What is it that liars want you to tell them? Like, whenever they say to you: speak the truth, the whole truth, and noth-ing but... What if those liars want you to go about telling them every-thing by way of the mouth? Including the truth all the time, and then letting them tell all the lies that they can find... out about? For you, even. But then again, we all know that that's not how things work, right, my friend? But what if it was a lie that they'd told you when they told you that thing? The thing that you're believing in, even now. "*What a sin, Ting*?" What if they're telling you lies now? What if liars were the ac-tors who had acted in making things out to be so fabulously fine for you when they were? "Mi blow-wow!" Because they knew all along what you never knew. Like, nothing, that's who, mi cous. Or even another try, like. You did not know that the lie is the guy. What if that fine thing you have become was because of the lies they already told? What if it has become way too fine for you and everyone else now, and is beginning to cause those actors some trouble, somehow? What if the boogie man you're looking at now is the result of those said actors reacting to that fluke of the past? The mishap that would have happened, that had them spooked, and now, they're here at last, acting again to correct the errors of their past doings on your ask? But then again, just asking, Sue Hingh, *geh mi pass*.

What if, after telling lies for a while, liars should wake up and dis-cover that there are virtues in lies? Just like how things are in love and war, for instance. Just for instance, guys. Would it be okay to use it in that way, and in such a circumstance? "Why?" "Well." Could this be the war-time that we are witnessing now? Or love time for that matter, such sorts of love times, somehow. Love times that could warrant the use of such methods? Just asking this, my love, send in those letters with the lettuce's love. Love letters for people like brothers, from above, even. People who may or may not include you and me, Steven. But, how do you know when a liar is lying anyway? Nephew has got the perfect answer to satisfy that and this, and it's sitting right by him to say, "Whenever their lips are moving." But I wouldn't take that to bed. "It has got to have more substance than that, to prove him," I'd said. More meat to the bone than that one, or those ones, to add up to however much more than you at once. Like, one or two times the chance. So I'll settle on the answer I took with me from home, the one that says: when one is caught speaking out of both sides of the mouth, Jawbone, but one message is diametrically opposed to the other on the way out, up, or down. If you can call him out on the inconsistency of the matter, and he goes right on to explain it away with yet another, you know, like, blobbering lie. But he continues doing this type of wrong all day long, and at night, too, oh my! Isn't that true? Yeah, I know. Yet he goes on doing so, until you want to puke at all his lies and half-truths, with things that you know to be the facts who walk those boots. But what if every one of that man's friends and companions were to rally behind him and sing the same backhanded song, defending his sin and his inalienable right to do these things wrong? Wouldn't the man mature into becoming a clan, with powerful clout to subdue the land? To establish a norm where to be right is to do wrong, but with all conviction? Just a few nonsensical questions to sling along, then go sliding a bloody finger upon the bladed fan. Look out now, Mr. Man. Keep a watchful eye on that one.

Here's a piece of spoken word poetry for you. Just a look at some things and the way I see them through, at the very least. This is a poem called:

## Liar, Just Another Poem of the Times

It was first published in my "Waters of Silver Spring" book on Amazon. Go take a look and move on.

Then there are liars and God-deny her... who are now fast becoming testifiers. Swearing on the bible, which they are liable to value less than marketplace flyers.

Seeking straight answers to their crooked questions. The truth, though, they'd skipped, sparsely their conscience pricked. This, too, they'd forgotten to mention.

Crooked technicians playing the fools make themselves busy designing tools. Then, with just as much vigor, they're making the rules that govern the game for everyone else. While they pile on the glory, wealth, and fame, but only for themselves, in the name.

Boastful dealers and custom stealers are all professing to show. How much they are savvy, and in the know. While busily manipulating things, the way they want them to go. Then there's that someone who gathers all the spoils, though it was another who did the labor, another who'd toiled. Thank you, my child. I'm out.

## Who Is Going to Speak for Joe Average and His Interests?

Note. The city of Montreal once promised to give city streets back to citizens so that they could get around better in their neighborhoods, knee-smooth. But then comes this, and it's good.

Getting around in some major cities nowadays has become perilous, to say the least, for the pair of us. Or more like, not getting around at all, on two feet. Not getting anywhere, one might say, while sliding to the fall on the knees, hooray, one is left to wonder. Who are these?

We were there chatting away, my friend and I that day, about such things as... like, coffee beans to the swimming pool, and on down to drownings on a bar stool. Seat belts on school buses, and other wrong things as such are, and is, and yeah, the right ones too. Mere moments later, my friend and I looked at you and saw out there on the crowded streets, flying craters. "Oh, the fury, look, the wind gods are furious today," he said to me. "They're tossing construction cones around to scare me. They're tumbling and rolling across the streets of town; do you hear me?"

"About time," I'd started to say, "that something or someone tosses them away, no?"

"Why?" he then asked me while staring into my eyes, as if at the show to see.

"Why? I'll tell you." Why must you be doing all of the work at the same time, though? Well, not you, I know, but "them," I'd said this to him and the rest of them, looking on and listening. Yeah! Our bright leaders and their friends were accused of this, too. Only not in their hearing at that time. "True."

"Yeah, man," I'd said. "I understand. Those other friends of theirs had goofed it, right?" Meaning, those who were there before them, and you, too, Fitz, bright. They fell on the job earlier, didn't they? "Yes." "I know." Those who were there postulating as someone special, or acting as something they never were, with the gal, my girl.

Collecting money under a pretense and presiding over crumbling infrastructure? "Makes sense." Until people started falling through the cracks and the cracked structure started tumbling down on some people's laid-back doors, near the fence. The chicken had finally come roosting, with the hens and cocks following behind and smooching. Things weren't going to get better from there on in. Patchwork won't cut it from here, my dear, Hingh, not this morning, here, have a beer. "Thanks."

Time for a total makeover, or face fines, someone said; they chose to walk the lines, mi bred. So, although that's a relatively fine building there on the corner lines, it has some history to it, too, enough to have been able to garner the Times' headlines and to phone you. The historical society had just a year ago petitioned to have it preserved and restored to its former glory... oh! It never made the cut to go tell that story, no.

"No?"

"No, but look out." The wrecking crew is moving into view and position today. Competing with the other construction crew there on the corner remaking the walkway, and the city's sewerage system too, under the clay. Traffic circulation slowed to a screeching, halting stop. But go, yes, go we must. On through the mud and the slush, negotiating flagmen's puffs. Like, their ever-present puffed-up fists of rage and cuss, at cigarette smoke shaking the dust from the tailpipes' cage, at us. But the pedestrian stream must be factored in, for their better days, and in between.

Look, look up ahead, look at the scene. Several traffic lights down the watershed where the Boulevard used to be, said… like, said to be, it's now a total construction zone, where such streets we used to see. Replicated on every block throughout this town and has been coming in recently.

"Why, but why?" I had to ask this guy, "Couldn't you say no to the developer czar on answering his re-gentrification skyscraper tar?" It was always coming from him to us, through her, Huss… band hands on us. She who has been closing out the sunshine from where you are, as it occurred. You mean, couldn't he, or she? Couldn't they wait it out just a minute more, like? Until your construction projects close out the door, no? "Yes."

Meanwhile, everyday-Joe kind of people like you, and yes, me too. We're the ones who bear the brunt of the see-through. Yeah, and on these walking my shoes, the same "we" ones who pay the bills and buy her lunch out of real wants, or tea. She pays us back by jeopardizing our jobs on the crispy crunch, like me. Multiplied the bleeding forces with cruel, heartless cops. To slow us down on the motoring streets, stop, and go. "Real slow now, no?"

"Yes."

"As I'd guessed." Steal our "me-time," and deprive us of our rested sleep, mankind. Making it perilous to muse and use our roads, preying on us, pickpockets are the new "How codes." Speaking of sweet sleep. "The city is going to give us back our street," they say. And I was heard to say, "Yay? Well, hooray."

They're going to postpone 40% of the road work that was planned for this year, and on for us. Planned by the city and its clerk. "Because?" I had to have asked. "Because of what?" No, not that. It's not because construction workers will need to go into lockdown too and go indoors to social distance with you, no. "The idea here is," they say. We want to make the city more peaceful, while people work from home in their neighborhoods, knee-smooth.

"Hooray! Isn't that good?"

"Yes, yes, Mahmoud." As you already know, that's the new norm for us to go into lockdown, on the alarm. So, they're going to give back the street to the citizens, from now on. "We're going to better manage work sites," again, they say this. "Yikes!" Sounds right, eh, nay, or yay? (Hiss!)

"But why, why now?" I was to be heard asking this of my friend, yes, that cow, again. Now that the citizens don't need to use them as much as before, those streets... Because they, the "leaders," have forced and compelled them and us to stay, yeah, in. Behind a closed door, night and day, Hingh. Neat, eh?

"Enough, man. No more of these, rough palms."

"But, but?"

"But nothing. You have to stay off the streets and social distance away from meat—"Like him, her, and me?" "Yes." So, as it now is, there's not enough of them and us for leaders like you to push around and slap about with fines, with the cops too, and the city bus, route plying. And block our paths through the park while we were on our way North.

By preventing us from getting where we wanted to go, and going too fast. We were trying to get there on time, you know, but not anymore, just fine, I'm sure, you go. So now is a good time to cut back on the planned construction work. Which "we," meaning you, not me. You're the person who's going to get it done, but you don't yet know the score.

Like, when the projects will stop, or even get to restart once more, after "we" close that door, to the rest of us throughout this town. Well, I could tell you when you know. If only you'd bothered to ask me how Hugo. Yes, ask me because that's easy, you see. How about, like, when things get back to normal? The type of normal that we're all here working on, even now, and formal. For you, me, and all the citizens to be able to breathe freely.

"And when is that exactly?" you'd asked. How about, like, when people get back to going out on the roads again, daily? Trying to get somewhere or nearly. To go get things done there and dare Leigh. More things than they were able to do during the times not so new. Like when they, them, and you were forced to stay indoors and home with Hugh, all because of the lockdown and corkscrew. The streets were rid of traffic then, and definitely, no construction work was anywhere to be seen going on, on them (no workmen.)

Because those workers were locked behind the doors too, just holding on to the door jamb along with me, and Hugh. It wasn't because our bright leaders wanted to give it to him, and her, and them. Like, to give the street back to us as it occurs, my friend. Yes, those workers and the citizens who were in lockdown, *fuss*, were off. That would have been a good time for that, no? No, *cuss*, don't laugh. Or on the other hand, like, for all that good work to get done, by those same workmen who were forced to sit it out at home, no?

But it would have appeared to us as if they had other ideas cooking in the pot, luck. The best time to slow people down on the streets is that. "Yuck." Yes, when people are out there driving fast, and lots of them, so that they may turn up the thermostat, to go off and tax the axes on the carts, off him. So now that they're in lockdown, we, you, them, and he, like, him; Keith E Mingh, go ask him. They're about to get a timely gift from me. We're giving them back the streets of town so that they can enjoy walking around in their neighborhoods properly again, Mr. Brown. See?

But as soon as the crisis is behind us, like, when things start booming again, like rice seeds on "door us" in the rain. When everybody is out and about, busily playing catch-up with potato chips looming stout. That will be a good time to recommence the road works, no? But of course, right, you are, Flo.

"Not to worry about losing money, though," they explained it away and told us so. Because "we" won't have any penalties to pay, since there were no commitments made to do that road work in the past anyway. "Yay?" I was left here to just suppose a question in laughs and say, "No commitments! None at all? Just your words as were given to us-ward, and to the fall?" Like, your words only, as given to us, like him, and me, the citizens to see, hear, and believe you when you say, "We're doing road work, therefore, the road will be closed, and you will be forced to find a way to get where you need to go, on the nose, however you can. Whenever you can, in whatever condition or state of mind you can, can..." Like, be in when you get to your destination.

"And, and why?"

"Because I said so, guy. That is why. My! Oh my."

And you wonder why it's getting harder for me to argue against my nephew's view on these things. Like, when he's there arguing that "they're fixing up to waste us painlessly and as happy-go-luckily as they possibly can, G-strings." Yay, yeah man, that one.

Go ahead, fren-a-mine, laugh as much as you like. Laugh if you feel like laughing, if only to stop yourself from crying, my offspring, for one night. No, I ain't lying, though I might want to lie... down, on the ground, dead floored.

**Ain't Even Sheet. The friendship poem.**

So, is that the way you happen to see it? That my family and I ain't even sheet?

Just because we haven't arrived at the money street, yet?

While you were already there, busily lifting loads of multicolored discrete, off the other folks' bundle of joy. And sorrows too, pick-a-boo-boo.

Joy was brimming with laughter while crying too, shedding tears of yet more joy, and a bouncing baby boy. And girls, in dancing ballerina shoes, but who do you?

That was just because you had happened to discover that my family and I haven't yet crossed over. Over the bridges and turnstiles, turning the corner.

That's where Wall Street's big shots' money garnered, was to show you that my family and I ain't even squat. Because, we haven't yet got, like, got it all backed up to the loading dock.

In trucks and backhoes, backed up with all that: Doe, Ray, Me, Fah, So... Yet. As you'd thought and afterthoughts long, long ago. When you had set out to become, and became, a friend. To me and my children, but then again.

Your plans were thwarted when the doe you had wanted wasn't to be forthcoming, coming, coming. And the friendship began a-doning, downing, doning, downing, done.

## How Writing Found and Changed Him, and Me

He was hardly even able to string six words together to order his lunch properly from the bredda, or tea, but...

A high school dropout, he was; ran away from home at sixteen and hitched a bus ride. After two wasted attempts at getting back on the higher-learning train, he decided to get a haircut and a job, no matter the degree of "real." Just like Bob, he went and got a job to pay the bills.

None of the jobs he got quite measured up to the mastery of the bills. He decided to get a marketable skill. It came in the form of apprenticeship training in custom-tailoring. Just as in the story of the wasp and the bumblebee, as soon as he was able to make the honeycomb, and ran off to phone me. That was enough, he thought, so he quit the learning process, too fast, yes.

Got himself a sewing machine and a house dress, at last. Started out passing himself off as a tailor, unsuspecting that many were to be hooked and dragged into the failure. Did that for well over twenty-five years. Well, you know, one tends to get better with time and enough opportunity to steer and practice. Even in such things as that, and this.

So, he wasn't too far off the mark after all. Migration was to eventually find him and become a viable option to call. Started traveling; straddling the islands in search of work, yes, that one he hopped upon was a jerk...

"Chicken?"

"Of course, he's in..." he did manage to find some, but there was still an inner burning desire for more. Somehow, life holds more than this for him and me in the stores. Those island-hopping roads lead further to North America. Speaking of roads, that's where he ended up earning that somewhat "livable" income, with love. He became a bus driver, which was to see him spending long hours on the roads and then some more in the glove.

Other side effects and things were to come with this, too. Like, Winsome and the chances of seeing how people tend to behave in certain situations, and with you, Ms. Love. Like, while operating a powerful piece of machinery such as an automobile, he got to see quite a bit of that in the deal, and yes, did some power-tripping of his own there, too.

Like, on those lots of high heels on the wheel while wearing away at his shoes. Among the benefits was that he had quite a bit of break time between each trip to rest and wait for the next trip time to float around. Being a person who was into reading before, he would use some of these break times to do just that and more, like read.

But then, one was to see the opportunity there to write, too, and he did. Started writing down those stories as he saw them, weekly. Or some of the more outlandish types of behavior that he would have witnessed on the road from time to time between friends, believe me.

"From the savior?"

"Said speed, mi likkle bredda pickney." Over time, he'd amassed a stack-pile of such tales documented. Not in any formal way, not with any plans or intent to do anything whatsoever with any of it to go and tell-say. I guess the gods were at work behind the scenes, or perhaps a soul had died long ago with unfinished business that included writing and making a mocking fool of something out of itself and him.

That soul seemed to have (somehow) bumped into him and gotten a rebirth. Whatever the case, he started writing (inadvertently, at first.) But then, here comes the wonders of the "online, internet age," and pushers pushing ideas through the wavy cage. Sellers who are always selling all sorts of nothings in Arcadia on the rage.

They sold him on the idea that: if he had ever written anything, or even thought of doing anything such the likes of these things. They could make it all happen for him, like magic on the ice. (Look at them spinning around the bride.) He bit the bait and ran. By the time he'd managed to realize what was happening, he'd spent way too much money buying into the idea that he was a natural-born writer.

Big things were waiting to happen just beyond the next payment from him to them and wider, from you and me, too, as they hid and bit the bait that bit a sumptuous bite out of her. But, of course, it never came. He was angry and disappointed. Couldn't stand to even so much as look at the stack-pile of papers that he ended up holding on to (the anointed). Beyond me, alright then.

But two to three years later. He couldn't suppress the swarms of biting bugs any longer. Furthermore, he still has those long breaks to contend with between bus trips. So, he picked up the pen again, like this. Well, it was really the phone; he would have quickly learned how to make use of some of those notepad apps on his phone.

Several stories have passed through his gadgets since then to find a way home. Yes, the more he writes, the more his craft improves overnight, I think. At times, he was at a loss to think that those things came out of him. Which was to further convince him that the ghost that had possessed him when he wasn't looking was really at it and working. So far, he has Amazon-published titles such as these and those:

How to train a wild puppy dog named Manley. Plus, the "Real Inky Trails" series, including,

New Hiking Trail Casts Shadow on the Tattooed

TWISTED TALES from the BIG FAIL

The Sword, the Word, and the Writings.

The Shirt Depot, and

Backsliding, amongst others.

All are available wherever books are sold; if you don't see it, ask for it; they'll get it for you and the household. Who knows, it could be where another story will take shape on his journey and be born. The moral here is this. If you were born for this, or, it for you? You can do it; however, nothing is going to happen for you unless you hop on the horse and ride. If and when you get thrown, pick yourself up off the backside near the tailbone, get back on the mount, and ride like the devil is at your heels. Because she probably is.

### Don't Ever Grow a Cow. A poem of the times, somehow.

Ever thought about what it really means to "grow a cow"?

So, something must have been wrong with the thinking of the banana man. How else could he have gone and thrown five she-goats in with a big black ram? One should never grow a cow to send one's children to school, not when there are so many other outlandish tools, like those that we gave to poor people like fools, and coming at them in the ways of the Robin Hoods. But what else can you expect from their hands? After all, they're merely those types of politicians, coming in to call someone. They promise you the world on a silver platter with no food in hand (it's improper), none at all, man. It's a terrible thing, "Yes I-yah," like the Mutant of a Barak cuter would say best to yah. Give it to her, though, she, that's our Mona Lisa for thee. She's pretty and is sometimes witty. She's a temptress, she's a lady. Every man wants to father her baby, well, maybe. But then again, maybe not. Perhaps growing a cow is not too lazy after all, on the lot, and getting fat.

"We have given them this," she said, "and we have given them that, we have given them a couple of chicks to put in the pot," well, perhaps. An offer of goats, too, was coming in ones and twos to go grazing on the lots with you. This was to come at the mouth of one who talks a lot, "Like who?" You'd asked. Surely, not you. But they, them, growing a cow to send their children to school, can't do it because it's against the rules.

Meanwhile, crime rates go nowhere but up, while they complain and apportion blame as to who is at fault. Which of the many is more responsible for that, on the asphalt? While the most fertile arable land anywhere under heaven's sun lay waste and bare, under an abundance of

Idle hands, and spent sun, there. Because the youths are made to think that growing a cow is stinky, not something to do to send one's children to school or to learn how to think... ee, like for themselves. But look at her working that dress, she's so pretty, it's like a sin to confess. As for the other one, they called Davion, he sure knows how to stir things up with his tongue. "Oh, come on! Put it down." "Okay." While she works that body to make heads spin, trying to see. As for the ears and what's in between there, though, as shallow as they come, or as one could ever hope to have seen bare.

"Oh, no."

"Yes, bro." As for those who would have looked past the dreams, she has grown proficient at selling. Boy, that woman sure is pretty and pretty good at pulling the woolen things over the eyes of lickerish, dribbling, watery-legged men... kinds of things like I'm here selling the little...itch. She, along with her friends, offered them goats and two baby chicks. Two tiny chicks and a day's worth of feed to go with it. That should be enough to satisfy them and their needs. "Oh, sheet! What a lovely breed." As for the dog and the pigs. Be on guard with these, because. *That's waa gwine nyam yuh suppa, after dem done trick you and lef you fei suffa.* They never could. Never did, never will, this is known by everyone, but still. Paying their utility bills is now the latest trick. They never delivered that promised land, zinc, or a brick. But if the rats, hawks, and mongoose of sorts ever get to those chicks before you do, to get them in a pot over the fire, cooking up a stew. That's probably what's going to happen to those cute little chicks, too. One way or another, it's coming at you from the father. I must go now, but remember to forget the cow. Don't ever grow a cow to send your children to school. *But a really waana ask Di I "dem suppn" now. Did the Mona Lisa's mama say this, about growing a cow*? Hiss. Well, now hiss again, and say, "Wow"! Cause, *dah one yah really tek da cake yah, yes, I-yah. "Unnu nuh hear the lady*?" As the Muta man would be heard saying it to me and the baby: Don't you dare cultivate a peppering plant to jerk a sow. Whatever you do, don't even try to grow a cow.

Here's another 5–7–5 haiku poem for you.
Pity the dumb king.
Left stranded in a bombed tin.
No man would save him.
Ever thought about what it really means to "grow a cow"?
Here's another 5–7–5 haiku poem for you.
Pity the dumb king.
Left stranded in a bombed tin.
No man to save him.

### Twist Again.

Twisting hard against more spinners in the soup for them. An outsider's view of big Earth from Moronia, where I come from first, every time, to look at it around here.

Spin doctors were seen doing it, twisting and spinning away at the wheels with you in it, but still. I had to ask them, "What's the deal?" This was what they told me when I was out there in the fields.

"See that cat?" Look at that. That cat came in when he first came, under a cloud of election fraud. Theft again, like they did last summer, and foreign interest meddling, in the yard down under, the one with a known name, yes. "Oh, Lord, I wonder..." On through to boldly inviting foreign leaders like you to be meddling in "Our" elections, to secure for you and him a win-jection of some sort of flashback from rejection, cash-trapt; no cash.

That would have happened just before they came into the campaign proper, from a slow dash. From that starting point to a place where the cat is now refusing to concede to that defeat (I ain't eaten yet). Eying them lying and saying that the real results had secured him the better feat. With threats and pledges to fight on for ages, or for however long it may take to pay these.

Threatening to take them to the Supreme Court, in a song, as the first option coming out of his mouth, against the tongue. But that was the very Court he'd just balanced more in his favor mere days before the election process got started in proper, down the stairways, mi bredda. Against the norms, better judgments, professional advice from babbling clappers, and all decency on the home-ends, Papa. Their days.

Although all indicators were pointing towards him losing again, by a far larger margin than that which he had (supposedly) won by, when he was said to have won an election from them almost a term earlier on, oh my! One which, until this very day, remains controversial (the least to say) about the lift-purse pal. Yet this same one is the cat painting the picture from here, framing the narratives as to the right versus the wrong approaches to such things, my dear.

"Calling the shots over there?"

"Yes," the same cat who was impeached for using the power of the office to further his own causes. Acting in ways to his benefit, supposedly so, but go on, he went, plotting against his opponent shortly before campaigning started to begin in proper on the home men. This he meant, and, raring to go, among other things, such as that cure, to show them.

The same catty person who'd popularized the verse things, in the phrase, "Lock them up," in those days, while speaking those things to keep this "Vic" of a licking stick off his opponents; Dick, Dickson, yes, all of them. Then, to get himself reelected as in the previous election, they "did." None of them whatsoever got to see the hind side of a jail cell, door jamb. Even under his one-term tough luck watch, the poor man.

He, though, barely escaped that fate so, like, so far. With cunning and clever maneuvers on one side of the bar, and some shabby workmanship on the other, blues slide guitar, probably. In both his election campaign periods, pardon me, there came those rhetorical, earth-shattering tremors of fraud. Loudly rattling up from the depths of the dungeon's yard to bother me.

Gladly took the win off them, but would not concede the loss he was dished out and given. He was heard arguing all along, saying that the election, like all other such things, was a fraud and a fake con. How does that even begin to make sense? Not in my Moronian yard behind the whitewashed fence.

Meanwhile, the country was going to hell in a sick, mal-handled crisis basket, to sell... "*Sheet!*" "*Yes, mi seeit.*" Only in Ulysses does one ever get to see things like this and these, or is it? Oh hell! Hardly anyone (if any at all) was out there calling him out on this strike ball. But I was looking down and in. That was when I began seeing some things going on with him, which left me wide-eyed and wondering. "How could they... how could they be there saying those things to him as if to pray?" So, I had to get away from there, to get a Moronian leg in here.

My eyes and ears, too, were zooming in on them and you. That's when I heard the news coming through, but not from the big-time newsmen, you know them, like, the "Who-is-whose," just the mocking comedians, and the open-mike fools.

Looking in from over there? I couldn't help but wonder and wide-eyed stared at them on the stairs. How come this is the same cat latecomer who's here now, making everybody else out to be crooked crooks, cheats, scammers, and election thieves? "Wow!" "Yes." Wielding heavy hammers over their bald and greying heads, in beads? Yes, please, but... Which of these narratives are we to believe? Which one are we going to take with us and them into the tomorrow-lands? "Mama Mia", come, run on over with an answer in a song. Tell me, wasn't he the one who came in on the plan under a cloud of irregularities and foreign interference like these? Wasn't he the same one who (throughout the entire tenner playing the fools there) was seen as acting in an unprecedented manner, in the block out doorways, on the hollowed sphere?

Wasn't he the tomcat little brat who was impeached for things like this and that, like, his actions? Including, but not limited to, trying to tarnish the character and reputation of his boss-man, the very person who was to be his opponent, yes, that one? Along with his family, plan? In ways that, before his time, it was never done to such a competition or opponent, someone?

That was the same one who ended up defeating him so very handily that evening, no? Yes, after several tests and trials at recounts from the thieving... well, no, I'm leaving that one alone (go, west.) Wasn't he the cat who openly solicited the assistance of foreign entities to help him secure a win in victory? Wasn't he the person who made lying straight-faced in high places a thing of no distaste as it was to me?

Didn't he go out of his way and worsen by trying to delegitimize the institutions? The very ones that were designed and enshrined in those places and times to facilitate and support the smooth running of the elections? Such things as mail services, even up to the last-minute courtesies? Yes, that's what my eyes were forced to see, yes.

That's when my Moronian jaw jumped back off the icy taw to ask this of Mister Mistar. "What am I missing here?" Well, as I was beginning to see some things and hear, the fake reporters of the day were the ones who were telling him what to do and say. Giving him fabulous workable ideas like this one, yay. Which was to have grabbed a choke-hold on my neck when they were heard asking him if he would leave the house (willingly) if he lost, (what the heck!)

I was sitting there in my highly perched position in my chair in Moronia, where I come from, to be near you, and musing. Courting a snooze and wandering around on the booze that I was accustomed to using, "What's up with that?" Somebody was supposed to answer me when I asked, but she walked out and left. The cat wasn't even thinking of such things before that wreck, but now? He is, that's for sure, the quiz.

"We'll see, we'll see," so said he, always, with everything they threw at him, on which to gaze, and then go grazing for what next to work on in those days. Then "go out too" is what he does and do-do... Gone about experimenting on the idea, and you. If it works, great. If not, that's what high-priced lawyers are for, and fat like an ape.

But wait, tell me, how does a cat like that get to be the one framing the narrative and calling the shots, on these? Doing so with a chance at walking away as the victim, with ease? The one who was cheated out of a big win? "By a lot, 'by a whole lot' at that?" Follow me along as we go retracing more of the life and times of the unprecedented tantrum, Pete. You'll see that I'm neat in no time. Look.

Pete is now firmly set into the Polly tricks and loving it just a little bit, like, too much for anyone's good. But how did Pete get to be that way with food? How did it begin, and where will it end? In the center of a lame turducken? Perhaps. From somewhere around Thanksgiving pots?

Again, we say, "Perhaps," but. "Hm, hmm, hmm," Um! I'm humming along and listening to the song.

"Will you shut the cup up and listen to me?" His friends were heard saying, trying to get him to see the logic and understand the reasons for the head we need...

"There's a bigger picture here for you to consider, man, whatever the outcome of this one, lose or win, you can serve only two terms, that's a given, and you've already completed one," hooray. However badly some might think of it and say. It's already done, good for you, "let's not spoil it now, okay?"

"But but, but why? Why can't I just keep on going since I'm here doing such a fantastic job, my guy?" an-an, and I — "Because you can't, you cannot serve more than two terms... that is, if, if you should somehow get reelected... You know that you've got to go back to the people at the polls for that to happen, though, don't you? And stop fooling yourself, you're not doing such a great job as you might think. But really, you mean you didn't know that? Have you been looking at the facts and the figures lately? Did you know any of the relevant facts relating to that and such other things before you got into hating me? How did you get in anyway?"

"I I I just walked right in, and the door was wide open, it's a tremendous thing really. I just got up that morning, walked down the stairs, and tossed my hat in the ring (all in). Which wasn't even a ring, come to think of it, just a mediocre, ah, a thing...

"Oh, sheet." Look at him there, flipping the finger ring in the air, while saying. "Full of those with political leanings on every side, doing partisan political things, badly if you ask me. Nice, nice, be nice now. Be sure to ask nicely, always. So, one cat doesn't have to know a lot. I figure that, if you say the right thing, the media will run with it and tell everyone, in writing, including you, me, and the daddy bad man, the right thing, right?

"Right."

Yes, yes, I knew it all along, look at me, see? They'll tell us what to do, so you don't even have to know a thing, nor two, just like the rest of them, and you. One doesn't need to know how to do it, really. And you don't have to pay them either, those fake newsmongers in the media. Only morons pay to get their stories heard. I won't pay a scented penny to those nerds."

Well, that was then, this is now, continuing on is how." I knew the right things to say, so I said them, and the people loved it. And, and, and I also know how to listen for what I want to hear and go bug fit. So, I know, I know... they will tell me the rest that I may need to know."

"So, you got in against your will, against your better judgment, right?"

"Well, yes, yes, somebody has got to do it better than them and best. If we're to make Ulysses great again, so I thought, why not? Why not me? I'm better than the whole bunch of them put together anyway, can't you see?"

"Yay, yay, whatever you say. Whatever the case, though, you can only serve two terms in this race. Half of which we have already done, um, I mean, not that good if I may say so, but with — "No, no."

"No-what?"

"No, you may not, you may not say that, ever. You're going to say what I tell you to say, and what makes me look good all the time, or I'll have you fired."

"You can't... um, you can't tell me what to do, Pete, what I can and can't say or do."

"Yes, I can, I will. I'll do the telling, you will listen and obey orders."

"Well, if you say so, Pete, you're my father. Go on, go eat your cas... Anyway, as I was saying, or going to say. With a little brushing up and tightening up of the "screws" here and there. Those that can be tightened up, like here, and yes, there too." Look at my friend who is there brushing up against his fake hairdo, all over and around the fogged-up square, too. ...And "and yes, there too. If we can get that done..." The brother kept blabbering on, "...we've got a good fighting chance with this one.

We may be able to hatch out a half-decent legacy for you now and going forward from here. That's what we're working on here, dude, your legacy, not food or beer. That's the plan. 'Don't, mess, it, up.'" Look, those words are dropping on the front of his shirt like his puke-up...

"You might do well to try and get some of your cat friends on board with us on this one, well, if you can. And those on the right side of the catfish wish of Christ, too, get them to the prayer line blazing for you. So that you may find favor with the savior, and whoever shall be sitting in that chair after you're done there, whenever. So that they won't be too eager to execute warrants on your meager... I mean, your, your... whatever and executing vengeance, petty grudges, and jealousy like — "No, no, there won't be any need for that show, we're going to continue on, this administration shall continue. We're going all the way, that's the plan (to tin you in.) We're going to continue with this administration, "sin tin." That's the plan, that's the plan."

"You have no plan, Pete, you just said so a moment ago, eat, eat. You walk down the stairs and toss your hat in there, in the ring, and your head then follows the, the... the thing, so I hear." (He was quick to say this and swore to swear on a head spin.) "You have no head," he said, "not a sober thought to take to bed. People... some people have been trying to find it, your 'head,' ever since. That's what I'm trying to do here, too, but you're completely unhinged, from the truth in the hut, I mean — "I'll sue them if they ever try any hanky-panky on this bus. I've got powerful friends and — "Uh! You've got 22 friends, Pete, count them, twenty-one now, twenty — "I'll sue you, too?"

"18 now, want to continue? Go, go right on."

"I'm going to sue all of, all of..."

"You've got 13 now, and sky-racketing, downward. Still wanna go on?"

"No, no, Howard."

"Thoughts so, coward."

Meanwhile, listen, your friends are on the radio again. The other friends, those fake news-monger friends of yours, they're talking to him. Yes, them. Listen to what they're saying. "The president of Kosovo, Hash them Tack-seat. A guerrilla leader in Kosovo's war for independence from Serbia has resigned because he doesn't want his trial to — "What a Pusey, he's a total and complete loser, sure not like me. I hate losers, how could he?" said the president of Ulysses.

"Shut up, Pete," his friend shot back at the wrong cat's feet, that other one, yeah, the president. Unprecedented though he might have been. "You talk just a bit too much, man, for your own good. You'd do well to listen some more, even to him, you might learn two, or one thing, coming backhanded to you, from him."

"When is the election? When is it again?"

"Don't rush it, things aren't going too well for you in that arena, my friend, you could... 'Oh shit, don't... no, I can't say this to him. But I must,' you could lose, Pete."

"Me? Lose to him? To the worst candidate for president there has ever been? Me, loose to him, to sleepy Gilchrist? They would never get me out of this, this... They would never get me out of here if I lost to him. Unless they drag me out kicking and screaming, like, like... that'd be the only 'waey.'" So he says, while spreading his palms sideways, like it was the norm for him to do so, in those days.

"What would I do next? I couldn't show my face around here again. What the heck? I would probably have to go awaey, I couldn't stay around here another daey if I lose it to Sleepy. I'm a winner, winning is what I do, it's easy for me, losing is the hard part. It might be easy for some people, like Gilchrist, for example, but not for me. I'm smart."

"Well, you had better start getting used to that idea because things aren't looking too good for you in this arena."

"If I lose, I'll sue them, all of them."

"Sue who?"

"Them, all of them." (Pointing around...)

"On what grounds?"

"On, on, on grounds of voter fraud for stealing the election. That would be an injustice against the people you know, and the nation, and I, I I will fight to defend them, the people, I always fight for the people over there, Hugo. They're fantastic people, really. I will throw everything at them, including the kitchen sink, just like I've already done to the rest of them, come to think... But, but?"

"But what?" fading out.

Meanwhile, on some other fronts, scrutinizing eyes were zeroing in on him and his past dealings via the witch-hunt. Here's what they found on the revealing, well, as it was to be found coming from among them, and the rest of the thieving... something.

In his media-manipulated business, he was heard saying: "Yes, yes, that will be all, that will be all, thank you, next? What. What's that? You're fired. Thank you, thank you, and go. (Look, lie add.) Thanks for your service, but no, yes, you were good, you did a tremendous job, but you're now fired, that will be all."

In school: continuing from further back with retracing the life and times of the unprecedented Tantrum Pete. Here, he's a young boy in grade school, look at him, and listen to the roll call.

"Donovan."

"Here."

"Pete, Pete, where's Pete?"

"Yes, yes, I'm here, too, I'm here now, and I'm not going anywhere anytime soon. Carry on, carry on."

"That's not funny, sit, sit, sit down, Pete."

In the end, after the election, after all the counting and recounts, surprise, surprise, a new president was announced. Some losers were heard swearing over there, "Hey! Why is the sink still here?" That was while he was being dragged out in handcuffs through the door.

"Move it, move it," said the lead one, wielding the big stick, as they were seen marching the cat out of all of that, and this. Bigger dreamers than he was numbered among those wielding the sticks.

"Hey, hey! Can you tone it down a wee bit?" said another to the whiney kitty-cat kit. "Careful now, mind you hurt somebody. Cut out the crop and move along, man. We've got work to do around here, dead-lines to meet and all and, and..."

### Questions for the Production Line Baby Generation.

Just a few simple questions were thrown out: To whom it may concern. A little thing called:

Questions for the Production Line Baby Generation, and it goes like this.

Did you not know that that is how the thing goes, did you not know? Did you not know that you are planted where the farmer wants you to grow? And that he will pluck you up whenever the reaping gets slow? Did you not know this, little one, did you not know?

Yes, he has fought wars, conquered nations, and handed over "lesser people," but those who were greater than you are, back to starvation. Then walked away with the wealth that once to you, belonged. Claiming it all for his 90th son's generation. Did you not know this, you simple one, did you not know?

But then again, what else did you expect? What did you hope to get? If you despise your forefather's land and give it all up to go off serving another man. Would that "other man" then respect your stance, and regard you as a part of his clan, with an equal share in his master plan? Would he? Little one, would he?

There they are, busy, very busy indeed. Debating truths and amending laws. Pledging loyalty to other entities. Swearing themselves into secrecy, with some other "someone" who didn't give them the key to the entry. Into the newfound powers that they now wield, in your name. Did you not know this again?

Did you not know, did it not occur to you that someone, somewhere, is trying to make a waste of you? He's sitting around, putting a value on your worth, deciding if and when you should or should not give birth. Or even be dead. Did you not know this, little one, as said, did you not know?

If you get your education in the other man's schools, where his scientists and technicians formulate the rules. Or appoint leaders for yourselves who answer to someone else. Wouldn't your destiny be wrapped up in the hopes, dreams, and plans of that other "someone" instead of in your own hands? Wouldn't that be how the thing pree?

What if you should find out what's happening now? In the laws and customs to which you bow? Where doing wrong in the name of rights, with scant regard for what's really right, is what they do, and that it's all designed to make a waste of you?

If you reject the God that you knew, and honor another for the things he does, and continue to do. Then call him up whenever men pursue. Would he then turn around and rescue you, would he, Mister T? Would he?

From primitive tools to shame and ridicule, as well as all the crafts that fall in between. Isn't it fair game for that "someone," if he's hell-bent on doing you in? Because he thinks that there are too many of you, and much too much of your kind, too?

Once he has gotten the numbers down to more manageable and sustainable norms, will he not then threaten with the wrath of God, in the laws he crafts, to bring you back? In numbers that will serve him true, and not make him feel afraid of you. Wouldn't he?

Did you not know, did you not realize that there's a seed of life placed on the inside? From the Tree of Life, yes, it's yours to protect and to bring to life, if you are going to be the next. Or be counted among those who'd survived, lived, and thrived?

If a man will give the right to you to do those things that you should never do. Would it not be very telling, too, just what he really thinks of you? And couldn't he be preparing tools, to waste, and plunder you? Couldn't he? Well, couldn't he?

## Holy Crocodile! What Do We Make Of That, And This?

Daring rescue of a wild beast from behind a crocodile's bad luck. But...

Some time ago, while he was busily doing nothing other than going through the WhatsApp feed on his gadget, the phone thing, you know, yeah, that was it. He'd happened to run into a video of an African wild beast being dragged by a reluctant hind leg to the feast. Yes, the leg was wedged into the jaws of a hungry Crocodile, my child, like this. The cattle beast's right hind leg was wedged up good and proper into the jaws of the Crocodile's clapper. While the beast was being drawn backward into the Lear and domain of the Croc, and to certain death, bad luck, in proper... Of course, it was there, in the deep waters where the beast (definitely) didn't want to be running off to, anywhere. He... well, let's assume it's a "he," he was resisting with everything in him, trying to escape the Croc's deadly death grip, Hingh.

Meanwhile, the stage was being set for another "Repent and be thou saved, oh ye sinful man," sermon. It was narrated by an emotional Christian brother; one would have known this much because of how he started out and then continued on to compare the whole scene proper, Leigh, to the life and times on the journey of a Christian like me.

God surely doesn't like ugly, boy. God doesn't like crocodiles either, so it would have seemed, probably because they are so ugly. It sure would seem so to me, yeah, I'm very mean.

In his mind, it would have appeared to us as if everything there with the breath, or even those without breathing breath in the nostrils to spew or spit, were there only to be used as props on the set. Designed to teach greater lessons to the believer, or even the unbeliever, who is to be the next one targeted to be converted into a receiver, perhaps. Well, everything other than for the Crocodile, mi pops. The Croc, for his luck, or even for the lack thereof, seemed to be likened to the devil's tools on the truck, or to the devil himself (tough luck). No one seemed to give a rat's assumption about anything about the life and times of Croaky the crocodile and its sin, so it would seem. But, as far as others are concerned, some of us have other notions about that, as was learned.

I, for one, have got a feeling about the Croc, and if you are a thinking person, more or less like the duck, or worse, you (probably) will too, because... After all of these happenings are done and over with, and many are gone to a forgotten land quickly, quick. I have a feeling that the Croc will still be here. Yeah, that sure is sick, my dear.

The Croc is a survivor; she has probably seen and gone through many such scenes in her own life and times before the divers, and her. Like, those other times when no human eyes were there peeping through the door and watching such things occur, nor cameras recording, and she would have lived it out.

Quite unlike how it was to be with some of her friends who did not live it out, like… Three of them came and didn't live it out, four of them came and didn't live it… Oh, wait a minute, no. I've got to stop this. Got this refrain going on in my headed brain, Fitz. Where did it come from again, and so quickly, um, I wonder?

Crocodile, though, had managed to live out a lot of things that could have been living, like still, and found her next meal shortly thereafter. "Chill." Yes, like I'm sure she did after those cameras were turned away from her saucer. Speaking of watching, some others were, be it of the people kind or any other greater or lesser creature kind, round and about those parts on the shore. They were there watching. Many may have been there and wearying themselves away, watching, until they couldn't watch anymore, because, well, look at him, you know the score.

They would have been trying hard to ensure that each individual: I, me, or even "we." Everyone among them would have been trying to ensure that, I, I, "I won't become the next victim," you know, like, the next meal for Croaky the Crocodile to go off fixing. But one of them will be, and soon, and then another and another, because, yes, mi goon. Crocodiles must be fed and shall be. Yes, yes, my brother, come and see.

It wasn't games that she was out there playing, like me. Like, stuck in the mud, or touch and run perhaps, or any other such thing as that. She was laboring for food to take back home to the pots, for dinner, for herself and him with spinners, and for her young ones. Well, if she has any, young ones!

According to the website, Pets on Mom. More than two hundred million years ago, crocodiles roamed the Earth among the dinosaurs. A combination of physiological and behavioral adaptations would have ensured the crocodile's survival through the ages, so the story goes on these pages. Croc, therefore, is a survivor who just happened to have lost out on the favor, like, the charm thing. No one gave her an arm swing to go and give it to him. If they did, it would have fallen off her and onto others from him, probably. And probably due to the Earth's over-warming and the overpopulation "sin Ting," or something. But what's up with all those scary-looking teeth on either side of her beak? Or those hanging on him, looking for something to eat. Like that long, curvy face, thing. Sure, doesn't help her or him any in this case, Singh, nor in winning friends and sympathizers in. Never was found lucky enough to have had many in her corner, clamoring to surprise her, shouting "happy birthday" in wishes and cheering her on, through the inside door. None to protect her from harm or from the threat of extinction.

But she'd managed to live it out, and many of the other kinds, too, roundabout him and you. She would have lived them out, those other species men would scout. Those who used to be, but aren't anymore. Like, those whose dried and well-preserved corpses would be lucky if found still hanging on some museum wall as props, or on a hunter's shelf, behind the door stops. Even them.

But Croc's God has been good to her and him, this I'd say on the risk of sin. She's still here and hanging on today, on a limb to prey, not on a wall, but on a "want to run away" hind leg. Which currently belongs to that beast who is finding with every breathy pant of his, that it can't, no, I mean, it cannot run.

But, as for you and me? Wake up and come see, yes. Now, tell me, who among you was he, or she? Which of you was there rooting for the Croc, urging her on and in for the killing, good luck, so that she could have dinner too, to go home and cook, and like, like, have a meal? Or to be fed along with her family in the deal? That's what she was out there laboring for, you know?

But I forgot, she's ugly like I'm not, huh-huh, why did you laugh? *Bwoy, clear off, and gweh yah.* So, as for the Croc, she should not be fed. Unless it's to somebody, and with bread. Right? Right, mi bred. That's just how things ought to be and go. No? Oh, well then. Over to you, oh. Such a shame, though.

**The Road is a poem about road death and safety.**

In solidarity with all who lost loved ones to the streets, it goes like this.

### The Road

Lilly white roses, yellow, pink, and red, freshly cut flowers piled high in a bundle. Monuments of sacraments amidst the flickering lights of the many burning candles. Heartfelt offerings from strangers and friends, for one whose life on this very spot met its fatal end.

I see them there, a teddy bear, on well-carved lawns, corner lots, I see them everywhere. Bouquets and crosses mark the sites of loved ones' losses. That bridge once crossed means innocence lost, and another mother cries. Papa sighs, crying, sighing, for a child who's not coming home. Much too soon gone.

Ghost cycle painted white, chained up against corrugated lampposts beneath city lights. There, on the corner where his last ride ended in doom. It's an exhibit there in memory of one, gone way too soon.

Holes burn black in asphalt that marks well, the spot. Twisted metals and debris there, I see fragments of the impact, which sends unsuspecting souls to yonder homes, never to return here. Dangers, they say, lurk on every road, some real, some imagined; beware, users, beware.

Firemen's hoses' powerful beams wash the bleeding down a sewer stream. Yet, while one walks these shiny streets, the bloodstain whines beneath the feet. Those trucks and cars with flashing lights, as seen from afar through the still-dark nights. Weary troopers, fast losing sleep, must reopen these roads, so with brooms they sweep. Mop, wash, and scrub the surface clean of all that's left of a mother's treasured dream.

Calvin drove his Cherokee Jeep down a ravine sloping steep. Into the icy cold water, it sank deep, nose first down, and bubbles came up. Then the snow fell down and covered him in. Yet the road just keeps on twisting, turning, winding along. She marches to the beat of her own tam-tam. She doesn't care much about all that vroom, vroom, vrooming along.

Honking, flashing, flipping, crashing. Rolling up in mangled, wreckless abandon of foolish exuberance, as wrapped up in the hearts of the simple and the young. She's just the road, friend, and foe of the wayfaring man. She takes one from point A to B and all other points in between them. Other than that, she doesn't give a damn.


**My Little Piece of the Dream.**

I wanted my little piece of the dream, so I skipped on over to the other scene, leaving all that I ever knew, and all who were familiar, too. When I got there, I'd arrived, I swear.

But while I was still there, many things I was to hear. I heard them talking ever so often, talking talks of what makes the place tops. I never did get out of the starting block, let alone out of the rut spots.

But as for them and how they plant, they can do whatever they want. I sure would like to do that too, but I never could find that foot of the shoe.

They never did seem to work very hard, at least, not quite as hard as my playing card. Yet they say that's what I ought to do, I obediently did just that too, and then, as for them.

They can just take off on any day, going on a vacation somewhere, so they say. Going to wherever, to do whatever, and whenever, but as for me! I could never, even though I'd like so much to. To do what they say that I ought to.

So, I worked harder and watched them get richer, and yet I could never get any further or anything whatsoever. Other than debt and waiting in the wings to come and swallow me up, and to get it, is death, always.

Even though he most assuredly knows that I don't really want to go, and yet. "Real," they say, is the dream. For whom, I ask them? For them, maybe, but as for me. This dream, it would seem, is not to be.

Note: Just a note to say "thank you" for choosing to read my book and for sticking with the story thus far; you must be liking it a lot. At this point, I want to ask you, my reader, to take a minute to post a review on the Sales pages at Amazon and/or any other such sales pages. This small gesture is so very much appreciated. So, go ahead and show the vine some love. Unlike what the one with the hate did. Don't keep it to yourself; be sure to share this. I thank you.

## Lead Sheet into Tug Life. Yeah, it's a long story.

They were friends and playmates, less than a day separating them from being the same age; one could scarcely separate them in the early days. Sigismund and Welton grew up together there on the island. Welton migrated to North America with the wild one, the other half of the timely twins, known to us as Welton and him, remained on the square, changed his name somewhat there, and ended up in a gang, leading it along.

Sporting guns and cars and girls as you are, and flashing cash, tainted cash for sure, and lots of it to help him score. Then came that fateful day when Welton, the expatriate friend from a long time gone, returned home to spend time burying a close family member and a friend of mine. Guess who showed up again, asking for financial favors from him, like handouts and such other things? Yes, Big-Sig it was, Sigismund the tug.

Siggy wasn't asking for handouts because he was cash-strapped and in doubt, like, needing a helping hand up and getting out. No, it was just the way things were done. Big Sig runs things around this neck of the hooded town now, and if you're to be even so much as passing through town on the way to Sunday school, as it was known. Chip switches to enforce his rules in his town and is careless enough to pass under Siggy's radar up the slide rule bar. Don't be found skidding back down the hot tar.

You had better be sure to have enough dough in your pocket row to pay the toll, at the get-go. Otherwise, be prepared to pass up on this week's quota of blessings from the hand of the Lord. Because she most definitely won't be receiving this week's incremental installments to pay the rent on such, she meant. Not for the daily feeding, nor for your handling, arms-length. It will be given over to care for the needs of Brother Sigismund's car and spent.

As is now the case with Welton, she most definitely won't be receiving that one from them, or whatever else the pay-up name would have meant. It's not going to be forthcoming this time, no, not at your hands, Welton, or nine. So Welton was in for a rude awakening from his slumbering journey. What transpired from there is the stuff that makes for a thrilling story, such as what is just about to be seen happening over there near Ghearny, where he used to live.

Welton handed off a handful of bills, trying to buy his way out of the sure bloody spills; the spilling of his own migratory blood, if you will. Good enough to buy himself a free pass, this time. But he'd better be gone quickly before Big Sig gets home to find out that those bills aren't the real free-flowing kind. They were specific to a particular shopping store line, like some sort of reward to get one coming back the next time. But Welton was long gone when Siggy found out what his friend had paid him to spend. Look at his reaction when he got home into the light and started counting it out that night, again. He was as mad as hell and swore that Welton had better not come back, or else. But he did, and that was when these things began to happen, on the skid.

It started much earlier when Welton was privy to witnessing a dusting in the early days. Like, in front of our very eyes, yes, before he'd gazed on him, and me. It would have happened when Siggy shook the lunch money out of Sean's stonewashed jeans and walked away with the entire "sunny means." Sean had to then lie his way out of another bout of beating and dusting of sorts, at the hands of his own sweet and dear loving father's lusting parts. "For what?" You'd asked? For losing his lunch money to a group of boys, or another such disgusting ploy. Surely not to just one very well-known kid named Big Sig.

Welton was in for another rude awakening on his next return trip home from foreign. What happened there is the stuff that makes up for this thrilling story here, and to go and share the comments when he gets back down off the air. Well, if. But he didn't know squat about that and this, as it was to have turned out.

...

Three degrees higher than yesterday, the heat has gotten up on the wrong side of the bed again today. Even in the shadow of the Poinciana tree, she felt as if she was bread in the oven baking patties for tea. Shannon could see the motorcycle approaching from half a mile down the road in, peddling his wares, trading, and coming towards them. Of course, it was him, Fudgy was riding his motorbike towards them, seated there in front of the luscious load, as usual.

She was quick to see him because she was standing at the half-open gate since, since... Just a little school gal, you know. The reluctant gate itself was resting on her backside all the while, while she was waiting, and looking out for him. As such, coming things were prone to be done, as shown to us on this very evening. She had been looking out for him all morning long, and into the afternoon song too. Readying herself to go about singing a sweet, showering refrain on you.

Trying to see a sign of the ice cream man walking the line and coming on through, or more like, riding. Riding his bike into view, just to get things she likes a lot, all settled in correctly, and not running headlong into you on the head block, Leigh. At the same time, she was in the middle of praying, yes, praying that today was going to be a good day's win, for her, of course, not him. She was praying that her mother was going to be a bit richer today than she was yesterday.

Most importantly, richer than she was the last time, when the ice cream vendor of class and flying high, on my end... and had happened to walk the lined path in and to pass by this way. That would have been last week at this same time of day. She was hoping then, too, with the same outcome on which to chew; nothing. However, she's super optimistic still. Hoping that her mama would be able to get her something soft and sweet out of that fudgy miracle box of his. "Cool, nuh man, just chill."

The box that he carries behind his back on the motorbike usually contains the creamy, delightful goodness that she likes and craves all the time. But can only hope to get a sign of some of the times. Like, more or less like when Santa pops into town at Christmas time. Yeah, man, you know what! That Santa friend of mine tends to be kind and caring like that. As for Fudgy and Mama's lucky charmer, though? Not so much so. Quite unlike how things are with some other superstar, as may be seen happening now with that Savia friend of mine, and hers.

Savia, Shannon's best friend to her, from her savior. Look, look at her and her misbehavior there again. She's dancing and skipping away gleefully at the hind side of her mother's lovely backside and hugging her waist above the bow-legged knee pulley now. Oh boy, wow! That woman is really blessed, yes, she was born with a golden spoon wedged up somewhere between her jaw, they say.

So far, all the evidence is bending towards supporting those claimed bear paws, okay? But now, look at her, she's standing up for the right of the good name there again, you know. Center-staged between the ice cream vendor and Skipadidoo dancing, Savia. She whose fingers and thumb were just a moment ago, merrily and brightly rampaging through that purse of her mother's and hers. Searching for the exact change I'd supposed, to pay the ice cream salesman or Fudgy the fee, for the tax man and me. Whichever one of those names one may choose to call him, half-heartedly.

The choice of name is probably going to be dependent on which treat from the box excites you more, in fact. That will probably be the deciding factor in which of those names one may choose to place on his door frame from the box, no?

"No, not on the door frame but on the head of the ice cream vendor and village clown named..."

The man who's riding the cycle with the motor and coming on down, is he. That box on the bike belongs to the same cycling salesman, not me. Look, it's coming up behind her, that's for sure the proper win to find her door, on the score. On any given day on Caymana's shore, he could be more. On one day, he may be fudgy, but on the next, he could just as easily be creamy. That's what Shannon is going to call him today after feeling me.

Savia's glad bag is just about ready to pop open and burst, as Creamy, the ice cream vendor, is doing his chores. Look, he heaves up the liberally charged cone of heaven's creamy delight, just high enough by way of a well-trained flick of the thumb to allow her to grip the filled-up cone and separate it from the empty ones to bite. Those who will be next in line for the same frozen delightful treatment of thine are left stranded on the stack behind. Ready and waiting for her mama's teeth mint, too, perhaps. Not mine, though.

Or, perhaps he'll roll the fudgy box to a stop or two down the street yonder by you, he meant to, and would surely love to do that, and that's the truth. But better than all that would be a mother's command for him to stop at Shannon's doorstep. Hmm-hmm, um, look at that. Savia's lips are now rapping a hip-hop hot chat up the charts, no? "No, not up the chart but, wrapping around a sumptuous mouthful, trying to chew, but it's freezing up her sick tooth." "True," while the other hand, instinctively, fell palm-up to the underside of the cone cup.

Right there, look, it's there where it appears as if, at any moment, the top-heavy scoop head overloads of ice cream could breach the code and fall off (high scream!) and onto the hot asphalt at her feet on the road. Of course, it could; it has happened like that before, and it wasn't good. But not today, no such chance of a score. Once is enough for such mess-ups of yours, no more. But still, she's not going to be leaving things up to mere chances. Not on mere will and the strength of the cone fill, or any other such nuances. Now, look. Look at those wiry legs faking the dances, yes, yes, my sis. But why shouldn't she? She's luckier than Shannon and me.

Shannon would have been dancing too if only she were as lucky as Savia is getting to be with you. Right now, even. Like, with her having the ice cream she'd wanted, and her mom as a friend there handling the man and you, not me, a rathid. But, as usual. Not so with the new gal, at least, not yet. Will she be getting lucky today, too, or not? The odds are biased towards supporting the "not." Because, Mavis, look at her there where she usually sat and squish-squish. Shannon's mother isn't rich, but she's sitting not too far behind her daughter in her tiny crevice.

She knew fully well that Creamy was on the way down to bold bully hell, trying to find her, as you can tell, no? "No." Well, let's just say, to get them sold on the sale, to sell refreshingly cool ice cream on a scorching hot daily sunbeam. He's coming down to quell the steam. Yes, look, he's coming towards her doorway, leaning now. If the call was to be coming in her favor, it would have begun to come already, and to save her. From the mocking, uppity head-spin, and wiry-legged dancing off Savia, if nothing else. But no, not so. So, run, run, look at her go, she's running.

There goes Shannon, running. Down to her favorite nearby watering hole in the river, drowning, she ran, pulling her clothes off with her hands, like, however, and whenever she can... can, anyway. Then jumping in... Well, she's not too focused on the "drowning" part of the thing this evening, as you can tell it even to the thieving, ugh, something.

"Whoa! Is the water really this cold?" Shannon was heard asking whilst shaking her soul, her teeth rattling up steam against everything... No, not really everything, I meant to say, each other. Just up against each other within. However, look, she's back out of the blue holey water now, and into the full glare of the mid-afternoon sun properly to blow-wow. In a minute or two, she'll be as good as new and feeling perfectly fine. Even as fine as me and you, but. As of now, the shake is on.

"Wow! I wasn't feeling this cold when I was in the water a moment ago," she noted on the sandy tippy toe. "Perhaps I should have stayed in, but. How is that even possible? Is this supposed to be happening? How come..." Ah, just then she would have recalled what Ms. Shirley Frass had said to them in class last week, yes, as a matter of fact, Mass Kid. Something to the effect that the inside space and the surrounding temperature, and some pressure, help to decide how one interprets the overall temperature.

"If your body temperature is warmer than the surrounding temperature in a room, for instance, then you'll be feeling cold (or colder) on your skin at that very instant."

"So, when you say, 'I am cold,'" asked David, son of the shepherd. "What you're really saying is 'I'm hot?'" Or better said than that, you're saying, "I'm warmer? My body temperature is warmer than the space in this roomy corner, right?"

"That is correct, David."

"Ah! I see," said David Shepard and me. Now, excuse me, please, I need to go and take a peep at these, like, I'm going to take a peep at looking at a pp-peeping scene in the lavatory.

"Who needs ice cream when there are blue holes in which to to... to jump and swim and spree?" So said Shannon on the run again, towards me, before plunging headfirst into the water and under the currently cold curse of current like an Olympic gold medal swimming prospect. Medals for the purse, yes.

It's getting dark now, down by the river, and Shannon is alone in the riverbed. Well, as far as she can tell. But she suddenly began to get the feeling of eyes watching her from somebody's half-hiding head. "Hurry up and get out of this freaking gully, girl," said Shannon upon a pulling action over the curls. She pulled up the Pum-pum shorts around the curves fast and shortened the work of the left hand at pulling on the pulley, nearer to the curls than the boss man, and me.

She bent down and picked up her sneakers with the same left hand, as she tossed the button-front shirt across her shoulder with the right one. Somehow, she didn't feel the need to wear the top, even after all that. And the sand felt really soothing under her feet and squeezed up through her toes. This was what decided the matter for her as to which way the shoes should go. Smooth and soothing is the light ahead of the way for her to show, leaving the bulk of the darkness with the river down there, and with whoever else might be there, sneaking a stare.

She can slow down and cruise into the harbor now, because she's in familiar territories again, somehow. Just about home, outside her house, to be exact. She placed the shirt on the curb and sat on it. Still wearing her bra as the only thing above the waist, Ted pit. The November sun, this far away from the river, still allowed for some heat and gladly delivered.

Now, look at this, here it comes. The car rounded the corner on the approach to her home. She knew right away who it was; it was him. "Yes, it's him," she said. No one can mistake it and separate that car anywhere, from him. Well, not around these parts on the drive-in, but then. Look, let's take a deeper look in.

...

Savia is in the hot seat again. It's Sunday evening, and she's out joyriding with her friends. No, oh no, not her so-called "best friend" Shannon, she's beginning to outgrow that sort of companion on the ship of friends from London, now. Well, so it would seem; she's beginning to find much more pleasure in the company of men much older, I mean. Particularly, that Damion fellow. But now...

Those same longtime friends of hers: Savia and Damion, as it occurs, are like a pod of peas lately, and a devil of a man is he. That's a sure thing for one to see and go talk to Shannon about me. Just in case she might... But Shannon?

They're doing the drive-by sing-along song again tonight. Just a promenading spin around the block, and along the scenic route off the posh neighborhood where the rich and famous folks around these parts live. Yes, on the waterfront near the bridge, port, of course. Courting Waterloo, where they go to do what they do when not doing the play-of-the-day and sporting the fee off you.

"We're robbing this one tonight," said Damion, to his friends' fright, and they laughed. But when at last they could finally recompose their body parts, and fully digest the weightiness of the impact. That was when they'd noticed the fact that Damion wasn't laughing. He wasn't joking as she had supposed, and thought, spin, he was as serious as serious could have ever been.

The mischievous glitter in his dark brown eye, like a splinter, gave little away as to just how serious he really was that day. Well, it was just about when the darkness fully set in to go play, after the evening had sulked, tumbled, and fallen off the Edgewatery Bay.

"Those eyes," she whispered and mused to her friend about the guys. Shannon's whispering surprise felt coming from warm breath beside... her, dripping the words down to fall on her inner thighs, sure. Well below the gaze of the man's eyes that were, at the time, overseeing them via the rearview mirror, but not close enough to overhear her words.

Aren't they the most beautiful eyes you've ever seen? Looking up at Savia, she heard it as it was said to her again, about him and his behavior, I mean... and she'd laughed. Laughing, giggles at how much truth was wrapped up within such talk, disheveled though it was, and still is, of course.

"But then again, how many eyes have you looked into to, to... Save? Eyes that were to be found at the time, upping the shades, and upstaging a teenage girl's lustful brainwaves anyway?"

"None other than... um, or maybe?"

"Maybe what?"

"Never mind that."

Quietness now, in the car seat out back.

She's looking in again tonight, or out. But squarely at him and his braided brain covered up, and tight. "Now, shout."

"So?"

"Yes, too tight as a matter of fact, for a 'man' like that."

"Well, perhaps, perhaps we could do something about that," said Savia, almost as a whispering thought. "That's not too bright, though, what you mean by 'we,'" Shannon remarked. As events and time would come to show, she was right. Yet, they laughed because it was funny, in fact. Except when and where it applies to the real truth about such things as that. Those who cannot face the daylight schemes of things. In such a case, it's not that funny. Shannon knew it. "Want to bet that on the money?"

"Yes, but, oh, those eyes again,"

"Those eyes, sure are bright, for real."

They're off to get a move on hot wheat bread, to go along with the fried chicken of Ken's fame, before homing it back home to bed, and the crib again. To go and get overly excited with them. He's got his sparring p... with him in the pan, and that was when...

Murder She Wrote. "Or was... wasn't it Red rum?"

Savia was standing there at the corner of the street in the square when she called out the slang of the week, "Red Stripe Beer," she said, so to speak. That's when they looked up and saw them, on the run, running away from the scene that night, and out of town. This was after she'd seen a police party approaching, coming on down.

Savia's stage show act was designed as a disguise so that those men (her friends) could make an escape and get away from them, guys. In time to go and hide their guns, bloody clothes too, those that were stained with the leftover spills from their games, from you. She was placed there to slow them down, yes, the police patrol, "If they should drop into town." By walking out into the street in her leggings and skimpy pum-pum shorts under her mini skirt, clothes of sorts. Those she'd picked up from the new store that had recently opened up on the corner, Victor's Reveals it was what they'd named it. Just next door to the old, Vickie's Secrets, but they couldn't keep it, that's why...

This act was designed for that very purpose, to slow them down, by showing off her buffs, knowing full well that they would want to stop and chat off their mouths with her guts. Trying to get a taste of the pretty pp...pea soup with the p-p meat of the week, you know. While giving the armed men time to get away and go home. "Sweet ee?"

"Yes, like marrow bone, mi pickney." Meanwhile, the men would have gotten enough time to run down the back alley and across the gully to make the getaway and make it safely home. Most folks around these parts knew these men very well; they have always known the score but will never tell. As everybody already knows, they don't work.

"They never do a hard day's work in their lives," some would confess at the point of the hidden knives. Yet, they're the ones who are always sporting coils of cash and such the likes. They drive the most expensive cars on the roads and bikes. They have all the pretty girls too, as you already know this truth. "Yikes."

"Like whom?"

"Like Savia, for instance, and now this little one in the room, still not yet fully grown to go the distance. What's her name again?"

"Shannon."

"Yes."

"Yeah, man! She same one, sweet Shannon."

So, the two girls were left there to their own devices, sitting there in the back room of the house, as the choice was. Sigismund and Damion had just slid out of the house to go and grab a bite of some kind of grub. Well, that's what they'd said to the girls, left sitting there, by the bed of pearls. Down at the shop, though, Sigismund and Damion didn't show. They'd gone to do other business somewhere across town, no? Yes, that was the reason why they were so long gone, as seen through the eyes of Savia and Shannon.

Welton was lying on the sofa, back down, battling the sleepy eyes that were just about coming on, while entertaining the late show on the television. Bang, bang, bang, came the battering sound, pounding on the door to try and break it down. "Open the door, open up. This is the police; this is the cops," but it was not, though Welton didn't know that. He popped the door open to his own demise; it came at him with such a great surprise. Damion and his friend both pulled guns and aimed, starting to demand "everything" from the trembling Welton. "Unashamed." He didn't know who the other man was, since he was covered-faced under his plan-tam, hands in gloves. Welton couldn't run, nor could he respond in kind. Like, to deliver in the same way as those intruders had demanded, at his shaking hands. He was home, yes, but his luggage was not.

They were to follow him today, or on some other day thereafter, and that was that. That was the wrong answer, as seen through the eyes of the gangsters. "You're a dead man, Welton," he said, before shots rang out, bang, bang, bang, and now, look, he's dead, yes, and gone to bed; now the crooks are running, armed, and scared, under droplets of his migratory blood, bleeding red, out of there.

Running now, towards their regular ways and means, to go river-wash them and get them clean. By the hands of none other than their regular girlie means. All done now, and back at home, drinking champagne, while sitting down, "Ice Cold" is the new name as it's known down home. But then again...

There she was, testing her ability to seduce him and trying to see if she could get him to fall in love with her, in the new scene. For the first time, even. "You're playing with fire," he said. Those words landed like truth in her ear, on either side of her head. She knew it all along (obviously), and he knew it too. But, yes, she wanted to be scorched by his flames, not you. That's why she followed through with the playing of the games. "The loss of a loving gaze from her papa, perhaps?"

"Yes, by any other name, it can surely do such damage to a beautiful girl, and the sane." This same smart one, too, if you'd asked me, but then again. "Mama never was..." Stop. She had to hit the pause button because of that, yes. Because she knew her mother wouldn't be too amused by such words in talk. Especially, not when it's coming from her own beautiful daughter in dishonor, since you'd asked.

Mother Mavis has enough of her own troubles with which to bother and try to fix. She's got her own pail bucket full of ash in the fire pits. Now and then, it would spew, like, whenever the pressure would build up to blow the top off a little piece of her piece of peace and you. While spewing ash on everyone in proximity to the hot fork, and yes, Fitz, on the crosswalk, no shoes. Shannon mostly so, she's always more than inclined to be the one in the direct firing line of it, but. As for her?

Look, Shannon is back there again tonight, so I hear. He was so very smooth and polite with the wrapping paper and the food, after the beer. He came up to her after pulling on the spliff and offering a puff to her. "Take a sniff," he said, cough, cough. Her neck hair raised a degree up, and spread sideways, out. "The long-awaited moment is finally here," she said, communing with the braids on her head. "This is where all reluctance will fall away," I suppose.

She giggled as he came over, kissed her neck in foreplay, and twiddled her nose. Those giggles again, on rapid replay. He gets goosebumps even now; every time he hears the sound, it happens. Her laughter melted him down. She sighed as the TV burst into more applause, jerking her back to attention for a brief moment, on pause. That was when she first took notice.

"He's probably stressed," she confessed, because his stiffness was showing up, as he began to lose control of his smooth. "Aah man! You're too rough," she said, just before the surrender, so I'm told, mi bred, near the veranda... I wasn't in there. She couldn't help herself; she fell in love, just like that. Listen, more giggles. Her willpower wasn't going to pitch in and save her this hour, no, not this time, and so. She tried to escape but could not. She didn't really want to, because... But then again, "Why now?" What a time to remember... She was beginning to remember what had happened when...

The last time she fell in love like this was with Save. Well, it was the first time, too. Few friends ever got as close as Savia and Shannon did in those days. Such good vibes led to sleepless nights, grinning from ear to morning coffee, and no shut-eye, on which to gaze. Couldn't forget how she looked at her then, and you? Nothing. Nothing came from that to fit her shoe. Not even to fulfill the promise of love, no such thing could ever do.

She knew that from the start and also knew that it would be the last time. But she still could not forget how she looked at her then, but now, this is quite another thing coming in at ten. Save isn't here tonight, just Shannon and him. "No, this is not good!" Something's not right, panic-speaking it in her head, "I've got to go," she said. But she did not. They were both much too eager to see, feel, and devour each other in total, like, on the spot.

But first, she's got to rid the heart and soul of the past and come clean. To try and "be real" with each other before that roll call comes chiming in, through each scene. To make things happen as she'd wanted; you know what I mean, right, kid? "Right." Like, to keep it safe and sacred to just them, them, and no one else coming in between. Trying to make it real, and to get it on. But then, she was gone. She got out and ran home to her mom. Got cold feet, you know.

She was the first to fall into it, head over heels in love with Savia in "Ochie." After all, they were first friends, with braids. "Nothing more could ever come of it with the power to stay amended and to fit". Somebody was heard saying "Amen" at this. Promised to keep it safe and sacred to the touch, if they're not to be "happening" in so much. So, they told each other about some secrets amongst themselves, and brought it all to an end, oh hell, tough luck. They were just trying to fill out some empty spaces with something crazy, well, perhaps.

"But, but what for?"

"I don't know, relax, man, relax, my star." Releasing the intense desire for merging, though, maybe that's going to be a harder nut to crack, no?

"So what?"

"Uh, well, let's continue with the talk." She was conflicted as to what to do next, so she waited as long as she could. Resisting the urge to go out and see him again, in the hood, but then... Went over to his place and found him there, alone. "Profound," she said, "but good". She found there that time, the privacy she needed, and also found much serenity in his every jest, as he did what he did. She encouraged more out of him with her every comment. He was becoming kinder to her by the moment, kinder than he had ever been.

Sublime lights spilled in through the drapery and shone up against his face, just as if to remind her later on of all the pleasantries of the place. "We are being called into the immediacy of the moment," she said. But instead? His manly presence was heavy, as heavy as lead. Overpowering her, unabashedly, she fell into the tub. Full-fledged in love, she was, just as she knew she would.

"The moment is here, at last." She whispered this in the inside talks. "This is the moment when and where all reluctance falls away, like crying tears." With no place left for her to run and hide, or to hesitate, in disguise, she took the plunge, much too deeply, as we're beginning to see things now through this side of our eyes, and coming in weekly. His response was quick; she couldn't help herself out of this. Sweet Shannon came forth.

When she arrived home for him, she arrived there for herself, too, first and foremost. But as for him? He'd sensed it coming from deep within. Something was coming out and over on him, from somewhere deep inside her shallow past; he wanted to shout for joy, but covered it up, masked in his mouth. It must have hopped over from her and onto him, yeah, that same ghostly something that I was talking about earlier this evening. Because as he touched her, he was shaking, hard.

Still, vulnerable as he knew she was, yet forcefully, he was coaxing her will along. "Oh, Lord!" The will to come on in and possess him completely. She held her breath, her face felt like fever, it was burning her hot from wanting to deliver. His stiffness showed up again, well, as she was beginning to feel things coming in. He wanted to try her on for size, you know, but this time, oh! Look, look at his eyes! "No!" she whispered, didn't let him, you know, like, stop. Couldn't let him stop, not this time. But then, that was when...

His manhood began sinking deep into her surrendering soul. Oh, Lord! It was hard, but she couldn't stop, all out of control. Sweetly penetrating her flesh, she gave way to her wrestling ways, with the inner powers of a woman being born into freedom. Her wings fluttered. She quivered and broke free from the cage. It was poetry in commotion, as in the phrase. Wetting, spots of warm crystal balls started sliding deep into her innermost being near the wall, to the bottom, even.

She melted right there on the floor, beneath him. Burst into tears, and weeping, then, it was done. Well, almost, but as for her? She was nearly spent. The tears ran down her face, she wanted something more to completely fill up the empty space, but, but, but. "What was that? He was not, like, not breathing heavily anymore. Or even at all. She rolled him over when she was too long done, waiting for him to move at her beck and call, and come. But as for him?

He still wasn't coming home, not anymore. With the wonder of wonders coming on more "some," she left him lying there, naked and bare, picked up her feet in her hands, and ran. She ran down the long path, out of there, and home. He was done, nothing spared. That hunk of a man, Damion. What went wrong? It will be someone else's job to find that out, among other such things, to search out and scout.

As for Shannon? She's long gone without, like, without — "What, a man?"

"No, without a word of mouth, because she's not speaking anymore, now. What she thought she had a lot of is gone a lot.

"Wow! Back, bach home?"

"Well, yes, that too, but not that alone, it's all gone and done."

As for Mama Mavis? She's gone on a different path than that, or this. Her worries have just begun to become a permanent fixture. "Because of that, and this?"

"Sure, yes, because of her daughter who will not speak anymore down sweet Jamaica way, I'm sure." Now, kiss me before... yes, kiss me, like this: hmm-mwah, yeah man, that's it, now, quit, I mean, stop it, because. I'm gone and done. Finish it, nuh man. Well, hmm, muah, again. Yeah, real Jamaican *yardie sin ting, suh, galang*.

Notes: Some lines and quotes in this work may be recognized as familiar lines from some well-known (or not-too-well-known) songs or persons. We lay no claim to the ownership of these materials and only use them on the assumption of a "fair use" basis. And out of pure love and admiration for the pieces, and in some cases, the authors. Thank you.

So why do I write? You'd asked. The answer is: I'm a guy of many words, but whose tongue is slow and heavy, and my words tend to come out awkward and clumsy, so I write because I always have something to say (I think). Which always tends to get me into trouble anyway, now, wink. The extra bonus, though, in writing, is that a pencil usually comes with an eraser. Just here trying to do the right thing for you and the savior.

How far would you go to save someone you love?

**In Name Only** | A poem of the times.

Everybody sitting around was sighing.

As some merely sat and rolled their eyeing.

Because you were there, a baby, crying.

"If you are crying," they were heard saying.

"Then you are not really dying."

It was Diamond Golding and his wife, named Crystal.

Whose daughter, Ruby, was fighting for her life in the sick stall.

But upon finding themselves both penniless.

And wanting their child to have the very best.

Went out and sold off all of their assets.

And yet the proceeds were insufficient.

That prompted them to sign off on the consent.

Which was what permitted the dueling picker.

That same one with the Sterling Silver Clipper.

To chop off her hair for money to pay the piper.

# PART FOUR

# Black Blood: Trace the Family Tree. A short story.

### Description.

Black Blood is a futuristic story depicting a close-up look at the life and times of a fictitious Jamaican police commissioner, Commissioner Watkins, and his many encounters with the count, Count Lasco: a trans-continental drug lord and wannabe Jamaican kingpin. The world was on a comeback trail after "The conflict" had passed, and the countries and peoples that were affected by it were starting to reinvent themselves. While many of those Nation's Stars were still falling in the aftermath of the conflict, other nations' stars were rising at meteoric speed. One such fast-rising country at the time was the tiny island of Jamaica in the Caribbean region.

Commissioner Watkins, aka "Shaky" Watkins, was the top cop of the Jamaica constabulary force then, and he was nearing the end point of his illustrious career when a series of never-before-seen types of crimes started flaring up on the then rapidly developing Jamaican landscape. The commissioner wanted nothing more than to crack the case before he demits office, would he? One way to find out. Come along with me, there are lots of what you want to see, hear, and feel in this story. We spared none of the gory details, lots of blood, thrills, spills, dark humor, and anecdotes. So, look. Go grab some comfort food, pull your feet up beneath the sheets, and let's go back to the future again, for this.

Note: Black Blood is a work of fiction. The names and characters depicted in this story are fictitious and not to be construed as real or associated with any person, living or dead. This, too, is a copyright-protected work. All rights reserved 2017.

B loodlines. The name is the link

There was blood everywhere. Sergeant Kennedy was tiptoeing across the pavement, trying his darndest best to avoid disturbing the scenes. He bent down and examined what turned out to be a spiff tail. "Rogers!" he called out to the young corporal, "Bag it," he said.

Corporal Vince Rogers, being new to the service, had only been on active duty for five days; however, he already felt as if he had seen enough blood and gory mess to last him a lifetime. He fetched a receptacle from the kit and placed the saggy bit of would-be evidence inside, then replaced the cap and set it aside. Vince, by then, was feeling sick to his stomach and was beginning to question his career choice. All of a sudden, the pulpit seemed mighty appealing to him. His mother, too, seemed like the wisest woman who had ever lived.

She had it all planned out for him from when he was a little boy. His mother wanted him, or maybe it was "The Lord," as she would always say regarding this, "It was the lord who had called him to be a minister of the Gospel." But Vince was more than half sure that the Lord would have made a big mistake on that call, too. As for the role model she always pointed him towards, in the person of the Reverend Richard Bultzer.

If she was serious about her son becoming a minister of the Gospel? That would have been a mistake of Titanic proportions on her part, too, to point her son towards the Reverend Mr. Richie Bultzer. Vince's thoughts of him were never very flattering, to say the least. His thoughts about the Reverend were that he was nothing more than a lazy, heartless, bloodsucking piggy-backing leech who "preys" on those silly women with low or no self-esteem.

"I'm not a sissy," he said to his mother, "I will go out and get myself a real job and earn my keep as real men do." So, instead of registering for Bible School, as she wanted him to, the police academy was to be the beneficiary of Vince's coming of age and his search for adventure. If one takes a moment to examine the facts concerning people like the Reverend Mr. Bultzer, and how they flow. One may well be on the verge of a healthy dose of get-with-it reality broadside, Vince was heard arguing on this wise.

Sergeant Adam Kennedy and Fenton "Fats" Michaud were partners in the early days, and they were friends too. But Fenton wound up dead, way before his time, and the sergeant would have gotten himself a promising young constable in his stead (or so it seemed) as his working partner. Sergeant Michaud was a very funny man, among other things. He weighed in at over 320lbs, but very fast was he, and as agile as a Tomcat on steroids, too. He will outrun Usain Bolt on a Sunday morning after a raving hot Saturday night party on the town, with you. Fats was implicated in an earlier shooting incident where he was said to have used excessive force to bring down a shooting suspect, a man who was clearly seen running away from him at the time, yes.

Folks said that the only advantage the poor guy had over fats was his size, and he used it to squeeze through tiny holes and crevices. Such as those that the sergeant could not go through due to the Fat-facts, all were in his getaway bid. "I've got something for you," said Fats, before he lit him up bright with a barrage of bullets and spilled his red blood. Well, so the story goes, but. He wasn't going to lose that one, not again.

"Fats died at his desk," so the official reports said, but we all know very well where officials and their reports stand on the final truth, as well as the trust and confidence index in the mind of the common people, such as you, no? "Yes." Folks said the goodly sergeant died trying to climb Mount Gallimore, on a bunk bed at the office. It was to take two of their strongest young men to pry him off it. Yes, the frightened Galli-mountain. May he forever rest in peace, as he very well might.

Meanwhile, Sadie danced. Silhouettes of dancing Sadie were floating down from the window and floating over the shoulders of investigators and curious onlookers alike. Her relationship with the deceased family needed to be examined, Commissioner Watkins thought to himself. He was going to do just that, that was for sure. The commissioner would have been the first to arrive on the scene after the call. He didn't stay very long, though, just walked around the peripheries of the compound and assigned roles to the next in command. On his way out, He cast his eyes up at the third-floor apartment and saw Sadie standing there, her upper body framed in the window, bracing her stretched-out arms against the windowsill, and looking down at the events as they were unfolding. Commissioner Watkins paused just long enough to survey the settings before moving along, shaking his head in the usual "shaky Watkins" manner. Sergeant Kennedy and the team then went to work gathering evidence.

Crime scene Analysis, these were what the forensic team was to have found and documented at the crime scene:

· Two dead bodies,
· One bloody machete,
· A bloody kitchen knife.
· A wet and saggy spiff's tail, and a trail of blood led from the living room to the front lawn, where one of the two bodies was found.

The trail of blood led them across the hallway, out through the front door, down the steps, and out onto the paved driveway, where the second body was found lying face down on the pavement. Just beyond the cordoned-off area, curious onlookers and tight-lipped neighbors alike were stretching their necks to sneak a peek across the fence. Many among them were probably the same ones who did not even bother to respond to cries for help in the night. Now they are out seeking a thrill, though. All that, plus a senior cop obviously perplexed beyond the norms at what he was seeing. Also, add those newspaper reports and thesis coming in all morning, and later on too. Dancing Sadie was to be called in for questioning and then released. The deceased's lifestyle, too, came in for scrutiny. The verdict was left hanging, for the time being.

...

While Sergeant Kennedy was skimming through the various crime scenes all over town, the commissioner was thinking, planning, and strategizing. He was also sharing anecdotes with his family back home, as he always does. He needed to review all of the incidents in detail, though, in order to see if there were patterns. Any link and tie-ins that could connect one to the other would come in handy. He would later find the connections, yes, but there was much work to be done before that was to come about, and the clock was ticking the time away.

**B**lack Blood? Too black to be that.

They stopped there for a quick coffee break; they weren't going to be very long. So they didn't bother to lock the door of the white Ford transit van. There was nothing in there for one to be overly concerned about, nothing other than those two dead bodies that they had gone to pick up, and those weren't going to be going anywhere anytime soon. They didn't plan on what was about to happen next, though. The crooks were Swift and surefooted as could be. While one of them was there keeping a watchful eye on the lookout, the other one climbed into the driver's seat of the throttling van and drove off. Slowly enough at the start, he allowed his accomplice to run alongside the van and then hopped in. The erring stooges, scampering out of the diner, were to be seen chasing the illusion that they would catch up with the speeding van and regain possession of their belongings, including the stiffs. Meanwhile, look at that, and this. A panicking teenager running out of the diner after them was chasing the two van-chasers while shouting at them to say; Hey, come back here, Sir, Sir, you did not pay me, you've forgotten to pay me.

Later on, down the road, two dead bodies fell out of a moving vehicle and onto the roadway. Or were they pushed out, as some had argued? Police investigators were later found frantically trying to piece together the chains of events that led to two dead bodies lying on the roadways. After a frantic call came in from a motorist who'd reported running over two dead bodies on the road, did he cause the deaths of those two, or were they already dead when he hit upon them? He was wondering. The investigation into that one continues. In the meantime, though, the funeral service people were making themselves very busy trying to keep it all under wraps. How were they ever going to be able to tell the grieving families that they had lost the bodies of their loved ones to a couple of corpse-snatching bandits? Or whoever those two should eventually turn out to be. Luckily for them, though, they had a few things going in their favor; the funeral home people were tops in body makeup artistry, and the bodies did not both belong to the same family, if you'd bothered to ask me. So, even if they should become somewhat suspicious of any inconsistency in the look and bodily appearance of their dead loved one, upon receipt for burial. It should be easy to explain it away, thought the expert funeral planners and embalmers. After all, how likely is it that any one family would have had to deal with burying dead family members to become so well able to tell how a dead body in a casket, ready for burial, is supposed to look? Not having another one to compare it with, or another disgruntled family questioning those very same issues at the same time as they are, and in their hearing? That put the odds squarely in favor of the funeral home people. Furthermore, they were not going to sit around and leave it all up to chance; they were already busy on the job of trying to smooth out the rough spots.

The narratives that were being played out in the public sphere quickly changed from one where a motorist ran over two dead bodies on the roadways. To become one where two men were (apparently) struck and killed by a vehicle that did not stop, and was then run over by a second vehicle. The driver of the second vehicle, thinking that he had run over two people who were there (for whatever reason) lying on the street, then called the emergency services hotline number to report it. He was later taken to the hospital, where he was treated for shock and sent home, the reports said, as is the norm. Someone, somewhere, was skillfully manipulating the facts and painting a different picture. Even though it was black blood that was sputtered on the scene (what little of it there was). That black blood was too black. It could not have been flowing through the veins of someone alive and breathing ten minutes before the impact that caused the spilling out of the black blood. Sergeant Kennedy and the commissioner knew it, but the other version of the story was what was being broadcast on the news all day and into the night. By morning, folks would have swallowed that version and moved on to the next topic of discussion for the day, which suited someone, somewhere, very well indeed; it would have seemed to me and my friend, Ingrid.

Chapter

H op on, we're going down Kingston way
Count Lasco and his crew were regulars for many years on the guest list at the jet-set reception country club near Stinson Pen. His entourage usually included the hippest and richest in the music (especially hip-hop music) and the black film industry. It was not always the same modus operandi, where Lasco would fly in with a bunch of his friends and cronies and party all night. Or party till they drop, however long that might turn out to be, and then leave. No, there was a particular style and flair to him and his clique. Lasco himself never spent much time at the country club. He seemed to use it only as a means to access the special privileges that were afforded to the jetsetters who were associated with the club. But he mostly used the club (as well as its well-streamlined systems) for logistical purposes, and logistical purposes only. It had been speculated that the Count had also been scamming the systems by selling (or subletting) certain privileges to other entities. Entities that got passed off as business partners and associates of his. In fact, he was peddling those privileges to his so-called friends and business associates for a substantial amount of money. So, there was always somebody around the clubhouse who was on the record books as being associated with, or related to Count Lasco, in one way or another, on any given day down Jamaica Way.

Though it may be difficult for some to envision it now, there was a time not very long ago when Jamaicans would have done anything to get out of Jamaica. It didn't matter where they were going; they just wanted out. Many did migrate and swore on their mother's grave (or anyone else's that they couldn't escape) that they would not return there, "Not for all the gold in the world."

"Even if they should find as much gold there as there are bicycles in Beijing," one was heard to have said, "I won't go back there." By the way, there are lots of bicycles in Beijing. Come to think of it, they're plentiful in Kingston, and in Montreal nowadays too.

"I will not return to that godforsaken place even if they should find as much gold there as there are bicycles in Beijing," she had said. But that was then, this is now, "Oh, how things have changed." While some of the very astute and forward-thinking Jamaicans in the diaspora were busily preaching the gospel of the return to the land of their birth, Jamaica. Appealing to them, too, to get involved and help in the building and rebuilding processes that were happening then. At the same time, the government and business leaders on the island were busily carving out new paths into the future. The doubters and naysayers, though, were just as busy. Yes, some were busily dragging their feet along, or holding fast to those long-time beliefs and pledges to never go back. The government and its economic growth teams, though, were making it their mission to go and build a new Jamaica, and build they did, and boy, did the people come? Yes, in droves. A strange phenomenon had started infiltrating the Jamaican psyche at the time. The concept of industrialization, doing things big, like big dreams, big plans, big business, and big money. Making plans about how to make all that money do the work for "us." So, gone are the days of sky juice, suck-suck, market stalls, shantytowns, and corner shops. Jamaicans now have a brand-new outlook on life. She now does things in grandiose style and weight, yes, weighing it all in on massive scales, big enough to be seen from outer space, and with flair and finesse too.

The Prime Minister and his government were stirring up another spirit in the people, a go-getter kind of spirit that sought to equip and encourage the people to invent and create. Rather than just going searching for survival at other men's tables and eating off their plates.

"Don't just think in terms of going out in search of a job, but I'd rather you think in terms of creating one for yourself, and for others, too, if at all you're able. Create something, invent something, and build something of your own, instead of just running around trying to find a job. 'That job which you seek,'" he told them, "If you are to find it, somebody has got to go out and create it for you. Why not be that somebody? Go right on out and create something," he encouraged the people with such words. "Because the other nations that you find to be so desirable now, 'remember this,'" he continued, "remember that they were not always like that, rich and powerful. But they invested heavily in themselves at some point, and what they now have is what you believe to be the best thing since? what? Slice bread? By building yours, investing in yours, developing yours; your own country, your homeland, yes, your little place on the rock. This will, (in like manner) bring about the very same sorts of outcomes." So, build they did, invest they did, develop they did. Then out of the mire, out of the gloom, out of despair arose the bright and shining new Jamaica that we all have become witnesses to, in these "modern days." Look, look at it. And then, one day, it finally hit home to them that "This is for real." Jamaica was not just becoming... something, but she was the place of choice for many to work, live, raise their children, and retire. Then, all of a sudden, everybody wanted to go and went by scores, or by the dozens. But it was too late for many because the purchase price for the property they had vaguely considered buying at one point suddenly skyrocketed out of their price range. Oh! The dilemma of delay. What a difference twenty years can make. Those were the best of times for Jamaica, but at the same time, those were the worst of times, too, on some other levels. With the massive influx of people from all walks of life moving in, there were sure to be some undesirables coming in amongst them. The don, Lasco, came right on in among them and set up shop.

Kingston was jumping like a mountain toad in those days; it was the place to be. The Renaissance was in high gear then, and people were starting to feel more optimistic and upbeat about the future. "The conflict" would have taken a heavy toll on Europe, Asia, and North America and had almost dragged the entire world into the whole mess. The mighty US of A, at the time, had its eyes focused on North Korea and its allies, as the two threw insults back and forth at each other. The insurgency of the longtime Middle Eastern enemies, in the meantime, snuck up their backside and caused never-before-seen havoc. By the time it was all over, and the Allied forces had declared victory, half a million people were dead, and the world was plunged into yet another recession. But all that was behind them at this point, for the most part. As for the astute and savvy leadership of the Jamaican government and people, they just shook it off like cold water on the back of a greasy duck and kept on moving ahead. More or less like the Energizer Bunny would have said, and the people kept coming, bringing their money in with them. Africa, too, (for the most part,) was being set up on the path for the big take-off after much realignment and reassignment. Many African countries were on an upward trajectory. Back home, though, Jamaica (at that time) was being highly touted as "The lost tribe of Africa." Being strategically situated in a regional trans-shipping hub, she, too, was red hot and ready for take-off into the big times.

The 51st president was at the zenith of her popularity then, a woman who was riding the high tide of popular approval. After the dismal performances of those other two earlier bums who, (for some yet unfathomable reasons,) would have happened to occupy the white house before her. 48th wasn't half bad as a president; he did try. However, owing to the mood in the country at that time and given the fact that the power base on the right was still very strong and on the attack. The poor guy didn't stand a snowball's chance in hell of making any gains.

At the same time, Jamaica was to be favored with the enviable pleasure of hosting its first Olympic summer games, and the reviews were still rolling in. The entire country would have breathed a collective sigh of relief. They had done so very much better than was predicted by the naysayers throughout the sporting world. Even the local organizers and committee members were very apprehensive and edgy throughout the entire period while preparing and hosting the games. But they all were relieved afterward, after it was all over and done with, and all the rave reviews started coming in. Everybody could "Just chill," and that was just what they did, in classic Jamaican style. "No problem, man."

In those days, you see, more and more countries were withdrawing from the EU. The United States was re-adjusting, revamping, and re-making itself, and the United Alliance of African States (UAAS, or the New African Union, as some were heard calling it these days) was fast becoming a force to be reckoned with in the modern world. The construction industry was booming over there; hotels were being built in all sizes, shapes, and star statuses. Just like it was happening here in Jamaica and on the home front. The Jamaican landscapes were seeing those sorts of growth activities, you know. Hotels, manufacturing plants, factories, apartments, and houses were being built all along the coastal areas, winding their way around the entire island and venturing sporadically into the interior parts of some regions. The rich and famous were moving into their first or second homes and luxury apartments there. The business class, students, lovers, haters alike, and those in search of the real Jamaican stacks (if you might.) They came, and Jamaica just kept on rising. Zimbabwe was the surprise upstart African country; it just seemed to have crawled up behind everyone while they were sleeping and caught them all off guard. She was the whiz kid in those days; no one expected that country to be doing so very well at the time, and in such a short time after Bobby Mac would have skipped the yard.

Bobby Mac was dead and gone, and the schemes and plans he'd put in place to try to cement his family and inner circle into the annals of power in that country would have crumbled right on the heels of his hostage and passing. After factoring in the ten to fifteen years it took for them to re-position the country's affairs, it has been outright amazing what they have managed to achieve since. The Congo regions were doing very well, too, despite the constant wrestling with the old colonizers and the transnational companies who seemed to want to cement their hold on the vast natural wealth of that region on the African continent. Cuba, by then, had made a dramatic turnaround and was seeing growth that was the envy of every Nation. Being mere minutes across the bay from a thriving Jamaica seemed to have factored in the reasons they did so very well. South Africa, though, had slowed somewhat in recent times due to the unsettled race issues; the rhetoric has been heating up again in some quarters of that society in recent times. What with all those nagging talks about the separation of white states from black states (or not). Even the total removal of all whites/non-transferable people from the land, as some were suggesting at the time. What else did you expect? All this ended up doing was to help set them back many decades, such a sad state of affairs. Man, deh yah must be turning over in his grave, even now, well...

In this modern Jamaica, they would have finally come to terms with over 90 years of tribalism, political fighting, and infighting. The criminal class would have given way to a brand-new, vibrant class of young professionals and a savvy and sophisticated "Other" class of go-getters. The Kingston trans-shipment wharves were doing brisk business, and foreign labor was then in very high demand; that was when...

When the Chinese first came in to start the building projects that laid the groundwork for the takeoff several decades ago. Some people did not like it one bit and were quick to make that known. They were regularly heard saying things like, "All these Chinese are coming in and taking away the jobs that should have been given to us, the Jamaican people." But these many decades later, most of those same people are thanking the Chinese. Those well-qualified professionals were trained by those Chinese, under the agreements signed by the governments on either side of the shining seas. They are now in high demand in the region and farther afield, as other countries are now getting on the building and re-building train running headlong into the bright future looming on the horizon. The skills they were to have acquired via on-the-job training had put them on the fast track to real lasting wealth and prosperity, thanks again to the Chinese. High-rise and luxury condos rose where there once were Shanti-Towns, roadside shacks, and shopping stalls. Poverty moved out, and wealth and prosperity moved in.

This story was recorded for a travel magazine and told to us through the eyes of Jason and Irene Toppings. Two Jamaicans from widely different backgrounds who came together in those times and started a family and a new life in Jamaica, as it happened. Jason, a young University business major, and Irene, a journalist and second-generation "Ja-merican," whose paths had happened to cross when Irene, just like half a million other young people from around the world, would have done. Like those who went to Jamaica at the time for the 2052 summer Olympics, and many of whom had (in addition to finding a rocking good time) found love.

This story was an attempt at chronicling the life and times of those two, through to the point where they were found sitting in rocking chairs in their hilltop luxury mansion, overlooking the Caribbean Sea, and reminiscing. Jason, the husband, father, and now, grandfather. Was from an average lower-class Jamaican family. A young man who had come up the hard way and, after graduating from university, decided to go into business for himself. He was to be found (at the time) running a hip, hot, and trendy nightclub called The Toppings Spot. Irene was born in the United States of America to Jamaican-born parents who had migrated in the mid-seventies, leaving the posh life they were accustomed to in Jamaica behind them. The new immigrant family was ill-prepared for the harsh realities of the life they were about to face in the new country, before they would finally get it all together and start prospering again there. But then came that once-in-a-lifetime opportunity for Irene to go and see the Olympics in the country that her parents once called home, and which she had longed to return to, and to experience for herself. Well, Irene, here it comes.

# Welcome to Jamaica

Welcome to Jamaica, the land of "Many Sunshines." The land of wood and water, or "the land of many peoples." Just like the travel posters say, "Welcome to Jamaica," was what everyone was saying in those times: "The greatest little country on the planet." It was the best place to live, work, play, and retire. So, down to Jamaica, they went, in droves, to cash in on the bonanza, the retirees' dream, with love. The Jamaican government was actively working to promote the country to those particular demographic categories of people: the rich, the returning residents (particularly the rich returning residents), and the rich and famous types from every other sphere of life, too. "You can retire in absolute comfort here in this tropical paradise, just like our subjects here today did, and enjoy every minute of it, too. Just like they are doing," said the reporter as the camera started to roll.

"Today we're going to hear from the Toppings as we try to get the perspectives of people who have actually lived 'The Jamaican dream,' just like Jason and Irene. But how did they do it? Let's go find out from them, let's ask the Toppings themselves."

Interviewer: So, who wants to go first?

Mr. Toppings: Irene will, she's the journalist and the talker in the family. Interviewer: Okay, so I understand that you were from the US. How did you end up here? How did it all get started for you?

Mrs. Toppings: I started out writing, that's how, from very early on in life, my dad used to say, "A short pencil is better than a long memory, okay?" Ha-ha, ha. So, I would write down everything. That's where it all got started for me. But I don't think that is what you want to hear from me today, today you are after the juicier kinds of stuff, I believe, (more laughs). Well, I was here to report on the summer games. I was an intern with the AASN, that is, the All-American Sports Network. Jamaica was hosting the games, you know, the very first for an English-speaking developing country of her size. It was a big deal then, and no better place for an intern sports reporter to be than at the Olympic Games in Jamaica. After checking in at the Jamaica Calling hotel that night, along with a couple of other young reporters, we decided to go out on the town for a while. We ended up at the trendy new hotspot, the Toppings Spot, which later became known simply as "The Spot." Boy! That place was hot, and I don't mean it in terms of the sizzling heat of the Jamaican summer sun; I mean, I mean, it was really, really "happening." Let's pause here for a commercial break, said the reporter while breaking away. To be continued.

The White Knight Rider (in the meantime) rode into town, and a trail of dead bodies was to follow. Many refer to Lasco as the white knight, but a more suitable name should have been "The white knife," because, wherever he went, bloody messes and dead bodies followed, and the place he chose to stop that time around was Jamaica; the outcome was to be no different. He followed the hip and trendy crowd who were (ironically,) trying to escape the likes of him in those cities from whence they had come, in the wake of his crimes, yes. He would have plundered and spoiled cities such as New York, Miami, Toronto, and LA. Since Jamaica was in those times the hippest place on earth to be, why wouldn't Count Lasco be there too? The police federation, and their top man, in particular, wasn't mincing words. "Jamaica," the commissioner told him straight up, "is an open and accommodating society. We're happy to have you here and will bend over backward to make sure that your stay here is a memorable one. But make sure that, all of that 'shit' that I hear about you... Those things that are constantly being said about you, and which are being associated with your name, or any part of it, that might (remotely) be true. Be sure to shake and leave it over on that side of the bay from whence you came." Lasco just grinned his gold-studded teeth and grunted, hmm-hmm, um. "No problem, man," in his best Jamaican Wanna-Be accent and tone, "The word is good," he continued. But the astute and very aware commissioner Watkins knew better than to hang on to any word spoken by anyone like Lasco. So, his eyes and ears were ever open to his every move from then on and after, so far as was humanly possible.

Meanwhile, Sadie's stars would have been going nowhere but up in those days. Her name was plastered in flashing neon lights atop the Jamaica Calling hotel. "She's 'the madam' there," some said. Others said she owned the damn joint. One way or another, she was not one known to be missing out on a chance to get a good time on. Since Count Lasco and his entourage had been "Making it to Jamaica regularly of late," and the Jamaica Calling, their Jamaican abode of choice. Sadie has opportunities aplenty to do what Sadie does best: she dances.

Let's pause here for a moment for another spoken word piece, folks. A little thing called.

Born for this. Just another poem of the times.

A glimpse into your pile of nothingness, at how futile your life has been. You're going to take nothing when you go out of here because you brought nothing in. You're a loser, there, I said it. You're just trying to save your very skin. But until you lose what is to be lost? You are never going to win.

You are trying, and trying so very hard, wanting so much to succeed. Just so that you may consume it all, in all of your envy, and all of your greed. But you're a loser, I know it, despite the social stairs you've been climbing. Until you lose what is to be lost, you are never going to win.

You've kicked the doors wide open, then steamrolled over haters, same as a loving friend. Yet in all of this, you can't venture beyond these. That someone who's standing right there, you see, is the same "someone else" who's holding the key. He's there to remind you if you'd but listen to him. That you're a loser, mister man, and there's a reason why you can't get in. Until you lose what is to be lost, you are never going to win.

You spread your feathers like a blooming peacock and boast of all the fine 'blings' that you've got. But what good is all of that to you, I wonder, when you're lying stretched out six feet under. Before that day finally breaks, it may do you some good if "Notice" you'll take... That you're a loser, my friend, born to lose in order to win. Except for losing your load of sin. You are never, ever going to win. Aug 2017

## 11

Chapter

asco rode into town

*"Think you've got trouble? Wait until you've got trouble. You'll see."*

It was an accident, everybody knew it, but the kid was scared, behind all of the tough guy facades, Sergeant Kennedy could see that he knew more than he was saying; he was fidgety and sweating rather profusely. What was he afraid of? Was it the pinch of dope over the legal limits he had on him when they brought him in, or was there more to it? Sergeant Kennedy gambled that there was more, and like always, this time too, he was right.

Lasco was coming out of the washroom, and the young man (as of yet unidentified) was going in. If only he had knocked before entering, like his mother had taught him to do, chances are, none of it would have happened. Just as The Count was reaching out to take hold of the washroom door handle to pull it open, the door was busted open fast. Knocking him smack dab on the knuckle, and nearly broke the middle finger of his grasp: you know, his favorite f-you finger. In a couple of minutes, he will be perfectly fine, but for the time being, it hurts like hell. The young man solemnly apologizes, repeatedly bowing his knees before "The Count," and clasping his hands as if offering up a prayer, like this.

"No problem, man," and a gold-studded grin was all he got in return from the departing stranger. The man he thought was just another of the many rich and famous house guests who, in those times, delighted in staying at the Calling. The young man then went on to do what he'd gone in there to do in the first place, while still sorry-moaning over what had just happened. He did not pay much attention to the two people who walked into the washroom next, just others like himself who were there to do the same as he was doing, he thought, but then? Somebody walked up and grabbed him from behind. While one of the intruders was covering the door to prevent others from getting in or out anymore. The other one covered the young man's mouth with one hand, the knife in the other. He (the intruder) reached down and then back up with the knife. Slashing through the young man's right hand, which, by then, had shifted from the support role it was playing at first. To attempt to protect "The family Jewel." The knife-wielding intruder took the jewelry, the chest, and all four fingers, yes. Along with a part of the thumb of the right hand that was playing the guardsman role. While in the same motion, slashing up and through the abdomen. Leaving the intestines a-washed in blood, partially digested food, and other bodily parts and fluid on the washroom floor. There was blood everywhere.

Meanwhile, the other young man, Robbie, just happened to have hopped in and seen it all as it went down. He was vending marijuana to help himself through college. In the age of the partially legalized status of the wisdom weed. Five ounces was what was allowed at any given time for a person. Anything over that, one would run the risk of jail time for possession and transportation, among other possible charges. Robby always tried to make sure that he didn't exceed the five-ounce limit. He would meticulously weigh and measure it to ensure he stayed within the legal framework of the limit. Although everyone knew he was vending, whenever he was confronted on this, he would always say it was for his personal use. Since he was, by all other accounts and indications, a decent, upstanding, and progressive young man, no one bothered him over a bit of the common weed. He, too, was to wind up dead in the strangest of manners, mere days after the departure of Lasco, after one of his (now regular) visits to Jamaica had ended. Lasco was (quite conveniently) off the Island at the time of those happenings. The young man was found dead with his hands tied behind his back, both hands tucked into the pockets of what were supposedly his pants, before wrapping the legs of the pants around his waist and tying the legs in a knot. Some theorized that it was a message to say, "Take your hands out of my pocket." Commissioner Watkins didn't buy that, not one bit; he had quite another theory. But...

## 12

Chapter

# Tracing the Family Tree

Shirley Houghton-Smith is the name of a second-generation American and one-time governor of Pennsylvania. She was not the first in her family to be governor, as was to be discovered later. There was an earlier family member who was governor in Jamaica, along with a few other folks in their bloodline who were rather prominent figures in society. Her son was to become mayor of Pittsburgh, too, four years ago, at the time of these happenings. Her bloodline was traced back to Mandeville, Manchester, and the roots get tangled and messy from that point on. But the record was to show that her great uncle, one Mr. Author Ferguson Matthaeus, was once a member of the legislative council (MLC) representing the parish of Manchester. His grandfather, before him, too, was governor. Governor Walt Baines was an Englishman, a plantation owner, and the king's representative in the colony. Governor Baines had a daughter named Aidah; she would go on to marry a sailor who was also reported to be a soldier in the Haitian revolutionary army, and who used to refer to himself as a thinker, sailor, soldier, and all-around nice guy. The irony of the whole thing, though, was that here was this rather peculiar family, a Jamaican family with connections encompassing a governor serving the British crown, and a soldier/sailor serving the Haitian government and army. Another family member was, at the time, serving the Jamaican state in a very high office. Yet others were serving in varying roles in the great big USA. But that is the Jamaican quilt for you, out of many, one strikingly amazing people, I'd say.

Author Ferguson Matthaeus did not have any children of his own; however, his sister Melda had two daughters: Elsie and Rhonda. Elsie married Marcus Peart and bore him two children: Lascelles and Lisa. Marcus died, leaving his wife with two young children to raise on her own. She did not grieve very long for him. Within a year, she was married again, to Orville Kennedy. She went on to bear him seven children: Rhonda married Alfred (Freddy) Houghton. They went on to parent many children: Author, Walter, Ann-Marie, Sadie, and Joe, among them. Walter Houghton, after migrating to the USA, married a Puerto Rican girl, and she bore him seven children, including Shirley. Shirley would then go on to marry Les Smith of Smith's Wood Pulp and Paper Products Inc. They have three children: two boys and a girl. She then went on to become the governor of the state of Pennsylvania. Her son Clinton would follow her lead into the political arena later when he was to become Mayor there too.

...

Out on the plains of Saint Catherine, on the approach into Spanish Town as one travels north out of Kingston, is the location of a large lot of land that housed the Jamaica Police Academy. The Jamaican State police training school is situated on a nature reserve donated to the government for that purpose, and that purpose only. It was donated by the matriarch of that very rich and famous farming and agribusiness family. Five hundred to six hundred young men and women from all around Jamaica and other Caribbean countries are trained there every year in advanced police technologies. Trained by the latest in a long line of very well-abled and learned lawmen, Captain Thomas McCook (Captain Cook as he was known), he and his highly sophisticated staff were running the show there at the time. The commissioner, too, was a part-time lecturer and contributor at the training school. The only problem was that there was an insurgent among them at the time, and few were those who even knew it. To make matters worse, another agent (or counter-agent) was also sent in to track him, watch him, protect him, and (if needs be) kill him before he gets busted. Who was behind the planting of these agents was anyone's guess, and guessing was what some were doing, not the commissioner, though. Let all others guess and speculate, but facts are what the commissioner pursued and utilized in his practice; he was not about to change his methods at the winding-up end of his career. As it turned out, that was the very last case that the commissioner had to wrap up before retiring from his career in law enforcement.

The 50-acre plot of land that makes up the nature reserve is to the far north of the plains in the parish of Saint Catherine, and borders on the south side of the neighboring parish by lush rainforest, sporadic villages, and townships dotting the landscape throughout the mountainous region. A river winds its way through it. Other than for the native peoples that live in those hilly parts, only by way of an aircraft flyover would the strangers or visitors to the island ever get a glimpse of those interior parts. To the south side, though, of where the training center is located, Preston Foster and his mighty clan laid claim to 260 acres, along with the circular mounds on which the barracks are built. P-Fost (as the locals used to call him) was not one known to mince words, nor would he ever miss out on an opportunity to remind the other powers that be just who was really in control around those parts. Preston, like his father before him, was a military man. Leon the senior Foster made it up the ranks to become a sergeant before he retired, halting on one leg. Preston fared an awful lot better than his father. He rose through the ranks to serve his country as Major General for fifteen years and retired without a single battle scar. That is, if one should ignore popular claims that "He was losing it." Many people said that he was mentally unstable.

On the massive acreage further south of the training camp is the city of Kingston. A modern, vibrant, and thriving city, she is ever-growing and expanding. Apart from being a tourist and transcontinental shipping hub. Kingston was at that time (and still is today) more or less like the New York, London, and Paris of the Caribbean regions. They came from all across the region to shop in Kingston and in Jamaica as a whole.

13 |

Chapter

# Home is Where the Heart Is

The commissioner was a very dedicated family man who just loved his family and did not miss out on a chance to spend quality time with them. As a matter of fact, the commissioner hardly had much of a social life. Other than serving his country in the office of the commissioner of police and going home at night to his family, and the stint he also did lecturing at the police academy. Other than for those things? Supervising the care of his beloved dogs, his church life, and his home life is pretty much all else that he does. His family was a rather large one, too, with seven sons and three daughters of his own, his wife, Sheila, and he also adopted two more children (siblings), a boy and a girl: Joel and Janie. Their eldest son would have followed in his father's footsteps in the Jamaica Constabulary Force and had been climbing rapidly up the ranks. He was head of the K9 unit at the time. Another of his sons, his sixth, had also followed suit and is a constable in the force. The commissioner's own mother lived just across the street from his house, but one might not know it since she spent a whole lot more time at the big house than she does at her own home. No one would ever complain about that, though; it suited everyone just fine.

It was dinner time at the commissioner's house, and the entire family (including his mother) was seated at the table. They were sitting there, eating fried chicken and potato chips (among other things, yes.) Grandma (she was Commissioner Watkins' mom, but everyone else called her grandma, including all the in-laws). So, Grandma was sitting there at the table, she was the only one with the bucket of potato chips (she just loved fried potato chips, and little else). Billy (the kid) was sitting to the right of his grandmother, who was the commissioner's wife, and who was sitting to the right of Grandma (her mother-in-law and the commissioner's mother). So little Billy was two chairs away from Grandma, who was there with the bucket of chips tucked under her hamper load of beads. We'll call 'em that, for the sake of making this point with a degree of ease, and subtlety that is. While grandma sat there stuffing herself full of Potato chips. She would have managed to pull the bucket out from under the bouncing beads. Look. The container tilted slightly forward and to the left of the center. She pushed it at Ferrari speed across their mother, sitting next to her at the right, all the way to the far end of the seats. Did you see it? "Yes." Then pulled it back quickly, then back and forth again, with the finishing point of the action, pointing straight at Billy the Kid's nose, as if she intended to say, "This is your only chance at even so much as touching, let alone tasting one slice of these potato chips in here tonight." So, Billy the Kid did the best that he could; he dipped a nimble right hand into the bucket very fast and settled for the first thing, or several things that he was to find in the grasp of his fist. Because he knew by experience that whatever he would have had in there when he pulled it out, that was likely to be what he would inherit from the potato chip-eating contest there that night. From Grandma's perspective, however, that was a very clever trick on her part, designed with several purposes in mind. She really wanted the kid to have some of the chips, but him, and him only. "Don't you get too smart though, kiddo," she was (probably) thinking; you're not going to deprive me of the lion's share of my comfort food here this evening. So, whenever you dig in, make sure that you get something, because I'll be making damn sure that it won't be much. Another aspect of Grandma's plan was to make sure no one would be able to accuse her later on of eating all of the chips and not even offering a bite to anybody. Like, "Not even the baby boy," oh boy! Furthermore, if they should ever dare to say that she only gave a single chip to the boy. She would be able to argue that the kid took what he wanted. The bucket was right there in front of him, and he took what he wanted. He could have taken as much as he liked. If he took only one, then, perhaps, that was all that he wanted. No? And I, "I didn't even see how much he took out of the bucket when he reached in any way." (Yay, I'm sure she did not, since her attention was focused elsewhere; she was actually looking the other way at the time). Wink, wink, my dear, no denying it. Furthermore, if they hadn't made a big point out of it and brought it up, and hence, to her attention, she would still be thinking that the kid took a whole wad of the stuff. All that would have been said with the straightest of faces possible on Grandma's part, but...

Chapter

**T**alk to me, People.

From the Toppings' beachfront home, the interview continues. Listen on.

Mrs. Toppings: Those were hopping-good times. On any given day, you could walk down any street in Kingston and bump into celebrities from YouTube stars (YouTube, as you already know, was the biggest thing in those days). To Hollywood, bally-hood, or even Nolly-wood (that was the Nigerian counterpart to Hollywood) stars. They were coming to Jamaica for work and play. Jamaica wasn't too shabby in those regards either. Jamaica had Jami-wood, yes, she was more than holding her own in the film industry. Adding to the already prestigious positions that sports and the music of the land were commanding on the world stage at the time. Jamaica was taking off into the real big time; there would have been ticking up moves in the entertainment business over here, and there, too, ever since the early days of the Renaissance. Their local stars were becoming well-renowned the world over. The terraces along Harbor Streets and Port Royal Streets were the walk of fame of the Jamaican stars, and so it is to this very day, as you can see. Name the star of the day, you would have been more than likely to find them there on Jamaica Way. You may sneak a peek at them, but don't you ever stare, it's just not cool, they say. We used to ride the train down to the harbor on Sunday evenings, to see the sights. As well as to sit on the dock and watch the big ships as they come sailing in or sail out again. Then, we'd go bolting in and out of the shops, just to be in there, you know. "Ooh, the sights and smells in those shops, fantastic, that was all we wanted. Nobody bothered us; we didn't bother them, they didn't bother us," (laughs). It was just life at its fabulous best. Not that it's any different now. It might even be a lot better today than it was yesterday, but we've moved on. "Maybe we should just 'go slow,' we thought, not so Young anymore, you know, you know what I mean, right?" she asked rhetorically. "We're leaving it all up to our children and grandchildren. It's their time now."

"Tell us some more about them; your children and grandchildren, since we're on the subject," the reporter continued, "how many are they?"

"We have three, two boys and a girl, and that many grandchildren, too. So far. Though they have not said so, we strongly believe that there is at least one other child on the way," Mrs. Toppings confided to the reporter while leaning in and lowering her voice as if to prevent someone from overhearing what was being said. Even though everyone knew that there was nobody else in the house but the news people and themselves. "I could always tell, you know? been around long enough to know a thing or two," more laughs.

Jamaica was the destination of choice in those days for people in search of premium medical and dental services. She was also a major hub for commercial activity in the Caribbean region and South America.

There was something special happening there that day, one could feel it. An unusually high number of limo zines were floating around the streets of Montego Bay. Helicopters were flying overhead, too, "must be something big going on," many were heard saying. Or someone special might be coming to town. Montego Bay was the home of one of the most sought-after medical care facilities, not just in the Caribbean, as it was, but in the world at large, in those days. If you've got money and you happen to get sick, Jamaica was (and still is) the place to go for world-class care. Dental care in Jamaica was right there amongst the best of them, too. Jamaica built it, and the people came. As it turned out, it was the president of the United States of America who was in town. Not the sitting president, however, but two digits back from her. But everyone already knows that, once a president, always a president, right? He was in town for emergency surgery because he was having prostate issues for some time, the story was told to me, and he would have tried everything that one could think of in the great big USA. Nothing seemed to work for him on that side, so all roads (or flights) led him down to Jamaica.

B lood was Everywhere.

There was blood everywhere, red, hot, delicious hemoglobin. It was being reported as a murder-suicide, but Sergeant Kennedy had his suspicions from the get-go. Ramah and Saeed were students there, yes, studying at the University of Jamaica in Montego Bay. Both of them were to end up lying dead on a dorm room floor; murder-suicide, the news reports said. But Commissioner Shaky Watkins, Sergeant Kennedy, and many of the locals had their suspicions. Commissioner Watkins just walked away, shaking his head at the incredulity of the whole thing, "No further comments," he said, brushing off a slew of reporters as he walked by their poky probing lenses and microphones. Shortly afterward he would have managed to wind up the loose ends of those things, he was to end his career on the highest note, yes, being awarded one of the country's highest honors; order of the Nation (O.N) As well as the many citations and commendations he was to receive for a stellar, squeaky-clean record of services to the country. Although the list of those who doubted that the Commish's hands were as clean as they were made out to be had been growing longer by the day, down Jamaica Way.

Ramah was an international student studying at a Jamaican University. She was from a Middle Eastern country, but most people mistook her for Asian. She just hated it when they called her the "P" word. Ramah would have met and fallen in love with Saeed on campus, a strict no-no for a Middle Eastern young lady already betrothed to be married on her return home from school. Saeed, also, being from the same region and culture, and having first-hand knowledge as to what it all meant, was taking things slowly, being very careful, and hoping for the best, you know. Ramah, on the other hand, was fast developing a taste for the wild and risky. She ran into suave and debonair Count Lasco and was immediately smitten. From then on, Ramah would alternate her time between campus life and the penthouse atop the Jamaica Calling, whether in Kingston or Montego Bay, where the Count had set up his little love nests. He was spending more and more time in Jamaica in those days. Ramah (he'd found out) was unlike any other girl he'd met before. Very caring and attentive, no one had ever made him feel as she did, and so, he was being drawn into her more and more every day. To the chagrin of Saeed, among others. When the semester ended in April, most of the other students turned their faces towards home, wherever in the world that would have happened to be. That summer, Ramah stayed on in Jamaica; she would have spent the summer in Jamaica, opting for extracurricular activities on campus. But most of her time was really spent at the penthouses. Even though Lasco was not there all the time, he would leave her there and take care of her needs for the duration of her stay. As a matter of fact, Lasco had long been taking on the responsibility of her tuition, too. Because it would appear as if Ramah's family was dropping the ax on her support system. Not good for young Ramah, but what does she care?

September morning saw the return of many to campus life and studies at Jamaican universities. Saeed was back with more than reports from home for Ramah. He wanted to resume the relationship with her. Abdul, the man she was betrothed to, who had (seemingly) given up on the prospect of marriage with Ramah, had begun looking elsewhere. As a matter of fact, the word was out that he had all but fully given up on her and was seeing someone else. Not seeing Lasco going on for four months was beginning to take its toll on her psyche, too, so the devil was in the mix from then on. Saeed's hopes mounted at least by a degree or two. Trouble was brewing on several fronts, though, and everyone knew it. Well, everyone but the lovey-dovey duo, until it was too late. After what had happened with the death of the kid who was peddling the weed, and then came these two students, both with links to the Calling hotel and particularly to the penthouse, the commissioner found it necessary to make another courtesy call on sweet Sadie. Just a bit of poking around, you know, so said he, to somebody. Like, picking her wits to see what he could garner. Trying to determine what she might have known, you know. Didn't get much out of her that time, but a portrait hanging from the wall did speak to him in an underhanded way. There was something about the picture that beckoned to him, inviting him into a further investigation. He could not quite put his finger on what it was, but it was there.

Meanwhile, look, Sergeant Kennedy was at it again. He was out investigating the gruesome death of rescue Roy when he met up with the commissioner, and the end. Yes, because he also met up with all of the doings of his own past there that day, everything changed from then on for the sergeant. Rescue Roy would have gotten himself roasted crisp when he tried to light up his smoke. The only real problem with that was that it was just after he was done rescuing fuel from Bernie's fuel tank via his suction hose. Roy was a very industrious fellow like that. Although times were good for the most part for many, some of the local people (for whatever reasons there might have been) were falling through the cracks, finding it harder and harder to get a foothold in the big boom of the day. Rescue Roy wasn't about to let little things like that get in his way. He was a survivor, and whatever it was going to take for him to survive, that was what he was going to do. He had always been a proponent of the virtues and writings of Marcus Garvey, whom he touted as being the greatest Jamaican who had ever lived. "Marcus said," was how he would always begin every argument, and he would be quick to remind anyone who would bother to listen of that fact, or his version of the facts. For example, he would say, Marcus said if you can't find a job, then go out and create one. Therefore, in whatever way one may choose to look at whatever it may be that Roy could be found doing at any given point in time, to make a living for himself. That was his job, which he may or may not have created for himself, but it was nonetheless his.

Lasco was back in town, and Commissioner Watkins summoned him for a meeting at a mutually acceptable spot; he obliged. Not much came from that, but they were to meet again, on the commissioner's terms. The ending was dramatically different at that time. Find them at the bottom of that gravel pit of mine, just outside of town.

16

Chapter

**P**arenting and the Job.

"The world is governed by rules, laws, and guidelines." The commissioner would often counsel his family, more specifically, his children, in this wise. The exceptions, though, are what grease the wheels of function, so favor the exception. "Someone once said," he continued, "If you are planning on the exceptional and the extraordinary, then choose the exceptions rather than the rules. The Count, Lasco, seemed to choose to live his life by that mantra, too. However, he seemed to have forgotten about the rest of that story, or maybe he'd just chosen to ignore it. That other part went on to say, "Don't make the exception become your rules because the law is an aftermarket, and her consequences and recompense are heavy-handed and unforgiving. They are designed, it would seem, with the assumption that: (a) If you got caught this time, you might have been doing it for quite a long while, therefore, it's going to be payback time for you now. And (b) if you are caught in a breach of the law, the rules, or the guidelines, you must be reined in and made an example of, so that others may see and fear in so much that they will not do as you did. Deterrent, they call it."

The Jamaica Sailing Club (Miami-Jamaica leg) boat race was beginning to take its place as one of the premier summer events anywhere in the hemisphere. After a rocky start where several boats were lost at sea, and a sailor died en route to and from the clubhouses on either side of the basin, the organizers had to go back to the drawing board. They suspended the event for four years. When they finally came back, though, with the new look regatta and a host of new subscribers from across the globe. The new look course and fields took on two more destination locations with the addition of Havana and Grand Cayman. So, the North Coast development strategy employed by successive governments would have seen the industrial sectors heating up to a fever pitch in recent times and thriving. Pushing the red-hot developing industrial sector and its class further and further inland. But the Jamaican people weren't going to take it lying down; they fought back rigorously. Forcing the government to concede and passing laws forbidding any further industrial-style development in the interior parts of the Island. "They can take the plains and the coastal areas," the people proclaimed, "but we will take the Rocky Mountains and the high hills," and so it is until this very day.

Meanwhile, the steamy hot industrial and commercial development continued on the coast. China Town, for instance, in the Martha Brae regions of Saint Ann, was becoming the modern-day Miami, and the darling destination of the Caribbean region and America. Shoppers from as far as South America become regular patrons and customers there. Olympic City in Trelawney has also seen its share of rapid growth and development. After the closing of the games that year, the developers went right on in, and a brand-new city rose out of the tracks, trails, and courses. That's now one of the trendiest little cities in all of the Northern Hemisphere, if not the entire world today. The North Coast tram and shuttle system never sleeps. The Jamaican coastline nowadays, too, is just like New York used to be; she, too, never sleeps.

# Meet-up With the Count.

*There's no security in job security; just wait until you want the security of your job. You'll see.*

As it turned out, the limo driver for Lasco and his crew was, in fact, an undercover cop, inserted in there by, well, you might as well guess. They had run (supposedly) into a roadblock, and a detour followed. This was said to have happened while they were en route to the north coast on a Friday night party mission. "Police operations," they were told. The detour took them on a remote and increasingly lonely road until they came smack dab into an ambush.

"What the fuck is going on here?" Lasco inquired, seemingly addressing the questions to the limo driver. "I don't know," replied the driver. "Turn the car around, turn the fucking car around," Lasco ordered. At the same time, the two bodyguards would have been bracing themselves for action and reaching for the backup weapons that they carried strapped to their lower legs. Although they were not licensed to bear arms while on the island, everybody knew that they did. It just came with the job. Then, out of the bushes came heavily armed men pointing their weapons squarely at the pusses... I mean, the car, and more specifically, the occupants of the car. Instantaneously, each man returned his weapons to the hiding places and sat back down, really still. "Put your hands over your head, put your hands over your head where I can see them, and get out of the car slowly, very slowly?" The instructions were coming at them fast and furious. They all got out as instructed. "You,

you get over here," one said to the driver. So, just like that, they separated him from the rest of the group. "Keep those hands where I can see them," the man barked at the driver, as well as Lasco and his friends. "Will someone tell me what the hell is going on here?" said Lasco again, but this time the questions were directed at the apparent ringleader, the one who was issuing the commands. "You'll know soon enough," said the big boss man in charge there, as it would have appeared, but then?

Out of the bushes walked more men, with dogs. Each man was holding his dog on a leash with no other visible signs of being armed, only the dogs on the leashes. But the amazing thing about that picture, as it appeared to Lasco, was that those dogs seemed so very well trained. Not even as much as a bark came out of any of them. They just bared their teeth at him and growled, more or less in the same way as Count Lasco himself would. The dogs bare their teeth and growl while bouncing off the leashes as they try to break free from the handlers and pounce on them. At the same time, look who's coming to the games. While the gun-toting gang was still aiming the weapons point-blank at Lasco and his men. Out of the bushes walked the commissioner, rather calmly and coolly, as if he were walking into a children's birthday party gathering at the dance, to fool me.

"Well-well-well, what have we got here?" Said the Commissioner.

"Is this some kind of a fucking joke?" Lasco asked, "No one is laughing, as you might have noticed."

"You know what, Lascelles, it really is nice to see you again, too." Lasco was taken aback, and for a very brief moment, the commissioner could have sworn that he saw him gasp. Lasco knew then that something big was up; no one called him by that name, "Lascelles," in years. The commissioner (he realized) has been digging, and (obviously,) he has got something. What else did he find out, he wondered. The commissioner took one step closer, "You know," he said, "I've been wondering what it was that had brought you here on our sunny shores in the first place, and what is it that keeps you coming back." He said this across his strides towards him, hands held up by his thumbs on the loop of his strap. "Don't get me wrong," he hastened to say, "I'm really happy that you came, you know, I like you, I really do like you a lot, but something about you gets me nervous every time, it comes with the job, you know. When are you going home? I mean, how much more time do you have here on the Island until your end of stay here?"

"For the life of me, I cannot see how that is any of your business," Lasco rebutted.

"Aah! But it is, it is, I've got to make sure that you're safe while you're here, you know, and it's costing me a lot of man-hours, as you can see. Your security while you are here falls squarely on my shoulders."

"In your professional opinion, Sir, how safe am I and my men at this particular moment?" Lasco asked again. While he was speaking, he turned his head slightly towards either side to identify each of the men and their presence there as his bodyguards, and to acknowledge them as his men, and noticed that one of them was shaking at the knees, and hard.

"I will bet you," said the commissioner, "that you, and your men, all of you, are still a lot safer here than, aah, let's say: New York, LA, how about Pittsburgh, Pennsylvania? Should be safer here than Pittsburgh, don't you think?" At that moment, those words were (seemingly) much too heavy for the shaky-kneed accomplice to swallow (me). He bent down and reached for his gun, which was tucked in his sock. At the same time, all the dogs bounced up on their hind legs and bared their teeth at him, while each dog handler took two steps forward.

"No-no-no, no," Lasco shouted as he turned and cast a scalding hot glance at each of his friends. But then, he quickly turned his attention back to the commissioner, to continue the discussion (seemingly). That was when the other guard, not Mr. Shaky Knee, that time, but the other one, seemed to lose it all and turned around and ran. The other guardsman then followed suit. Lasco, now splitting his attention between the departing guards-turned-friend-turned deserters, and then back to the Commissioner. At the same time, he turned and saw the now purposefully advancing canine brigades, handlers and all, bearing down on him.

He, too, turned around, and just like his two friends did before him, he ran for all he was worth. Whatever doubt the commissioner might have harbored up to that point that Lasco was, in fact, Jamaican, to some degree. All such doubts drifted away as he watched that sucker go, adding it all up to make them three.

"Aah, ah, yep, that's a Jamaican boy right there for you," the commissioner mused. "Son of a bitch was born to run." Even though the other two did get at least a full New York minute's worth of jump on him, he would have caught up with them and then proceeded to overtake them in a flash. So there they were, the retreating gangster in full flight, fleeing with the canine brigade in hot pursuit. But abruptly, a barbed wire fence met them and mounted up to their waist. All three leaped off the ground and scaled the waist-high fence. Nothing wrong with the takeoff, I'd guessed, nothing wrong with the airy flight over it, but then, there was the landing to be reckoned with. Unbeknownst to any of them, that barbed wire fence they had just breached in a tiger-cat-like leap was a peripheral barrier around a very deep, mined-out pit on a decommissioned quarry.

Later on, it was reported in the media that three young men fell to their deaths in a gravel pit when they tried to run off without paying the fare for a taxi ride.

"They got out of the car and ran across an open field," the reports said, "and then when they came up onto a barbed wire fence, they jumped the fence but were surprised to find that there was a mined-out pit on the other side."

"Those poor things," some were heard saying. Others were not so pitying, understanding, and supportive; they got exactly what they deserved, were their verdict as they saw it. Darned thieving sons of a...

The findings of the commissioner's year-long investigations into the carrying on of Count Lasco and his men saw him tracing the family tree deep into that rather extraordinary family. Count Lasco's real name, as it turned out, was Lascelles Peart. Sadie was named after her grandmother, who was Freddy Houghton's daughter, also named Sadie. One of the two young men who was killed at the house across from where Sadie lived turned out to be her first cousin. The commissioner, after much digging and prying, was to find out these things, among others; he then began the task of making all the other connections, which he'd intended to use to bring them to book. So, sweet Sadie was not too far removed from "The Count" on the family tree as it turned out, neither was Sergeant Kennedy, nor Vince Rogers, for that matter, who knew? In the end, the only aspect left hanging regarding the series of killings that could not be linked to Lasco and his gang was the gruesome murder of those two students on the University campus. So, the spotlight was then shifted from their prime suspect to start focusing on other possible suspects. There has just got to be another explanation for what took place there, though, because try as they may, they could not connect those killings to Count Lasco.

Sadie must have felt the hangman's noose tightening around her neck after the reports of the deaths of Lasco and his cronies. Because she was found on the pavement in the parking lot below her penthouse dressing room window, mere moments later, her well-manicured and waxed-to-a-shine body, in liquid form and shaking like a pound of liver. Some said she jumped, while others (including the commissioner) think she was pushed. Isn't it funny, though, how this particular circle of friends, or family, or whatever the ties might be that binds them together (on me), they all just seemed to go in somewhat the same gruesome manner? Every single time.

Then there was Serge, with the rest of the chorus. Sergeant Kennedy had gone to investigate the death of Rescue Roy when the commissioner and his team showed up, and it wasn't to assist in that investigation as he had assumed (shut up). The Commish was actually there to book him on a barrage of charges. Including but not limited to, obstruction of Justice, aiding and abetting fugitives and criminals, and attempting to pervert the course of Justice, among many others (at the seminars).

"You're making a big mistake, Sir," protested Sergeant Kennedy.

"I hope so, I really do hope so for your sake, my friend," he replied, "but if I were you, I'd call my lawyer, and then..."

...

Mayor Clint Smith was the fiercest warrior in the fight to make and keep Pittsburgh the cleanest city in all of America. Not only in terms of employing those great men with brooms, but he also meant it in terms of employing the greatest and most capable minds of men and women with other tools of the trade. Like, "vroom, vroom, vroom." Some among them were mightier than those used by the broom brigades. His plan had been so very successful in getting a handle on the narcotics trade that most of the other cities and mayors have been employing it, to the chagrin of characters such as Lasco and his kind. Therefore, Lasco had been trying to reinvent himself and his business, hence his many treks to Jamaica, the land he dearly loved and the birthplace of his not-too-distant relatives, and more, much more.

The insurgent agent who'd infiltrated the Police academy turned out to be a plant, sent in by none other than the count himself. His mission was to search out those who appeared to be on the fast track to leadership positions in the force and to spare no expenses or effort in converting them over to his (Lasco's) ways of doing things, of course.

"If all else fails," he was instructed, "then do what you have got to do, and be sure to do it well." As for the other trainees, "desensitize them from what the school is teaching as much as possible and introduce them to an alternative way, our way." That was the instruction from Lasco to him that day. The counteragent's role was simply to lie low and keep a watchful eye on him (the prime agent). "If you see the slightest sign of trouble," he was instructed, "desertion or treason. Then certain protocols must be followed, which ranged from a phone call to a halter call, or even a cold old morgue stall." His list of instructions was laid out in playbook formats: If this, then that. That was the roadmap as laid out and presented to him. As it turned out, and as was to be discovered later by way of the investigations, Lasco was planning to return home to the land of his forefathers. So, he was in the process of setting up shop there ahead of his arrival, since the heat was getting a bit unbearable in the land of Uncle: you know him, right? They call him Sam, or some other name, the likes of that one. But the count must have found himself messing around carelessly one time too many, tripped over me, and fallen, and then, he was gone, way too soon to have been able to foolproof his strategy and reset his line of command. So now his business is in limbo and ripe for the picking, which suits some entities very well indeed. Watch out, all you pickers! They are still moving in for the kill.

The United States government, through its many and varied governmental departments and agencies, in recent times, has been sending gifts in cash and kind to the Jamaica police federation. The central government, as well as various civic groups, too. Some said that this was meant as a thank-you gift for getting the Lasco mess off their hands. Meanwhile, Jamaica continued its upward moves.

# 18

## Chapter

**F**ather Knows Best.

Carol wasn't quite himself that evening; he was obviously in some kind of distress, or was it just simple stress? Carol was the second son of the Watkins, a shuttle bus driver at the University. "What's going on with you?" his father asked."

"Nothing, I'm okay."

"See, that right there is why I hate that fella so much!" said the Commish. That got everyone's attention focused on the commissioner. What was he talking about? Who is this person that he hates?

"Nothing. 'Nothing' is that fella that he hates," Carol updated them, to a great burst of laughter. There was a marked improvement in Carol's countenance right away, so he opened up to tell them his story.

"I love my job," He reminded them, "I do, but there are days when some people and their attitude and behavior just get to me and rub me the wrong way."

"And today was one of those days, right?" His father prodded him with the question.

"Yes, this girl almost got me into trouble, or some sort of issue with my employer."

"How so?" asked his mother.

"She wanted to get on the bus that was already full to capacity, and would not take no for an answer. The rules said I must not carry more than 48 persons at a time, which is the normal seating capacity of the buses."

"So, what's the problem?" asked Marie, his sister, "Once you have 48 persons on board, you close the door and go, no?"

"It's not as cut and dried as that, Sissie. There are rules and guidelines to follow. 'Did you know that the bus cannot be early?'" Carol added further. This got everybody else's attention, all those who were sort of just there and hanging on the sidelines. All of a sudden, everybody was involved in the conversation.

"What do you mean by that, 'the bus cannot be early?'" Chelsea (his niece) asked. "When you get to school on Monday," said Carol, "ask one of your young friends, they will tell you why." Everyone but Chelsea laughed; she was blue in the face, angry at him for showing her up like that. The bus can (for any number of reasons) be late in arriving at a bus stop or the destination. Carol continued to agitate... I mean, educate her. But you are not supposed to leave early; even if you already have a full load, you wait for the proper departure time. The reason for this is that if you leave before the proper departure time, someone can say that they were at the bus stop on time and the bus wasn't there.

"Oh! I see," said Chelsea, as three pounds of weight fell off her brow and onto me. "Tell us more about what happened," his mother prodded him on.

"So, this girl came running up to the closed door of the bus, passing four or five other people standing there. She started to tap on the door, so I showed her via my usual signal that the bus was already full."

"What signal is that?" Chelsea (again) wanted to know. So, Carol showed her: it's my cutoff sign, it goes like this: I fixed my fingers and thumb together like, somewhat like a duck head, and then pointed it at my neck and moved my hand from side to side like this, so that they would know that the bus was full.

"OK, I get it, go on, continue, tell us what happened next," said Chelsea. Yes, even with that, the girl continued knocking on the door and begging: Please, please, I have to go, I have an exam in half an hour. At this point, yes, after hearing about the exam that she's got to go and sit, I cracked the door partially open and told her verbally that the bus was already full. "Oh sheet!" She said that she could stand. "Not on my bus," I replied to her (although some of the buses are equipped with arm bars and straps to allow for it, mine wasn't.) I further told her to ask around if anybody on the bus would be willing to yield (give up) their seat so that she could go, since she had an exam in half an hour, as she had said. She responded that she could not ask someone else to do that for her. "Really now, nobody but me, right?" So, I closed the door and began to move, slowly, of course, since my departure time had by then rolled around. The young lady kept banging on the door and on the side of the moving bus while shouting, "No, no, I have to go, don't do this to me."

"So, what did you do next?" His father asked. I stopped the bus, closed the engine, and sat back. I wasn't going to run the risk of running her (or someone else) over and getting myself into trouble, real trouble. I have all day, I reminded myself. Yes, I could sit there as long as I needed to, to be allowed to operate the vehicle safely. So, when the others on the bus saw that they were going to lose time and run the risk of being late themselves, some started acting up and speaking up. One young lady got up from her seat, where she was, way down near the back, took her belongings, and started walking up the aisles to get off the bus. "Hey," she said, "she can have my seat, I will catch the next bus."

"Not so fast," was my reply to her, the questions were asked earlier if anyone was willing to give up a seat so that she could go and sit an exam, as she'd said, no one offered, but now after she started throwing a tantrum and behaving badly, and dangerously, everybody is ready to give her what she wants. That's not how it works in the real world, Aunt. You all came on the bus (I assumed) because you intended to go somewhere. None of you wanted to give up the seat when asked. If you truly wanted to help her, that would have been the moment to do so, not now, not after her rude and childish tantrum-throwing behavior. Eventually, the young lady in question seemed to realize that either that was not her day, or that her steamrolling tactics were not going to work on this bus driver, on this day. So, she stepped aside and allowed us to get on our way. But since then, I've not been feeling too great about my actions; how I handled it, you know. Maybe I should have given her a break. If the other girl hadn't offered up her seat, I wouldn't mind it so much. But she did offer it, and I forbade it. It then puts the onus squarely back on my shoulders, and now I'm not sure if I did the right thing." His father, at this point, sat further back in his chair and was slowly stroking the place where a beard once used to be, my dear. While slightly shaking his head in an up-down motion, quite unlike the to-and-fro sideways motion that he was known for, whenever he was bewildered or amazed, like me. Meanwhile, nearly all eyes were then focused on him as if (automatically) they knew it was his moment to speak, and speak he did.

"I once heard it said that one can never go wrong by doing what's right," said the Commish, "even if and when doing the right thing is in correcting the wrong that such a one might have done previously. With that said, I will give you my thoughts on what we have just heard here. You know," he continued further, "I once issued a ticket to a motorist. 'For riding in an automobile without wearing a seat belt,'" I'd said. One of the guys, the driver, if I remember correctly, wanted to know why they were pulled over in the first place. Which seemed to imply that he thought he was being profiled and discriminated against, or something like that. I didn't argue with him. "For the non-use of seat belts, while operating or being in an 'automobile in motion,'" I told him.

"How did you know that I, or anyone else in the car, for that matter, wasn't wearing a seat belt?" He wanted to know further. "Because..." I told him again, "Because the car manufacturer of that make and model car you were traveling in, whenever they send them out on the market, they come equipped with five seat belts. I could clearly see the bodily outlines of six people in the car you were driving, which means at least one person wasn't wearing anything. Shut him up really quick." (Laughs.) So, did I hear you say that some of the buses are allowed to carry more than 48 people? He asked his son.

"Yes, but not mine; those other buses have handlebars and leather straps on them, which the passengers can hold onto for support. I don't have that on my bus."

"I see, my son." He continued: Law is an aftermarket; the effect and weight of the law are brought to bear mostly after the fact, after some breach would have occurred. What you need to do is know exactly what is required of you in the execution of your duty and do it all the time. Don't worry about what the other person says, unless the other person is authorized to give you instructions on your job and on how you carry it out. If they say don't carry more than 48, that's the cutoff point for you every single time. And I will tell you why. Don't ever bend the rules, is the takeaway for you here, and here is why. There will never be enough of what people want, so there will be no need for them to want anymore. People always want more, be it money, food, or even services (such as a bus ride), so there will always be ample reasons to breach the rules. As is the case with your bus ride story here. Five buses serviced the routes, with departure times at very regular set intervals. Every one of those passengers knew, or at the very least, should have known when the buses leave, and to a lesser extent, when they arrive. Of the five buses, two of them (we are told) were allowed to carry people standing, up to a limit of twelve. That is, one standing passenger would correspond to each row of seats. Such buses, therefore, may carry up to sixty, still a limit at that point. Why two, and not all the buses, one might ask, and that's a very good question. I don't know the answer to it, but I have my suspicions as to some possible reasons. Anyway, if the buses have set departure times, one has good reasons to believe that the passengers knew the schedule well. Why would one person run up to the bus stop at almost the departure time, and see several people standing there in a line, a bus parked on the stand? This person then proceeds to walk (or run) past those who were standing there in line, to then go banging on the closed door of the bus, trying to get in. Did I just hear someone say, 'Special case?'" Learn this, and never forget it, my son: Dangers are always hidden in the fine print, tucked safely away, they will only come up to judge you on your calamitous day. Look at it this way. Suppose you were operating one of those buses which were equipped and able to carry up to sixty passengers, just for argument's sake, and you were on the stands and found that: after being full. Two other passengers wanted to get on the bus, the driver (you in this case), then had two choices: (a) Give in and take them on, or (b) Stick to the rules and leave them there. If the driver chose option (b), by sticking to the rules and leaving them, then there is nothing to worry about. If he goes for option (a) and takes them, though, there are two things for him to worry about. Either it all goes well, or things could go wrong. If it all turns out well, there will be nothing to worry about, and you will likely want to do the same thing again and again, until something eventually happens to get your attention. Like, if it doesn't go as well as you would have liked, and you have an accident, for example. Then you will start realizing that you don't have quite as many options as you had before, and this is called "a problem." You might even have to interact with the police, and they are going to want all the relevant facts and statistics, which will include how many people were involved; that's a problem. Why were there so many on board? Problem. The insurance company, too, is going to want those, among other statistics. You were told that the vehicle you were operating was equipped, licensed, and insured to carry 48 passengers seated, plus 12 standing (in some cases). For a maximum of sixty passengers, you were carrying sixty-two at the time of the accident. As it turned out, sixty of those passengers were checked and certified in perfect health with no injuries arising from the accident, great. But two were injured, the insurers will not take on the responsibilities for that, based on a breach caused when the number of passengers exceeded the limits. They successfully argued that the excess weight on the vehicle did affect the stopping distances of the vehicle and that, if the vehicle was not overloaded, it would have been able to stop in time to avoid the accident (as the road did). Or at least, reduce the effects of the impact. They won't pay, your employer too, won't pay. Because they did everything that was required of them. Including, but not limited to, informing you of all of the rules and guidelines to follow. On this occasion, as we're seeing via the outcomes, you weren't following, at least, not all of them. Somebody was at fault for what had transpired, somebody messed up, somebody was responsible, somebody will be made to pay. Who is that person? If it wasn't the insurers, wasn't the employer, then who do they have to focus on next? Yep, guess who is in the hot seat now? Never forget this, my son: Life is an aftermarket hack; the essentials take effect after the fact. In the same way, you weren't thinking about any of those things before you were confronted with the sobering realities after the fact? It's the same way it works on the other person's part, your passengers in this case, but... They aren't thinking about the "bad day scenario." They know that they are at point A, and need to get to point B, and you're that person who is in the position to make it happen for them, in their minds. So if it will take only a bit of persuasion to make it happen for them when the odds seem to be getting somewhat against them. That's when they will try persuasion, without worrying about the consequences. Nine times out of ten, everything will work out just fine for them and you. But it is the tenth time that one needs to pay very close attention to. Again, I say, "Dangers are hidden in the fine print, tucked safely away, they will only come up to judge you on your calamitous day."

## 19

Chapter

# Relapse into Normalcy

The commissioner's response to his son's concerns seemed to us to hit the correct margin on everyone's acceptance-measuring grids. Chelsea wanted more, seemingly. She, out of the blue, remembered that she too had been having some issues she needed to get his advice on. "Very well," said Dad. Chelsea, like everyone else in the household, calls him dad, even though he is, in fact, her grandfather.

"Can it wait until tomorrow, though? Because it's already almost your bedtime, little miss, and I have a feeling this might need quite a bit more time than you have remaining for us to do it justice tonight. So, what do you think? Can this one wait until tomorrow?"

"Well, I suppose so, I think it can wait that long, but no longer than that, okay?"

"Promise," said the Commish with a palms-up seal, as Chelsea, as well as most of the others who were there in raspy attentiveness, being witnesses to the conversations, started shuffling around and moving about. This was the indication to us that this part of the show was over, and it was time for everyone to move on to the next part of the evening. Chelsea, for example, went to get ready for bed. The Commish, though, at the end of the sit-in, while everyone else got moving about in preparation for bedding down for the night. He was left there by himself, still sitting on his La-Z-Boy. Yikes! It was then that it hit home to him that this could be a snapshot of his life and what it would look like from then on.

Chelsea came back down to hug them and kiss them, both the commissioner and his wife. She came over and kissed them goodnight before she went off to bed. His wife poured them two glasses of wine like she had been doing for decades. They then sat back and chit-chatted while sipping the wine, as was the norm. After the children had all gone to bed, they would indulge a bit, well, usually. Especially as it applies to the younger ones, and me. They had never taken more than one drink at a time, but that night, Mr. Watkins wanted a second. For some reason, he was feeling a bit nervous and apprehensive. His wife, though, reached across and placed a reassuring hand on his knees and rubbed it. "Relax, dear," she said, everything is going to be alright, things will work out just fine, you'll see. That didn't do much to appease the Knott's he was feeling in his stomach. Because it had (apparently) just started to settle in, in his mind that that was the first day of the rest of his life on the outside of the police commissioner's office, and the police force as a whole. He won't need to get up early and go to work like he used to. He could sleep in if he so chooses to. But he could not begin to see himself lying in bed after the sun had risen unless he was at the point of near death. His wife reminded him that he had promised Chelsea a hearing the following day. Not that she thought he had forgotten, but rather to make a point: you have got that one to look forward to, and then, who knows? It might be Joel the next day, and then Jane, and after her, it may be Jay-Jay.

He did get the point, but she continued to tell him anyway; Honey, you have got the most enthusiastic and adoring bunch of people right here to train, educate, inspire, and equip for the task of living life in the world in the current age. You won't have time to notice that you won't need to get out of bed that early and go to the office in town anymore. You can go right on and set up shop here and continue doing what you do best, which is training, educating, and inspiring people. Especially, the people you love and who love and adore you in return. She was right, he knew it. He was stimulated and buoyed by the gesture; was that a harbinger of things to come? Yes sir.

The police federation and the police officers' club would have gone about putting together a retirement package for him. A package that included a Caribbean cruise trip for him and his wife. The commissioner instructed them to cash it in and donate the proceeds to the Children's Hospital Benevolent Society fund. "I had planned on taking the ride of my life," he said, "but it will be centered around the home and family." Yes, the family with whom he still, (after all those years,) felt as if he hadn't been spending enough time with. Well, all that has just been changed, make way now, for the new and improved Shaky Watkins, commissioner, still.

Calling all Teachers.

The age of the youth is now in full bloom, young people are staking out their claim in almost every sphere of life, and in almost every corner of the globe. Jamaica is not to be left out of this trend; Jamaicans have always been among the trendsetters of the world, so nothing strange here. The political class has been going through its fair share of makeovers in recent times on the Island, too. The old-school politicians and their times have passed or are passing on, and taking a lot of their old ideas with them. Mark you, not all of those ideas were bad, nor were they all good. But the modern Jamaican man (and woman too) has seen and heard enough from that passing class to know what to latch on to and what to leave well alone. The current prime minister is still a young man in his upper thirties, although he is serving his second term in office. He is the youngest person to ever occupy the office in our country, knocking his predecessor from that esteemed spot. He was the youngest at the time when he took office, but that didn't last very long. That PM, the one just before him, had served the country for well over two decades and retired, some say, only because he didn't believe he could win again. The mood in the country was changing; many were calling for change (time for a change, they say) as if we'd never heard that one before. So, he retired, handing over the reins to his deputies and more. The election that followed those events shortly afterward saw the very young and articulate finance minister, who, at the start, no one thought was able to take on such a big job. But he did, and prospered gloriously.

He is now well into his second term and still riding the high tides of popular approval. Another young person is at the head of another big entity in the country, too. The Jamaica Constabulary Force is headed by a (relatively) young and well-capable woman, Commissioner Evadne Maine, and by all indications, she is doing a fantastic job.

Taking up from where the previous Prime Minister and his team left off was no easy feat for the young PM. "He has surely got some very big shoes to fill," many were heard saying regarding him. "And the twenty-second century is looming large on the horizon." The country is still thriving, the people are prospering, but the crime issues will not go away, and the age range of the culprits and criminals seems to be getting younger every day. So, as of late, the government has been targeting a shift in its focus. Whereas the focus was on the rapid development of the country in the previous years, like the creation of jobs, jobs, and more jobs for the people, under the mantra that the devil finds work for idle hands. Therefore, if those hands are put to proper use, there will be fewer idle hands for the devil to use, and hence, the crime monster will become a thing of the past, well, so they thought. It didn't quite work out that way. However, now that most of the other big-ticket items have been taken care of, this new government is focusing a lot more attention and resources on getting the crime issues under control. The call has gone out now: calling all teachers, counselors, mothers, and fathers, too. Father seems to be the centerpiece of this government's plans; they want to put fathers back in homes and into their children's lives. A very handsome package has been put together to assist and encourage father to remain a part of their children's lives, in the formative years and beyond. "Our children are our most valuable assets; they are our future," said the PM. We must love and care for them, treat them well, and teach them well. Let us prepare to take a moment now and go back to the past a little. Just long enough to see what we can learn from our elders and our ancestors, both the good as well as the bad aspects of their experiences. Then, when we've done that, and will have seen the outcomes. We must decide on what works well for them that can still work for us today, then take what is good and apply those to the current situation. What is to be left alone, though, leave it well enough alone. We are under no illusion that this will be easy; it won't be a walk in the park. There will be haters and naysayers. There will be busybodies, too, many who will want to run over here to tell us what we should and shouldn't do. But there comes a time in the life of every person, every nation, every people, when and where they will have to decide for themselves where they want to go in life. What they want to do with their lives, and then get up off their rear-ends where the wives... and go get it done. This is where we are now, as a nation. This is where we are as a people. We are moving forward from here to a much brighter tomorrow. We will not be daunted, we will not be discouraged, and we will not be defeated, so today we are calling all teachers. Today, we are still calling all of you builders; today, we are calling all well-thinking Jamaicans. Come along with me and let's continue the push forward in building out this great Island in the sun: Jamaica, land we love. I thank you all.

That was, (in essence) the speech that the newly re-elected Prime Minister delivered on the day of the swearing-in of his cabinet, and the whole nation is once again all revved up and ready to go the next mile on the road to real prosperity. Long live J A, Jamaica land we love.

The End.

This poem was written by special request, to honor the life, work, and times of someone very dear and special to both me and the person who'd requested it, and dedicated to "the principal," principally speaking, and to all teachers on Teachers Day. On another note, the name "Delivered" was a chance encounter. After finishing the first draft, I was about to send it off for approval by the person who had ordered it, under the caption "delivered." It was then that I noticed that it fits quite well with the subject matter. So. Here for you is the poem, "Delivered."

Delivered.

You planted the seeds long ago and were not sparing with the water. You cultivated and watched them grow, cause that's who you are, a planter.

You'd tilled the soil and sunk them in, beneath the rays of a golden sun. For them, you've burned the midnight oil, your days were long, and the work was never done.

They'd sought you out and called you up, ten thousand young minds to mold and teach, your feet were swift, your hands were mighty. To find them and to reach.

Time and talent from your abled helpers, those who'd participated and invested. All had their own special part to play; you'd surrounded yourself with the very best...

The best of minds, that is. Able minds, stable minds, because what's at stake, you knew there and then, were pliable, impressionable, and inquiring minds.

Many sons and daughters, too, you bore on your strong shoulders to enlightenment. So, here's to you from all of us, this, the haughtiest of Thank-Yous, on this very day is sent. From all of us to you, principally speaking.

A good time for another spoken word piece, or two. Like this one called. **Hair**

Hair, oh beautiful beloved hair. Be very careful where you choose to grow. Not all regions are going to be as friendly, you know. And allow you to prosper and freely flow.

In some regions, they are waiting with sharp edges to cut you short, and will not hesitate to cut you low. At other times, their tool of choice. It is to whack you hard with a no-no, to where no hair ever grows.

Whether tied up in knots beneath nets and hats. Or let loose and hang low. Dare not you brush against bare skin. Or you'll be open to getting tossed to and fro.

Hair, oh, lovely flowing cascade of keratinized protein. Creeping out of someone's scalp and skin. To adorn the head on which you grow. And frame the face in virgin thin.

With oils and creams and methodized machines. Applied in temperatures hot and cold. Their razors and shavers, scissors and clippers. Will comb and brush you till you roll over and fold.

Take ye heed and listen well, you, tiny fiber of a hair. Every time you wake up and get a bit shaken up. A heated comb is likely to be waiting there.

So don't be eager to plant your roots around, in every lofty place or farrowed ground. Take a little time to ponder and beware. Cause someone may be itching to press you with a waxy mat, like this one, and that. And pluck you screaming out of there. 2017.05.16.

Here's another 5–7–5 poem for you called "The Teenagers."

She was just sixteen
When she befriended six teens
She wed the sixth teen.

# PART FIVE

**"7**6" Clancy's Journey: A Jamaican schoolboy's story.
Set in the early eighties in a small town in Jamaica. 76, Clancy's Journey tells the story of a gifted Jamaican schoolboy who was well on his way through high school and heading straight into university. Young Clancy was fast becoming one of the country's topmost schoolboy football players, but then, his idol, Bob Marley, died, and Clancy's life took a drastic turn.

Note: Some names, places, and events in this story might seem familiar to some, but this story of 76, Clancy's Journey, is all a figment of the author's imagination. Happy reading.

## 21

Chapter

**T**he Motorcade.

He was sitting on the low-hanging branch of the huge star apple tree. The emphasis here is on the "hanging" more so than the "low," since no one wants to fall from this height to the ground. He leaned his back up against the dominant trunk of the tree, resting the left hand atop the other, much smaller branch that grew out of the tree right at the level of his armpit, as if it was cut to fit the measure, just for him. His head was propped up by the round of his palm under his cheek, the tip of his fingers at ear level. His chin was cupped in the palm of his hand, behind his knee, which was pulled in front of his chest. The sole of his foot was resting flat on the same limb on which he sat. He wasn't sure if it was the sound of the music that filled the air that had woken him out of the sweet little nap he was having, or if it was because of the pain. It could have been that. A piercing, sharp pain that was running up through his armpit and over the shoulder, yes, it was probably that. The red, green, black, and gold Tam he had placed between his armpit and the tree limb had fallen out while he slept, leaving the bare skin rubbing against the hardwood. He eased himself up from the lower branch, hobbling on one leg, because the cramps in the right leg that had been hanging all this while would not allow him to put his weight on it. After the feeling came back into his leg (a little), he picked up the T-shirt he was sitting on and climbed down. By this time, the music was beginning to get closer and clearer, so he joined in with the lyrics; *I hear the voice of the Rasta man say, Babylon your throne gone down...*

In the distance, he could now see a couple of automobiles rounding the corner like little marbles as they rolled into view. He had positioned himself strategically halfway up the hills of Mount Rosser, where one could see the approaching vehicles as they passed just outside the town of Linstead. It was clear by then that the funeral procession was approaching. He could feel the throbbing on the side of his neck, and his earlobe was heating up by several degrees. "It's action time," he said to himself. The late great Robert Nesta Marley is being buried today, said Clancy, the funeral procession is passing right by this way. I may not be able to go to the funeral in St Ann, but nobody is going to deprive me of watching the procession as it passes this way. To make himself more comfortable, Clancy reached into his pocket for his pocketknife and gathered some dried banana leaves. He spread them out on the ground, then lay flat on his stomach, resting his propped-up chin on top of his folded arms, and then waited.

Clancy O'Connor was the name his mother gave him, but everyone calls him "76" because of the number he wore whenever he played football with the renowned Dinthill Technical High School team. His fame has been spreading throughout the island (in recent times) as he blossomed into one of the most prolific goal-scoring machines the island has ever seen. Not just in schoolboy football but at the club level, too, and he was constantly being compared to the great Allan "Skill" Cole. To say that Clancy loves the game of football is an oxymoron; however, he secretly cherishes another burning desire, of becoming an entertainer, someone like Bob Marley or Dennis Brown. He particularly liked Dennis Brown's style of singing. He thinks and agrees with those who say that DB is a better singer than Bob. For those close enough to Clancy to hear him sing, he seems to beam with pride when they say that He sounds like Dennis. "Maybe someday I'll be belching out hits just like DB, Clancy reasoned within him." But for the time being, Clancy is all about football.

Two motorcycles were leading the procession as it made its way around the corner, just before passing right by Clancy, who was joined by two others. The new arrivals on the scene were: Devon, with whom he was quite familiar, as they both attended Ewarton Primary School together. Devon now attends St Jago High School in Spanish Town. The young lady with him was not familiar to Clancy, but she had a rather cool and refined appearance, he noticed. "A foreigner," Clancy immediately thought to himself, "this might be his girlfriend." He was interrupted in the middle of that thought as Devon introduced them; Hey, he said, meet Debbie, my cousin from London. Debbie, this is Clancy, my longtime friend from primary school. Hi! Hi, they exchanged greetings with handshakes, then quickly reverted to focusing on the steady stream of automobiles rolling through the winding uphill climb of the street. But Clancy was quietly mulling over the multitude of thoughts in his head.

For the next 45 minutes to an hour (or so), while watching the happenings. Mount Rosser was transformed into a sea of cars, trucks of all sizes and shapes, and motorcycles, most of them being ridden by Rasta man and his pillion rider. Many of them wear the trademark: black, red, green, and gold Tam (headpieces). They were looking around with an inquiring gaze, trying to see the appearance of the hearse, which they had not seen yet. Or did they miss it somehow? They were wondering.

The traffic stream was beginning to thin out, signaling the end of the procession. But Clancy, as well as the other two with him (he could tell by the puzzled look on the faces of his two companions), was thinking the same thing: Where is Bob? The closest thing they had seen so far to suggest that there was going to be a burial (other than the vehicular procession) was a few cars and pickup trucks laden with floral bouquets and wreaths, and somewhere wedged between them, one van draped over by a top hauling. All three of them had the same puzzled look on their faces as Devon turned towards the others while pointing in the direction of the tail end of the procession and said, You don't think that... that's him? Simultaneously, they all burst out, no o o. Yes.

22

Chapter

The Girl in His Mind.

It had been a full year by then since Clancy first laid eyes on Debbie. He knew there and then that he really "dug" her, as he once confided in his friend Devon. She is sitting across the table from him now and sipping a Ting Jamaica grapefruit drink over ice from a plastic straw. Clancy, meanwhile, was working hard at pretending that he hadn't noticed her dark and mysterious eyes watching him.

Clancy was not yet of age to be admitted to a bar; he had another 10 months to go before turning 18; furthermore, it was not his idea to be there. But Dinthill had just finished beating up Veer Technical High School, all but driving them out of the championship. The fact that "76" had a lot to do with that wasn't lost on anyone. He'd scored two goals and an assist to lead the team to a 4–2 win. Not only the 6ft 2 inches, 220lbs frame he carried around on his toes, but his whole bodily features far more closely resemble that of a grown-up, than a teenager in the hoods, he'd owned, and besides, who is going to say no to the great "76"? The band was playing softly and low, as it all blended in with the ambiance, chatter, and laughter that filled the place. The band had just struck up the song "Blue Moon," which got half the audience singing along. Clancy joined in and was singing too. He slowly faded out when he noticed more than a dozen curious, gazing eyes zeroing in on him. Then slowly, the claps and chants rose; 76, 76, 76... Clancy hesitated for as long as he could, but the unrelenting mob was not letting up, so he gingerly walked up front to what was a sad excuse for a staging area.

| 207 |

He took the microphone handed to him by Baggermouth, the crooner, MC. Band leader all wrapped up in one. Clancy clumsily tapped on the microphone to make sure it was in proper working order. That caught some of the people off guard, especially those who were sitting directly in front of the speaker boxes. "Oh-Lord!" When he finally spoke, the chattering went down by several decibels. "I don't know what it is that you are all trying to do to me here," he said, "what am I supposed to do here?"

Singgg! The response came as if with one voice. After what seemed like an eternity to most of them, some of whom were reacting as if they were ready to pounce upon him like an anxious battering mob, Clancy raised the mic and spoke again. Okay, he said, I'll sing, but on one condition: that I get to choose the song. Without waiting for a reply from the audience, he belched out the words: If I have the world, I'd give it to you. "Pull-up," the crowd responded in classic Jamaican style. Promptly, the band struck up the backing rhythm to that song and then broke crisply, as Clancy directed them by an up-down swiping motion of his hand into a clenched fist, like this. Again, the crowd roared and shouted. He eventually got through the first verse of the song. Upon re-entering the chorus, the crowd joined in. That was when he bent down, placed the microphone at his feet on the stage, and walked off. To rousing applause, clapping, cheering, and calls for more, more, more.

He sat back down at the table across from Debbie, picked up the glass of drinks, and raised it to his lips, then gulped down a huge mouthful of the brew. Which, by this time, was just a degree or two below room temperature. After placing the glass back down onto the table, just a little bit removed from the round puddle of water where the glass had been before. He began manipulating the round spot into a hippie peace sign hanging from a long "necklace." The top of which conspicuously pointed to the side of the table where Debbie was sitting. Still drawing his finger through the now thinning water, Clancy uttered under his breath; Would you even want it though? After what seemed like a lifetime in dog years without so much as a breath in the form of a response, to him. Clancy looked up from the tabletop where his eyes had been focused ever since his return from the stint at the mic.

Debbie's sharp eyes were watching him. The fire inside her gaze was piercing through him as if straight into his soul, while she chewed on the tip of the plastic straw. She was slowly spinning it around in her mouth with her fingers. She didn't answer in so much as a single word.

Debbie collected her belongings; well, it was just her handbag and a scarf that was sitting on the bench behind her. But right in front of Clancy, who was keeping a watchful eye on them, along with the other belongings they had placed there: Clancy's sports bag, and Devon's neat "Murse." That's what Devon called it; everyone else calls it a Man-purse. Clancy rolled the window down and looked back at Devon while he was running his finger over a "suspect" spot on the car's bumper. Devon climbed back into the driver's seat and hesitated a moment before pulling out. To look back, perhaps at the amount of space he had between the two vehicles to maneuver, before settling himself in and closing the door. As soon as the car moved out of the parking lot, Clancy stuck his head out the window to look back. Maybe at the pick-up truck again this time, maybe at the club. Debbie, in a quick analysis, summarized that it was the club, the place where he'd just debuted as a singer/performer/entertainer. Whatever happens hereafter for the Clancy "76" entertainment brand, this will go down in the books as the time and place where it all got started and began.

# Hit the Road.

While he was looking back with his head out the window, Debbie said in a low tone of voice; What took you so long, though? Clancy pulled his head back inside the car and looked across at Debbie, who was now looking out the window on her side of the car so that Clancy could not see her full face or her eyes. He looked up at the rear-view mirror in the center top of the windshield and saw Devon's eyes looking back at him before turning to look on either side of the vehicle via the outer rear-view mirrors as if nothing mattered more than the observance of the proper driving instructions that he'd learned in driving school.

Devon was the first to speak when they were on their way toward Ewarton. "You were awesome tonight, dude," he said, "you absolutely nailed it."

"Yes, 6, you killed it," said Debbie while planting a soft but firm hand on Clancy's thigh just above the knee.

"6?" Clancy inquired, "What team have you been cheering for? Nobody calls me 6, at least not anymore."

"What do you mean by 'not anymore'?" Debbie asked.

"That's what some folks used to call me until it started to cause confusion between me and Richie Reid; he plays for CC, that's Clarendon College." He hastened to say this before Debbie, who was... Look, look at her there. She's fiercely protesting now, assuring him she knows what CC signifies. "I'm not so dumb, you know," she said.

"That was not what I was implying, I just wasn't sure that you knew, seeing you're not — "Not what?" Debbie chimed in accusingly.

"Hold up, hold up," Devon butted in before either of them got into saying things that they'd come to regret later.

"I'm sorry," said Clancy. Debbie didn't respond. "Not from here, I wanted to say..." Clancy continued.

"I am from 'here,'" Debbie shot back, "Jamaican born and bred." Clancy did not utter another word; he realized there and then that he didn't know enough about her. Should he have asked, or tried to get to know her better before... is that why she was so upset? She's probably right to be, he thought to himself.

"You know what I was thinking back there at the club?" Ask Devon, attempting to break up the silence and ease the awkward tension, perhaps. "I said to myself that it must have been that Heineken beer you were sipping on that had loosened you up. I never thought I would see you drinking beer again after — "Hay, hay, don't you even go there," Clancy interrupted, but Devon was not about to stop before filling Debbie in on the juicy details. Debbie was now sensing that she was about to be privy to something fantastic and was all ears (and eyes), focusing on her cousin Devon.

"The first time he ever drank a beer, no, tasted a beer is the correct term here. We were on our way home from school one afternoon. It was a group of us walking home from school when we saw his dad in a bar with some of his coworkers from Alcan. They were drinking in a bar. His dad called him inside and offered him something to drink, "Give the 'young man' a beer?" he said.

"It was a Red Stripe beer," Clancy interjected, but Devon continued rattling on. He tasted the beer, planted the bottle back down on the bar counter, and ran out of the bar spitting as he went along, wiping his tongue on his shirt sleeve and spitting some more. When we asked him why, he said that it was because that thing tasted like piss.

"How do you know how piss tastes?" Debbie turned towards him and asked. "That's what we all asked him at the time, too, to which his response was, it tasted like how piss smells." Laughs. Clancy, with his head now thrown back onto the back of the car seat, was not saying a word more. Perhaps it was because he knew he wasn't going to win in this. So, he thought the best response would be to step aside and allow both of them to exhaust the tickle, or for the tickle to exhaust them.

*"Yuh naaw goh a yuh yaawd bwuoy?"* Devon asked, which means, in layman's terms, Aren't you going home? Or, as it is in this particular case, get out of the car, you're now home. Prompting Clancy to straighten up and look out of the window. That was when he realized he was sitting in front of his house on Charlton Drive. Clancy reached for the doorknob and cracked the door slightly open to get out of the car. While sliding out, he grabbed his bag that was resting at his feet on the floor, "See you guys sometimes," he said, "Well, perhaps." Before closing the car door, Debbie leaned over and said, I suppose I'm not going to get an answer to that question, eh?

"What question?"

"What took you so long, dumb ass?" Devon shot back, before hitting the gas pedal and speeding off. Clancy threw his arms up, letting the bag fall at his feet in the motion while he watched the car go. He knew they were laughing their faces off in the car, though, because he could see the outlines of their upper bodies through the windshields. Ably aided by the streetlight up ahead, which suggested they were having the time of their lives. At his expense, of course. The car turned the corner and went out of sight. Clancy picked up his bag and went inside.

That night, although he was very tired from the events of the day, Clancy could not fall asleep, at least not right away. What an eventful day it was, he thought. The game was tight, down to the last minute, but we'd managed to pull it off. Sergio, the goalie, was exceptionally good this time, too. He stopped not one, but two shots in the closing minutes of the game, which could have easily tied the match and forced overtime. The man-of-the-match award was well deserved by him, despite those who thought it should have been Clancy's. The bus ride back home was rather festive, too; there was still a large group waiting and ready to party at Dinthill when the bus arrived. But the team was exhausted, and most just wanted to go home.

Devon and Debbie were sitting on the front doorstep waiting for the arrival of the bus. They were as excited as all the others when the team exited the bus, but seeing how the crowd thronged them, they decided not to add more pressure on the boys. So, they remained seated until Clancy navigated through the crowd to come over and join them where they were. They both fell on his neck and hugged him, then slowly walked together towards the parking area while Clancy exchanged pleasantries with the many adoring fans who (seemingly) just wanted a little piece of him.

Not until the car pulled into the parking lot at Club Jamaica did Clancy realize that they were not going straight home. "Just a small pit stop," Devon assured him. The coach was there, no mistaking him, but other than for his brother, who was somewhat like the extra man on the team (he's always there somewhere around the team). Clancy was the only player there, and the coach didn't waste any time reminding him, "Hey, no drinking, you hear?" From that point on, it was like a cat-and-mouse game between them as Clancy tried to conceal his drinks, no, it wasn't a Heineken beer, wink-wink. When the coach caught him at one point with a glass in his hand, Clancy said it was a Baby Sham. Hmm-hmm, said Coach as he walked away, turning around about halfway across the room to look Clancy square in the face while pointing his index and forefinger at his own eyes and then at Clancy's as if to say; I'm watching you, chum. Clancy and his friends later reasoned that that was directed at the onlookers around and about, who may later accuse him of allowing the boys on his team to drink alcohol, rather than being directed at Clancy personally. There was never any further intervention from the coach the entire evening. Clancy had a great time at the club, including being put on the spot to sing, but he had to admit that he enjoyed it. Not so much for the ride home, though, he'd missed what Debbie was saying to him and looked rather clumsy in the process. He almost allowed them to drag him into a quarrel with her.

Then, they have their belly full of laughter at his expense. But it wasn't all bad, Clancy deduced. Debbie didn't leave for home, still mad at him. He knew that because of how she seemed to enjoy the jokes, and if there were any remaining doubts. She'd asked for the answer to the question of the earlier evening as the last thing before leaving for home. This suggested that the question was still relevant, and the answer was much desired.

24 |

Chapter

**I**t's Break Time.

It's been three days since Clancy last saw (or heard from) his two friends. This was the early '80s, living in a small town in Jamaica, only the well-to-do had a home telephone then, and those were reserved mainly for dealing with important matters. This was the case in the Logan household. It wasn't like Devon was hindered from using the phone, but contacting Clancy by such means was not possible since he (Clancy) did not have a telephone at home. The other ways and means by which he could make contacts would be for him to call. Just like he'd done on a few occasions when he would have called from the pay phone by the post office in Ewarton Square. This time, however, Clancy was not so inclined as to make any contact, at least not yet. He needed to process the details of the previous weekend in his mind first because he was torn between anger and admiration for Devon. Why, he wondered, was it that Devon seemed to be setting him up for ridicule at times? However, those other times when he was clearly defending Clancy were certainly not lost on him. Perhaps Devon was waiting for Clancy to call or come over to the house. But he was the one with access to a car, even if the telephone was not feasible. For Clancy to get to Whitehouse, where Devon lived, he would have to walk all the way or part of the way there. If he were lucky enough to get a taxi from Charlton to Ewarton, he would still have to walk from there to Whitehouse or pay extra for the taxi to take him there. Clancy was in no mood to do either.

It was Monday evening, and Clancy left school at the final bell; he did not stay over for practice, as was the usual on Mondays. He just wanted to get out of there. On the way home, while walking out of the school compound towards the gate, he noticed the blue car that had pulled up and stopped. He thought that it might have been a taxi, "Let it go," he said to himself; there will always be another one coming, a taxi, that is. Exiting the school gate, though, he noticed that the car was still there. Clancy did a double-take; that's when he realized that it was Devon's. He sidestepped the line he was about to join and went over to the car. Devon got out upon his approach and walked around to the rear of the car to meet him. "What's up?" he said. They exchanged hugs, slapped palms, and bumped shoulders.

"What are you doing here? Clancy wanted to know, as if he didn't know and really wanted to.

"Just passing."

"This doesn't look like 'just passing' to me."

OK, so I lied; what's up with you, dude? You just dropped out on me; on everybody, it would seem.

"I saw you on Friday evening; the beginning of the 'weekend,' the emphasis being placed on the 'weekend part,' and who is this 'everybody' that you are talking about?"

Well, not quite "everybody," but you seem to be copping out on your teammates right now as it is. Clancy did not answer at once; he turned his head the other way and gazed out the window. "That was a low blow, dude," he muttered under his breath.

"I'm not trying to beat up on you, buddy," said Devon, after pulling the car off onto the side of the road and stopping, blocking someone's driveway in the process. "I'm not out to get you here," he reiterated while looking Clancy squarely in the eyes. "Believe me," he said, "I'm your friend. Perhaps the only one that you've got left, and although it may not seem so now, I'm looking out for your interest. It is said that the worst thing that one can say sometimes is actually the truest thing that one can say, and I'm telling you now, you've been acting like a punk-ass kid these last couple of days, and you'd do well to grow up and start acting like a man. 'If you are,'" he hastened to add after a brief pause.

"I'm a man," said Clancy, again under his breath.

"Well, you are starting to make me (and some other people that I know) begin to wonder."

The rest of the journey home was dotted with low-key conversation until...

Upon the approach to the house where Devon lived with his family, Clancy turned his attention back to Devon, after noticing the car parked in the driveway, and said, "Seems like you've got company, dude."

"Why?"

"Because there's a car parked in your driveway, a strange car that I've never seen before."

"Well," said Devon, "That's the surprise I told you about earlier, parts of it, anyway."

"And what's the other part?"

"Parts," Devon corrected him.

"Parts?"

Devon, after bringing the car to a complete stop, shut off the engine and braced himself back. With both hands on the steering wheel, he said; Clancy, this car that you're now looking at, is my dad's new ride.

"Really! Wow," said Clancy, as he cracked the door partially open to ease himself out. He wanted to get a closer look at the car, you know. But then, after sitting back down again, he turned to Devon and said, "What's the 'other' part, or parts?"

"Parts," said Devon, "part 2 is, this car we're now sitting in, is my ride."

"Whoa, whoa! Congratulations, bro, well, you know, to both of you; your dad, and yes, you too." I'm not too big on the bug, though, whispered Clancy while pointing at the VW Beetle parked in the driveway in front of them, and then looking back at his friend. They both chuckled. "Dad said, it's very reliable and economical. Furthermore, now that the family has grown and is starting to fly the nest, he no longer needs a big car. Definitely not a 'four-door.' This little bug right here," Devon continues, "suits him just fine. It's perfect for the two of them, Dad and Mom, to ride around town. My sister, Junie, seems to agree with him too; she's gotten herself a Datsun, two doors, of course." They were laughing again as they went inside the house.

June, or Junie as she's affectionately called, is the eldest of Percival and his wife's (the other Logan's) three children. "She's the brain of the family," they all said. A 3rd-year law student at the University of the West Indies (Mona campus). She used to travel daily during the 1st year, but that was starting to take its toll on her. That was when the decision was taken for her to stay in town, by Uncle Dennis. Yes, that Dennis. The Halls are on Mom's side of the family. Nowadays, Junie only comes home on the weekends, well, some weekends. Sometimes two or three weeks may pass without her coming home. That's usually when Mom and Dad, Mom more so than Dad, will drive into town to see her and the rest of the family. Jacquie is the baby of the family. At 14, she attends Charlemont High School, not too far from home. Devon, now 18, was the only boy sandwiched between them.

...

The meal was delicious, and the conversation, delightful, as usual. Clancy was somewhat apprehensive at first, not because he didn't like being there, or the food, or any such thing, no. But more so because he didn't want to "waste" his mother's cooking, as she'd often chide him. But Devon had promised a "part three" of his series of surprises, and that included them going somewhere after dinner. Clancy had agreed to that, and he was getting a bit anxious to find out what the surprise was. He'd further convinced himself that his mother would not be overly worried about him today, because it had become customary of late for him to get home late-ish. Due to after-school team practice. Since he did not stay over for practice on this particular evening, and she didn't know that. He was, therefore, ahead of time; he had some time to spare. As soon as they'd pulled the car up to a stop at the gate by the house on the hills of Mount Rosser, Clancy immediately began to suspect what the third part of Devon's three-part surprise plan was. He knew the place quite well; this was the very place where he'd met Debbie about a year (or so) ago. The only difference was that it wasn't at the house itself on that occasion; it was just a little way down to the far end of the property.

Devon tooted the car horn, to which an unfamiliar face appeared in the 2nd-floor window, and then disappeared from view again. A side door opened up, out of which came a middle-aged woman wearing an apron and looking rather dusty indeed, all over.

"Sorry about my shabby appearance," she said, as you know, I'm in the middle of my renovation project... who is this fine young gentleman with you?

My friend, Clancy, Devon replied ...you two have met each other before, Devon continued while looking back and forth at both of them.

"I did, did I?" said the woman. "We did?" said Clancy. Both of them seemed somewhat surprised at Devon's declarations.

"You both met at the funeral, don't you remember?" Devon reminded them.

"Oh, yes," said Clancy, "Mrs. Logan, your uncle's wife?"

"Widow," whispered Devon.

Ronald Logan was the elder brother of Devon's dad, Percival. He'd migrated to England in the early '60s with his family: his wife Myrtle, sons David, Lance, and Debbie, the lone girl at the time, and who was the baby then. Two other children were later added to the family on the other side of the pond: Wendy and Greg. All the children are in London except for Debbie, who is here with her mother now and seems hellbent on staying put. Ron Logan had died in London; in keeping with his wishes, his remains were brought home and were to be buried in the Ewarton cemetery. Shortly after the funeral, the family, as well as all the others who came with them, returned home, to wherever in the world it was that they had come from, all except for Debbie. She stayed with her next-of-kin in Whitehouse, while her mom, brothers, and sister all went back to England. Her mother made it clear to them then that she was coming back home to Jamaica, for good.

This is a good place for another break, so here's a poem called: **Born for this.**

A glimpse into your pile of nothingness, at how futile your life has been.

You're going to take nothing when you go out of here, because you brought nothing in.

You're a loser, there, I said it. You're just trying to save your very skin.

But until you lose what's to be lost, you're never going to win.

You're trying, and trying so very hard, wanting so much to succeed.

Just so that you may consume it all, in all your envy, and in all of your greed.

But, you are a loser, I know it, despite the social stairs that you've been climbing.

Until you lose what's to be lost, you are never going to win.

You've kicked the doors wide open and then steamrolled over your haters, same as your loving friends.

Yet in all of this, you can't venture beyond.

That someone who's standing right there, you see, is the same "someone" who's holding the key.

He's there to remind you, if you'll just listen to him. That you're a loser, Mister man, and there's a reason why you can't get in. Until you lose what's to be lost. You are never going to win.

You spread your feathers like a blooming peacock and boast of all the fine blings that you've got. But what good is all of this to you, I wonder. When you're lying stretched out six feet under. Before that day finally brake, it may do you some good if "notice" you'll take.

That you're a loser, my friend. Born to lose in order to win. Except for losing your load of sin. You are never, ever, going to win.

WritingElk.

## 25

Chapter

M ansion on the Hill.

Although Clancy would have been there before, he had never seen the house like this. The main living area where the Logan family lived was on the topmost floor. That's what Clancy remembers from being there in the past. He would have gone out there with Mr. Logan (that's Percival, Devon's father) a few times. The house was rented out then, and Mr. Logan was responsible for maintenance, upkeep, and collecting rent. So, Clancy and Devon would have gone "for the ride" with them on a few occasions when they went out there. The lower floor was under lock and key then, that space was a grocery shop when the other Logan's family was still here. Well, so says Devon. Below that, there was an empty unfinished space; this, too, is now a space under construction. Mrs. Myrtle (as Clancy took to calling her of late, trying to avoid confusion between her and the "Mrs. Logan" which he long knew to be Devon's mother.) Mrs. Myrtle said that these two spaces will be used for income generation when finished.

Clancy sneezed and wiped his eyes with the back of his hand; the dust in the place was affecting him in more ways than one. Mrs. Myrtle pointed to the small box on the windowsill, "Take a dust mask," she said, "Oh dear, I'm so sorry, it's very dusty in here, I forgot to tell you." Devon (as well as Clancy) both put on a dust mask. Clancy then brushed rigorously on his pants to try to remove (at least) some of the white dust that had accumulated and settled on his uniform. It was only Monday evening; Clancy usually wore one suit of uniforms for two or three days each week. At this rate, he knew that he would have to change those clothes come tomorrow. On entering the second floor, Clancy quickly looked around, being careful not to touch the walls after being warned by their host, and further, by the signs that said; Wet paint. But Clancy's eyes were secretly searching for something else. As of yet, he hasn't seen Debbie, and the way Devon's eyes were zooming in on him seemed to suggest that he was picking up on the anxiety of the moment, too.

The flip, flop, flicking sound of slippered feet descending the concrete stairs just outside the open louver windows got both young men turning around to see. They watched as a pair of legs, clad in grey sweatpants, got longer as they descended the stairs. Disappearing (for a brief moment) behind the walled-up spot between the window and the door. The latch rattled, and then Debbie followed the opening door to enter the room, "Hi-ee," she said, as she hugged Devon and Clancy. Her mother reenters the room from somewhere in the back where she'd gone earlier,

"I thought you weren't coming down," said her mother.

"I'm here now," Debbie replied, "actually, it's you who should've come up since we live up there and not here." They laughed, they all laughed at this.

"So, did you guys come to work or what? That's what we have here," said Debbie, "and lots of it."

"Actually," said Clancy, "I was just thinking of leaving for home, I've got a lot of things to do over there too; not the reno types like these," he said while swiping his right hand in an arched semicircular motion, "but work anyways." Just then, Devon glanced at his watch and then at the door.

"I did kind of want to talk to you, though," said Debbie, "perhaps we could link up, sometime 'soon,'" the emphasis being placed on the "soon."

"What about?" Ask Clancy.

"Nothing for you to get too excited about, but... Yes, it's important, anyways?"

"You could come along with us for the ride, if you like," Devon suggested.

"Are you coming back here?" asked Debbie.

"Yeah, I'll bring you back home."

"Okay then, I'll come along."

...

The curvy descent down the winding roads of the hills of Mount Rosser was as exhilarating as always, and having Debbie sitting next to him (at Devon's command) suited Clancy just fine. The only problem with that was that it was too short a ride, but no one was complaining, well, not quite. Clancy was not about to miss the opportunity to at least test the waters again, so...

"You wouldn't happen to have a Cafenol on you?" He asked. "Are you okay?" Debbie asked, all alarmed, now and ready to pounce into action on somebody's behalf.

"I'm alright," replied Clancy, only that...

"That... what?" asked Debbie again.

"It pains my heart so much, not having you in my corner," Clancy complained. The pun was not missed by the other two, who burst out laughing.

"I'm in your corner, Clancy; I've always been in your corner. It's you who either could not see it or, perhaps... perhaps it was you who were too chicken to grasp it."

"So, we are on the same page then? So good to know."

"Speaking of knowledge, or knowing," said Debbie. "I have some news here that you need to know about. I have here this proposal for you from Club Jamaica. They want you to join their entertainment team to perform with them on Friday night's happy hour, in particular."

Oh no. I can't do that, not at all. All of a sudden, everybody's popping up and out of the woodwork, with offers and proposals. I can't deal with that, not now.

"Does that mean that you will deal with it later?" Debbie wanted to know. "I could help you here and there if you'd like," she continued.

"How are you planning on doing that?"

"I could manage things for you, I could become your manager, that is, if you want."

"I don't know, man; I really don't know."

"Who are these, everybody?" Debbie wanted to know. "You said that everybody is now popping out of the woodwork. Who is this 'everybody'?"

"The clubs," said Clancy, the Major League clubs have been calling with offers and proposals.

But that's good, that is a good place to be, Clancy, having choices and all that. It's just for you to make the right choices now, the ones that are best for you, do you know what I mean?

"Look, I need to think, and I definitely cannot think clearly now. I'll see you guys later," Clancy said as he reached over, took Debbie's hand, and placed a soft kiss on the back of her hand. Debbie pulled him in towards her, threw her arms around his neck, and kissed him right back. Only, this time, it was smack dab on the lips and... and... "I'm here for you if you need to talk," she said.

Phew! Night, Debbie. Devon, I'll see you, man. With that, they parted company for the night.

That night, Clancy's mother was the next to chime in on her son's latest dilemma. She would have noticed the concerned look on his face and altered countenance. Yes, she was more than happy knowing that her son had become so well sought after of late. However, she was not bubbling over with delight at those developments, and she lost no time in letting him know that. "I'm sending you to school to get an education; a proper education, so that you may get a regular job like regular people do. People who earn their keep in a real and regular world." She then went on to lecture him on how an athlete's life is a very short and tiresome one. "Don't go about depending on your muscle, use your brain," she said, and this entertainment, singing bit? Even worse. All that it has to offer you is drugs, illicit sex, and money, tainted money. Clancy did not see things that way, though, but he knew better than to argue with his mother; that's an argument he knew he could not win.

There was never any doubt that Janet Johnson loved her son and wanted what was best for him. However, she would much rather it if he would become more focused on self-empowerment in the form of elite education. That's the priority, as she would constantly remind him. But if all else fails, then get a marketable skill. Using his father as an example, she pointed out to him how he, though not a very educated man, had managed to secure for himself a very good job at Alcan working as a millwright.

## 26

# Chapter

**T**his is Friday Evening.

It's Friday evening, look, Clancy is on his way home after school. He's taking the taxi from Linstead to Ewarton for the first time this week. As part of the arrangements he had with Devon, he's to go home, shower, change, and be ready for the evening out. "Why?" Clancy had decided to take up Mrs. Myrtle's offer to join them for dinner. At the same time, he wanted to hear what Debbie wanted to say to him. Clancy would have practiced with the team every evening since Tuesday, but today... Devon stopped by to watch the game on Thursday and then dropped him home.

He arrived on time and found Clancy all ready and waiting, which was somewhat surprising (even to Clancy himself) since he was always one to be late and slow to get going. But not this time, perhaps he was trying to get out of the house before his mother got home, Devon thought, which could be any moment now. As a matter of fact, as soon as Devon turned the car around and pulled up at the gate again, they saw Ms. Johnson a little distance away, walking towards the house. Upon seeing his mother approaching, Clancy decided to wait for her to arrive home. He would much rather come clean with her about his whereabouts, like what he was up to, upfront, than to have her worrying about him, and then have to face the brunt of her wrath later on. She was somewhat reserved yet pointed in her response to his plans for the evening.

"You are of age," she said, "to be able to make adult decisions, but be prepared to accept the consequences, as well as the rewards, if there be any," she quickly added. I've tried to raise you to be able to find your way through this world, and I always knew that I would have to let you go someday; I just never thought that it would be so soon."

"Mom, I'm going out on the road with my friends, it's not like I'm going to catch a flight to some foreign country or something like that."

"Yes, my son," she said, "I know, but just remember what I said, it's a great big world out there, a great big world indeed."

"Okay, Mom, see you later," Clancy replied rather sarcastically as he went and sat in the car, and then, they were gone.

Mrs. Myrtle was to prove once again to be the most charming of hosts, smart, bubbly, and very well-informed on the latest trends in both music and sports. She'd challenged Clancy on some Marley's music trivia; she also knew more than the average person about football on the world scene. "Manchester United," she said, was her team, and had dared Clancy to go and play with them. Her cooking was world-class, too, as all three sitting at the table agreed. After-dinner activities and conversations were (obviously) designed to try to get to know the real Clancy, and to see where his head was. Apart from a few nervous moments when he almost choked, he was very pleased with himself in the end.

Debbie wanted to continue the conversation surrounding the question of the performing gig at Club Jamaica, and that was not all that she was up to. She has been very busy wheeling and dealing, so it would have seemed. Other than for the club Jamaica gig, which (by the way) Clancy had begun to warm up to by then. She also made some mentions of a series of shows, doing the hotel circuit on the north coast. That got Clancy's attention. "Like what! like A.J. Brown and others before him, perhaps?" Clancy thinks he's got the wherewithal that could make a real impact in this arena, on those same levels, too. Or even to a greater magnitude than theirs. The evening took on an air of excitement and great anticipation from then on. As they walked inside the club, he was bubbling; he was going to do it; he was going there to try out for the "Club Jamaica happy hour." Clancy was more motivated by then, much more than he had ever been before. "Even if I should mess it up," he told himself, "It will still be a plus for me, because…"

Because he was beginning to see it all as training sessions for greater things to come, however, messing up, or "goofing around," wasn't on his mind, "not tonight," he told himself, and his friends. On the way to the club, Clancy rehearsed three songs in the presence of his two-person adoring audience; You think I Love You for just one thing, and Debbie had also requested that he do the one that he did at the club the very first time; if I have the world, I'd give it to you, the last one was Bob Marley's one love. Mrs. Myrtle would have used that one to challenge him earlier that evening.

It was as if everyone knew that he would be there and performing. They all were eagerly anticipating his arrival, he knew, due to the wolf whistles and screams when they walked in. Bagger-mouth, who was there doing his usual "thing," proceeded to acknowledge him, "Known to many as 76, some people liked to call him baller, Clancy O'Connor is in the house?"

Few people knew Clancy's full and proper name. So he was more than a bit surprised that Bagger was one of the few. Clancy just nodded and waved as he began to nurse the cold drink that was placed on the table in front of him. Debbie left them sitting there to go somewhere in the back. Since it wasn't the restroom, as Clancy had assumed it was going to be, then it must have been to go and speak with someone. The manager, perhaps, regarding the audition. She came back grinning from ear to ear, as she announced that they would put him on as soon as he was ready. Clancy gulped down a mouthful of the brew and patted his lips with the hanky he was clinging onto for some form of support it could not possibly provide. "I'm ready," he said, to which Debbie gave her thumbs-up signal to the MC, who then proceeded to make the introduction. After a huge mouthful of chatter, painting Clancy as this great up-and-coming star, a singer, entertainer, etc., etc. Most of which,

Clancy hardly even heard, anyway, he heard his name: Clancy 76xxx-ahh. Clancy took the microphone and got right into his first song, which went over very well. Before getting into the next song, he told them the story of how he'd just gotten beaten by an old lady, "Sorry, an elderly woman." This was designed to appease Debbie, who was about to shoot him dead with that look she gave him. He then dedicated the song to his new best friend, Mrs. Myrtle. The last song that they heard from him that night was, yes, you've guessed it right, "If I Have the World..." The response left no doubt in his mind that it was good, very good indeed. For the next few weeks that followed, Clancy compiled a list of 10 songs that he said he could use as materials to fill a slot without falling into staleness or boredom.

It was just about five weeks remaining before school would be out for the summer holidays, and Clancy was looking forward to it for more reasons than one. A week from this coming Saturday, he is going to Ocho Rios to audition for a slot on Saturday or Sunday nights at the San Souci Hotel. He hasn't yet decided which slots he would take should he manage to land the deal. For the moment, though, he has secured for himself that spot on Friday nights, along with an option to do Saturday nights also, at Club Jamaica. All he needed to do was say the word. Debbie was the driving force behind all the happenings there, but Devon was not to be left out of the reckoning. He was the backbone of their success, being a friend, chauffeur, bodyguard, all-around right-hand man, and go-to guy for the group.

27

Chapter

They Took the Show on the Road.

Clancy had been working with the backing band at Club Jamaica and would have done so for the duration of the stint there. They would practice on Saturday evenings, the most inappropriate day of the week, come to think of it, with it being just a day after the actual performance day and all. But it was the only day and time that all the elements could come together that allowed it all to happen. So far, though, it has been working out just fine.

The band (for the most part) seemed interested in his pitch to have them join him on the North Coast venture. All but Bagger seemed interested and enthusiastic about the prospect. Bagger-mouth, however, (as is to be expected) was concerned about the likely fate of the club Jamaica brand should the guys get up and take to the roads.

"Time to step up the game, guys," said Lukie, the bassist, attempting to help the others make up their minds. After which, they all got it together and decided to go.

...

Clancy got up from the table and turned around to open the refrigerator door, which was right behind him where he was sitting. He reached inside for the container of orange juice and poured some for his mother, and then some for himself, before sitting back down at the table. The juice container still rested on the table in front of them now, as if to bear witness to the proceedings.

"You're not going to finish my juice, are you?" His mother complained.

"I'll go pick up some more for you when I'm done here," Clancy assured her. "Hmm hmm." It's been several months since they had sat and eaten together as a family, and this one comes with a lot of nervous tension. Both knew what was to be said, but neither wanted to be the first to open up the conversation.

"So, how are things going with you and your... um, music thing?" She heard herself saying.

"Pretty good, Mom, pretty good. As a matter of fact, that's just what I want to talk to you about, that, yes, and a few other things. 'Mom...' he continued, "I'm sorry for letting you down."

"Letting me down?"

"Well, yes, I know that this wasn't what you had in mind for me, but it may not be as bad as it would appear at first sight. Mom, I'm doing okay, we are going to be alright, this includes you, Mom. You know, everything I do, I do for us; you, me, all of us." Both eyes came together and locked in on that phrase; "all of us." Ms. Johnson was to have caught a glimpse of the deeper meaning of those words right away. "What do you mean by 'all of us?'" she asked.

"Us, as in family, mom, our family is growing? My family is growing."

"What are you saying, Clancy?" Ms. Johnson inquired further. After a brief pause, Clancy, looking aside now to avoid the direct gaze of his mother's soul-searching eyes, said; You are going to be a grandmother soon, Mom.

"What, what did you say? What have you gone and done now, Clancy? Is this what I sent you to school for? Is this the way I raised you to be going about dropping off babies here, there, and everywhere, all over the place?"

"Ma, ma, will you stop? Ma, stop and listen to me, please. It's not like that, no, it's not like that. Debbie and I are..." "So, it is her! Silly me." (Rolling the eyes now.)

"Ma, hear me out on this, please, thank you." As I was saying, Debbie and I have come a long way; we have been through many things together. Ever since the day when we first met? Ah, ha-ha. He smiled. It was on the day of Bob's funeral that was when I would have seen her for the very first time, yes. Nothing has been the same since.

"You telling me!" Ms. Johnson interrupted, rolling her eyes at him. "As I was saying," Clancy continued, things changed and then changed some more. He took a deep breath and then waited. "I, I love her mom, I really do."

Miss Johnson bit her lip, almost to a bleed; she had a thousand things to say, but she was now somewhat committed to hearing him out, though painful it may be.

"She's the one who has been behind all of this," said Clancy. She made it all happen, made me believe that it could happen, and believe me, Mom, it is happening, for real. He was waiting for her response, but quickly realizing that it wouldn't be forthcoming, he continued. I know, I know; I shouldn't be mixing business with pleasure, that's what you are thinking, but it's not like that. Well, before all of the business part, I was in love with her. It was a long and winding road that led me to a place where I could finally acknowledge it. But that's where we are now, and moving forward into bigger things.

The silence that followed was broken with the words, We are to be married soon, Mom. Gasp! ...and I? I mean, we. We're looking forward to having your blessings and participation in this. Make it quick, though, because we haven't got much time; the wedding is in five weeks.

"Five weeks? Did I hear you correctly, or am I going deaf? You must be crazy as hell."

"Calm down, Mom, calm down."

"Don't you tell me to calm down, you're the one who needs to calm down, way down. You're moving way too fast for me, for everybody, as a matter of fact, but none more so than for yourself. Who in the entire world plans and puts together a wedding in five weeks? What is this, and why the mad rush?"

"Mom, there is no need for panic, and who said anything about planning a wedding? It is you who needs to calm down, Mom, take a deep breath, relax, and hear me out on this, that's all I ask of you, will you? Thank you. I did not come here to fight with you, Mom, so here is the deal: Debbie and I are a couple, and we are going to have a baby soon. But before the baby arrives, we want to be married, hence the urgency. Debbie and-and... yes, she again. Debbie and her mother are the ones who are taking care of everything, and no, that's not a slight of any sort on you. It's just how it's done in their family; the bride's family takes care of the wedding. The groom's side of the family will take care of housing? You know, where we are going to live afterward."

"Ugh!" Ms. Johnson gasped again, "And where are you going to put her? Your wife and baby?"

"I'm coming to that, Mom, and that's the good part."

Waiting for the big declaration, this has got to be good, she thought to herself.

"I'm buying a house, Mom, it's all good and settled. I've just bought a house in Runaway Bay."

"Where do you get money from to, to... to buy a house? She asked softly, counting the words away."

"Glad you asked, Mom, glad you've asked because that's what I've been trying to tell you all along. It is working, Mom, all of this, the whole thing, which seemed so foolish to many; to you, even. It's actually working out all right. I'm paid pretty well for what I do, Mom, and I want you to stop worrying so much and start enjoying this with me instead. I want to treat you like the queen that you are. Will you let me, Mom? Will you?" He asked again with steadfast earnest desires seeping through the barriers his mother was building between them.

"I need to think," said Ms. Johnson as she raised herself from the table with such great effort as if she had taken on 30 years to her age in the mere minutes since they had been sitting there. She looked tired and listless, and Clancy's heart ached within him. He wanted so much to make her happy, to see her smile, to hear her laughing those big, haughty, unmistakable laughs that only Ms. Johnson had been known for, but...

Before leaving for home that evening, Clancy gave his mother a cassette tape, "listen to this when you get a chance," he said. He hugged and kissed her on the top of the forehead; she gave him (reluctantly), and then, he was gone. On the way to his next destination, Clancy would have been trying hard to decipher the day's events in his mind. It had been a tough year so far, as he recalled. Ever since he and the group started doing the hotel circuit that took them from Ocho Rios, through Montego Bay, and on through to Negril. It mushroomed. What started as a weekend thing quickly developed into a full-time job employing the services of all of the boys in the band. They even had to have added more voices along the way, in the form of backing vocals, plus the wicked input of Myrna "The Divine Deva" in her own right as a cabaret performer. All ably managed by Debbie, via her company, High Climb Entertainment Inc. She would have managed to impress a lot of folks in the process of doing this, by what she does and how she does it. But none more so than Clancy himself. She was always quick to remind him that there wasn't any magic to it, just logic, hard work, and the right education, which she was fortunate enough to have acquired while in England.

Clancy did not tell his mother where he was going next. After "The talk" with her, he has one more stop to make, one more person to talk to on the matter.

Clancy had a very good working relationship with his father, although they had never lived together. Mr. O'Connor lives in Rose Hall just outside of the town of Linstead with his wife and daughters, all of whom Clancy got along very well with, indeed. He may have found such favor with that part of the family because he was a boy and the only son born to his father.

Mr. O'Connor had a reputation around those parts as being some sort of a lady's man; he had been reported to have fathered no less than five other children (all girls) for a total of eight. Of course, he admitted to fathering only three.

## 28

Chapter

Family-wide.

Mr. O'Connor was not at home when Clancy got there, but the girls and their mom were. The girls, both in their twenties, still lived at home with their parents. Clancy had just turned twenty and was about to be married, though they did not know it yet.

"Ma, look who is here," Vickie yelled through the big living room. The sound carried on a slight echo, noticeable only by the most discerning of ears, such as those with which Clancy was blessed. Helen came running, even though Vickie's call was to her mother and not her. Just the mere mention of his name was always enough to cause the excitement level to spike in his sisters. Mrs. O'Connor came through the living room towards them. They were still there, bubbling and bouncing around just outside the front door as the siblings hugged and giggled. Clancy lifted each girl off her feet and spun them around, for as much fun and laughter as he could squeeze out of them. The stint on the north coast had taken him away from most of his longtime friends and family, so it was well within reason for his sisters to be a bit more exuberant in seeing him this time.

One could only see the leg from the knee down of the navy-blue slacks that Mrs. O'Connor was wearing; above that point and up to the waist was covered by a white apron. A white T-shirt completed the upper half of her bodily adornment. She was wiping her hands with a kitchen towel as she came towards them.

"Clancy," she said, "good to see you, come on in, come on in and sit down," while waving the right hand towards the sofa as if to say, specifically, take a seat here. She did not follow the lead of the girls and hug Clancy, not because she was not as enthusiastic about seeing him, no. But more out of being somewhat self-conscious that she was not yet in a state of preparedness to be greeting and entertaining anyone. She was in the middle of preparing supper.

"Your father should be home any moment now," she said over her shoulder as she headed back into the kitchen. "Come on and give me a hand here, Vickie, will you?" She had hardly finished the sentence when the sound of breaking wheels on the hard pavement brought them to attention. Mr. O'Connor's Range Rover had just pulled up into the driveway.

"*Waah gwaan sah*?" Said Mr. O'Connor (which means, in real-people terms, What's going on, son) as he lighted out of the vehicle, "What have you been up to of late?" He asked.

"Dad," Clancy replied as he met his father on the step just outside the doorway. "I haven't seen you in a long time," he continued, as they shook hands and shoulder bumped.

"So, you, you just quit school, pick... picked yourself up, and left overnight, why?"

"Long story, Dad, but it's all good; moving on to bigger things, you know."

"Bigger things?" Mr. O'Connor shot back at him. "Wha... wha... what bigger things are there than getting a good education, which... which is what you've just given up on, to go chasing after... after god knows what."

"I'm following my dreams, Dad, and it's working just fine; can we go inside?" Mr. O'Connor shook his head, "Kids nowadays," he said over his shoulder as he walked through the living room holding on to his briefcase loosely. The handle was across the lower joints of his fingers, but the thumb, proud and rebellious as it was, hung aloft, refusing to even so much as touch the leathery contraption. "You all seem to think you know everything."

Mrs. O'Connor remained out of sight all that time since her husband arrived home. Clancy thought she was still inside the kitchen, but she must have slipped upstairs while he was greeting his father. Because she came back down looking splendidly different than she was ten minutes earlier.

It was Mrs. O'Connor's idea that whatever it was that Clancy had to say should wait until after dinner, but his father wanted to hear it, right in the middle of eating.

"Might as well," said Clancy, "as time is of the essence here. I, I, I'm getting married and I'd like to have you all in attendance at the wedding." The gasps that followed were almost unanimous and deafening, coming in all at once from the ladies. Mr. O'Connor froze with his fork in his hand halfway between the plate and his mouth as he stared at his son in disbelief. It appears as if he was seeing Clancy as a little ten-year-old kid. Clancy must have read his thoughts because he followed up with; Dad, I'm twenty, not nine or ten. Helen giggled, with the back of her hand covering her mouth.

"Wha? wha? What did you just say? Mr. O'Connor stuttered."

"I'm getting married, Dad, and I'd like to have you all in attendance to share the occasion with me. With us. My wife-to-be, Ms. Debbie Logan, and I are cordially inviting you, all of you, to share with us the solemnization of our love in holy matrimony."

"When is it? When will it be?" Vickie interrupted.

"Sooner than you might think, in five weeks from now."

"Five weeks?" The chorus came chiming in again, from the ladies, of course.

"Why the mad rush?" Mrs. O'Connor asked.

"Well, it's not so much a rush," Clancy corrected, "delay is more like it. Why did we delay so long in letting you know? We have been planning this for quite a while, but due to our busy schedules, and all. It's only now that I've gotten the chance to come and see you, and let you know what's going on. Furthermore, it's not that big a thing, just family and close friends."

"How is your mother taking to that idea?" asked Mrs. O'Connor.

"Not very well, she's fuming mad, but she'll be okay, I'm sure." Mr. O'Connor remained conspicuously quiet from that point on, but he had more to say, though, Clancy could tell. He'd asked if Clancy was going back tonight, to which his reply was, Yes, I've got some things to get done tonight, and Debbie will be waiting up for me.

Before leaving, Clancy gave them a cassette tape, which Vickie latched onto as if it was automatic that "Anything that comes into this house intended for the family belonged to me." She ran back inside to stick it in the tape recorder. Clancy sank into the driver's seat, powered up the engine, and moved out, honking and waving as the rest of them stood in the driveway and watched the car as it went.

## 29

Chapter

**H**ear it on the Radio.

Ms. Johnson was busy doing chores when it happened, the knock on the gate. This was then followed by a voice saying, Ms. Johnson, Ms. Johnson, are you listening? Your son is on the radio.

"What, what did you say?" Ms. Johnson said, as she opened the door and saw four or five young children, all excited and bubbling with glee, in front of her gate.

"Clancy is on the radio," they said again. She did not tarry; she'd heard enough to figure out what they were saying (she thinks). Clancy being on the radio could mean only one of two things: either her son was live on a radio show (probably doing an interview) or his music was being played on the radio. It was the latter, and although she did not recognize the song, the voice was unmistakably Clancy's. The other thing of note was that she only got to hear the ending of the song; together we are harmony so very right, my music and I? Tell me who can separate the music from me now.

"Ho no," she whispered, as she looked out through the window again, and upon seeing that the kids were still there, she went back to open the door. The children were eager to fill her in on the details. "Clancy's song was on the radio, did you hear it?"

"No, not all of it anyway, but I will be listening to it the next time that they play it, thanks." She was taken aback at the slew of emotions that permeated her mind and body. Seeing that she wasn't all that keen on the idea that her son had given up on the prospect of a promising and respectful corporate career that was his for the taking. Just by pursuing the education that he was well-positioned and capable of acquiring, to went off chasing after some elusive dreams. Firstly, he would have gotten sidetracked by the sports program, and now he has gone and given up on that one, too, she said. Disappointments and frustrations are the terms best used for filling in the voids surrounding those accounts in the record books for her, regarding her son's choices. But at the same time, excitement and joy were there, which she couldn't deny. She was excited to know that her son was (seemingly) reaping success at the things he chooses to do, be it by playing football or, as it now is, singing. Instantaneously, she remembered the cassette tape that he gave her when he was there a few days earlier. She searched for it and found it there on the center table where it had been ever since. She inserted it into the slot on the tape recorder and hit the play knob, and voila! There it was, the song in its entirety, plus an extra track without lyrics, which she was to find out one possible reason for. When the song was released as a single later that year. The lyrics sound to her like the rantings of a drunken sailor. Well, that was just from the perspective of a tame and well-mannered Christian mother who had raised her son to adhere to good moral ethics. Otherwise, the song was just conforming to the norms of the times: come on over and do me a favor, come on over and do me a favor tonight. Those were some of the lyrics in the chorus of the second song she heard from her son at that time. She did not bother to listen to the rest of it, at least not on that first encounter.

Yes, I Do.

The wedding day was fast approaching, and nothing seemed to be even close to ready. All around, everyone's nerves seemed to be fizzing, except for Mrs. Myrtle, as a matter of fact, she displayed a striking sense of composure that led Clancy and Devon to wonder if she was aware of the remaining time. Or maybe she knew something else, which none of them knew, yet. Devon went with Clancy to the tailor to fit and (hopefully) pick up the tucks. He didn't want to wait too long for them and did not want to have to go back the following day to fetch them. Devon had been the one driving the BMW all week long. Clancy was in no state to be driving anything. Well, except for driving down his blood pressure, perhaps, which seemed to be heading for Venus over the past couple of days. "Calm down," Devon would say to him, now and then, but to no avail. They were in luck, the suits fit like a hand in a glove. After running a few other errands in town, they swung by the O'Connors in Rose Hall before heading back to Club Jamaica on Devon's suggestion that he would do well with something strong to calm his nerves. His dad must have thought that that was a brilliant idea, too, because he was there with them stride for stride. He ordered and footed the bills, too. Clancy did not object to that, and there were some other things he didn't do, as Devon had observed. He did not refuse the drink; he did not run out, leaving the drink on the table, and most certainly, he did not puke.

"One is enough," Clancy insisted. He was not planning on staying out late, and he did not want to feel tired and "druggy" the following morning. His father was heard bragging to a few of his friends about his son's achievements and the fact that he was about to be married. He hadn't shown that much enthusiasm when he'd first learned of this at the house in Rose Hall. "Hmm, I wonder why," Clancy mused.

"What I can't figure out is why," said Mr. O'Connor. Why would you give up on your education and a promising career in sports and then go chasing after grandiose dreams in the entertainment industry? Furthermore, why the mad rush to go and tie yourself down by getting married so young?

"I'm not that young anymore, Dad."

"You're nineteen," his father shot back.

"I'm almost twenty-one," Clancy corrected, "in a couple of weeks, in fact, I'll be turning twenty-one."

"Maybe so, but the world still sees you as twenty until then? And this woman, how old is she anyway?"

"Not that it should be of any concern to you, but she is twenty-three."

"Twenty-three?" Said Mr. O'Connor, "Why, but why, couldn't you at least find someone your own age?"

"She is my own age, Dad. The 20–30 lousy months difference is no big deal. Can we change the subject, please?"

"Suit yourself," Mr. O'Connor said as he rested his case.

"You're going to be a grandfather soon, Clancy declared after a long pause."

"Oh? So that's it. Now it's becoming clearer; it all begins to make sense. Well, well, congratulations are in order, I suppose." He took the hand Clancy offered him and shook it, then shook it again while pulling his son in closer for a big bear hug.

"I'm happy for you, son, really happy. Despite what you might be thinking of me, what with all this, "Probing and antagonizing," as you called it, I'm mighty proud of you." Not wanting to risk spoiling all that good vibration and goodwill, Clancy signaled to his friend, who was busy there nursing the jukebox as a front to allow the father and son some family time, that it was time to go.

# As Busy as a Bee.

The big day finally arrived, and everyone and everything were bubbling in the Logans' household in Whitehouse. Well, everyone except for Clancy, even Devon, was up and about, although they were together all day long and went to bed at about the same time. Clancy had no appetite either; they were practically begging him to eat something. "It's going to be a long day," Mrs. Logan reminded him, "and though you might not feel it now, you're going to get hungry, really fast." That must have worked because Clancy managed to "down" three of Mrs. Logan's fried dumplings along with her world-famous ackee and saltfish (salted codfish). The real actions, though, got started before Clancy could finish his breakfast. Mrs. Logan read the "to-do" list, which included them picking up several items in Linstead, Rose Hall, and elsewhere. They were also instructed to go get the page boy in Bog Walk on their way back. The groomsmen were being housed at the Logans; Clancy had no idea where the girls were, but wasn't overly concerned about that at this point. The house appeared to him to be bursting at the seams.

Debbie's brothers and a cousin came in from London on Thursday and were being housed there in Whitehouse. The addition of the page boy turned the place into a perfect "bullpen". Other than Mrs. Logan, there were only men in that house. Clancy was pleased to learn later that day that Debbie's sister and her sisters-in-law were staying at his mom's house. Before leaving to go back to Linstead for more pick-ups,

Devon warned the guys to go shower and be done with the bathrooms before they returned. The only people who should be using bathrooms at that point, he pointed out, should be Clancy and himself. Clancy would have settled on having Devon and his father, Mr. Logan, pitch in and offer to play the role of chauffeuring the men. But he was pleasantly surprised when his father showed up at the house, all dressed up to the max in his fanciest nix nax, to announce that he would be chauffeuring the groomsmen. Everything was falling into place, he thought to himself. For what was supposed to be a "small" family gathering, the wedding was turning out to be a grand splash as Clancy was starting to see it. Him being an only child for his mother and having only been in any kind of relationship with two of his (supposedly) many other siblings, Clancy's idea of a family event would have been, somewhere in the region of ten people, twenty at the most. But so far, he has numbered well over twenty-five, and they had not yet gone to all of the venues where folks were supposed to be staying. There might still be a lot more folks coming, he thought to himself.

Chapter

L et's go to Church.

Linstead Baptist church was "The place to be" on what was turning out to be a bright, sun-drenched Saturday morning. It had been raining a bit earlier on, but it would appear as if all that hustle and bustle of the day's activities thus far had served to consume all of the moisture in the once foggy morning air. Devon dutifully mopped at Clancy's brow to banish the small beads of sweat that were appearing at regular intervals. He turned around to glance at the crowd that was steadily streaming in and being guided to their seats by Mrs. Logan and Mrs. O'Connor.

"The perfect ushers they are," Devon remarked, as he dabbed at other beads of sweat and smiled. Devon's two sisters were sitting across from them on the right side, and an empty bench to the left was reserved for the rest of the bridal party. At the other end of the seat, between the bench and the three-rung stair that mounted up to the platform, was a bare passage that led to a door that Clancy now wished that someone would open up to let in some fresh air. They kept it closed for some unclear reason, but when the signal came and the bridal party came marching in, as they walked to the far corner on either side of the platform and positioned themselves, Clancy exhaled, "It's action time," he whispered. The organ struck up the tune of; Here Comes the Bride, voices joined in, and the side door opened to the great relief of Clancy as well as others who welcomed the rush of fresh air.

"Isn't it a bit premature to be singing that song at this point?" Clancy inquired.

"I don't know," said Devon, "I'm not quite sure how these things work." Clancy stared at the open doorways with great anticipation, but nothing happened. Well, other than... They were still singing, following the cue from the people whose attention was focused on the aisles straight down the middle of the hallway. Clancy turned his head just enough to see the approaching of the flower's girl, then after a long pause, the bride's clear, angelic voice came piercing the silence of the room with a song not too well-known but very appropriate for the occasion: You are my treasure, and my darling I possess, the world's greatest treasure, the treasure of happiness... she was stunning. Clancy was not expecting to see her like that; it was supposed to be a small wedding, and she was going to be wearing a simple but somewhat elegant dress. "We just want to get it over and done," they'd agreed. Instead, she was now all decked out in white, princess-cut, tails, trails, and all, white gloves above the elbow, and the biggest bouquet ever. The oohs, aahs, and whispers were heard coming from many within the gathering, "She's beautiful," some were heard saying, including one of Clancy's sisters to the other. The minister did his usual thing, too slowly, Clancy thought to himself.

"...and with the powers vested in me as a minister, I now pronounce you as husband and wife, Mr. Clancy K O'Connor, you may now kiss your bride." His shaking hands reached up to pull back the veil for a clearer and closer look at her beautiful face and luscious lips. He then leaned in and obliged her begging, with a hot, lingering kiss. Once again, the ooh, aah, and clapping were to have followed, and then came the whispers, again. Clancy clearly heard the word "fat," and distinctly heard someone say; pregnant. From the corner of his eyes, he could see his sisters in a whispering debate, though still unsure what the issue might have been, he thinks he has a fairly good idea. Helen's countenance had been somewhat altered from that point on and throughout the remainder of the evening. Clancy would have been searching for his bride's (now his wife's) face and body language, for tell-tale signs, you know. Trying to determine whether she might have heard what was said and to see what effect (if any) they might have had on her mood, but she didn't seem the least bit disturbed.

It's Party Time.

Bybrook Sports Club's reception hall was the place to be on that evening in mid-July 1984. The atmosphere was charged to dizzying heights, and the air smelled of savory delights. Drinks of varying sorts flowed freely while chattering laughter floated in the air to be heard from a long way off. The bridal party would have taken another route from the site where they had gone to do photo shoots as expected, but... The gathering was beginning to get restless while they waited for the arrival at the hall. It was a long and tiring day, people were getting hungrier by the second, and the smell of all that savory food wasn't helping one bit. They finally came streaming in and all breathed a collective sigh of relief. The MC, too, (seemingly,) relishing the thought, announced that meals would be served right away, and that he would proceed with the program while "we" ate. The speeches and jokes were jovial all around, and haughty laughter became the order of the night. Clancy was seen mopping at a tear or two at several intervals throughout the evening. His mother's speech touched him profoundly, and Mrs. Myrtle's likewise left him, as well as his new wife, teary-eyed. It was obvious that Janet Johnson had come to terms with the way things were turning out for her son. Even though she still would have preferred it should he had gone on with his education, "What good," she said, "is a good education compared to being really happy sharing one's life with someone, in love." She'd had no doubt, she said further, "that Debbie and Clancy were in love, 'for real.'" They laughed. Mrs. O'Connor, too, would have surprised a lot of people just by speaking. But what she said was the talk (and whispers) of the evening.

Getting Debbie to agree to go away for the honeymoon was like pulling teeth. She wanted to just go straight on down to St. Ann immediately after the wedding to get on with the job of settling into the new house.

...

"I have to get my office set up," she said, "and the house itself needs a lot of work to make it habitable." Clancy was having none of that: "It's our honeymoon, dear, there is no way in hell that we are going to be working on any house or office or any other such thing on the heels of our wedding day." Both being strong-headed as it were, some other choice words were used during their squabbling over the issue before common sense prevailed, and she agreed to a four-day, three-night stay at the Mallard Beach Hyatt right there on the north coast, their regular stamping grounds. Which suited some people very well as they were to discover sometime later.

## 34

Chapter

# Too Short a Timeout.

Debbie yawned and stretched as she propped herself up with pillows on the king-size bed. She could not remember ever being this tired, and all of a sudden, that Caribbean cruise seemed like the greatest idea anyone had ever had. Too late for that now, she and her husband have to vacate the room by 10. That leaves them with just two hours to spare. Clancy was already on the case, though, the shower was going, and he was heard singing in an inner voice, probably trying to avoid disturbing Debbie or a neighbor next door. Debbie realized there and then that she had not been able to get some rest and relaxation in years. She had to cut short her term in college because her father had fallen gravely ill. The pressure was mounting on her mother, and although she protested vigorously, Debbie insisted that she would take a break from her studies to help her out.

"I can always pick up on my studies later," Debbie assured her. But when she got to Jamaica for the burial of her father, her mother announced that she was planning on "coming home for good." That's when things began to change. After she hired the contractor to get the renovations done, Debbie decided that she would be moving back home, too. As a matter of fact, she hasn't gone back to England since. Those few months while she was staying at her uncle's place in Whitehouse, she filled her days with varying activities, trying to shut out the great loss of her dad, but then. The next closest person to her was her mom, and she also, for all intents and purposes, was gone (back to

London). She was more than comfortable staying there at her relative's place. But at the same time, she was also playing the role of project manager for the renovation project on their own home. Then came that fateful day when she rode with her cousin Devon to see the motorcade as it passed through Ewarton. At least that was the plan, but then Devon said he had a better idea.

"There's this perfect lookout spot where we can see the whole thing for miles," he said. That spot he was talking about turned out to be her very own backyard. Debbie had not been able to survey and discover the surrounding areas of the house she'd called home as a small child before migrating with the family in the early 60s. Since being back, she has not been so inclined to do either. On that fateful day, however, when she went down the path to the back end of the property with her cousin and saw that stranger encroaching on their very own property. When Devon did not raise an alarm and chase him away and out of there, or even threatened to call the cops. When, instead, he greeted that stranger cordially, and when he, in turn, greeted her, he shook her hand firmly and self-assuredly. Most importantly, when she looked into those big brown eyes, she knew there and then that it was destiny. Yes, the gods of love had just smiled at her; she knew it.

"We've got to get going, honey, our ride should be here any moment now," said Clancy as he walked out of the bathroom, wrapped in his bathrobe. The clock on the night table, as well as the prompting of her husband, were all saying, "It's time to go," but...

Devon was right on time as usual. They wanted to have breakfast at the diner across the street, but Devon advised them to go "lite" on it because he had something planned that he thought they would like. Debbie was still thinking about the Caribbean cruise she should have gone on, but she would not mention it, since it was her insistence that had caused them to settle for this. Not that it was lacking in any way, as a matter of fact, it was a great stay at the Mallards. Clancy must have sensed what she was thinking because he was just in time to suggest that "we" should probably take things easy for a while and not be rushing back too quickly into work mode.

# 35

## Chapter

H omeward Bound.

Going home means a lot of different things to different people on different days, and on that day, for the young couple. They were going home for the very first time as husband and wife. They were going home to their own brand-new house, and they were going home to start their own family. Which, (as a matter of fact,) was already growing with a child on the way, though many did not know it yet. They were nearing the house, and the adrenaline had begun to flare up within. What awaited them beyond that point, neither of them had any concrete idea. Neither of them had walked that way before, and it was now all theirs to do, with no one in terms of family and close friends within miles to call on, if they should run into trouble. Clancy reached over for Debbie's hand and squeezed it reassuringly, as they pulled up within sight of the sprawling new housing scheme and, hence, nearing home. Devon had said earlier that he was taking the couple out to a cozy little spot that he'd found nearby. But he'd urged them to drop off the luggage first. He pulled the car up in front of the house framed by a neck-high concrete wall, corrugated steel with square thinning points atop.

"That's gross," Debbie whispered.

"What?" Said Clancy.

"That fence, we're going to have to do something about that ugly fence, and soon." Devon popped the car trunk open and quickly got out, walking around towards the rear where the luggage was stored. He grabbed a suitcase with one hand while fiddling with the keys in the other, as he walked towards the iron gate, inserted the key, and opened the gate. Stepping aside, he allowed the others to enter, and then, from behind her, he walked up beside Debbie, and placed a hand around her waist, "Welcome home, cous, he said, to your very own home. They waited on the paved walkway just before mounting the first of three steps up to the front door. Devon rested the suitcase down beside him and placed the other hand around Debbie, encircling her slender but firm body. She lifted her own hands and placed them onto her cousin's, at navel height. She then turned to face him, looking straight into his eyes, she said; Thank you, cousin, for everything.

Clancy climbed the three flights of stairs, shook the bunch of keys Devon had just given him, and tossed them up about nose high. Then, upon catching it again, he did a little shuffle. His stance widened with a sort of left, right, left planting of the feet. He turned around, looking back briefly at the other two who were there, giggling with delight. Inserted the key into the door lock and turned it; click. Slowly, he looked back again over his shoulder, smiling from ear to ear. "Welcome to my humble abode, you fine thing, you," he said. Debbie was cracking up laughing with all of that. Clancy slowly pushed the door open, not looking inside the house but at the two who were laughing hysterically in the yard out front. Well, Debbie was laughing much harder than Devon at this point. But then! The smile fell off Debbie's face like a brick, as she screamed out loud, covered her mouth with her hands, and her knees buckled beneath her. Clancy's first reaction was to run to his wife's aid, coupled with the loud noise coming from within the house. All surprised, he tried to coordinate his legs with his thoughts, but to no avail. His legs slid out from under him, and he fell backward in a twisting motion across the handrail that ran by the side of the steps. Devon was just in time to push back against him, preventing him from falling over, which could have easily spelled tragedy for the fellow. The sight that greeted him when Clancy looked inside the house appeared to him like a bouncing, bubbling blob with grinning white teeth, all around. Debbie was still down on the pavement with her legs buckled beneath her.

Clancy recomposed himself somewhat and ran to help her up. Are you okay? He asked. By this time, the crowd was steadily streaming out of the front door and was converging around Debbie. One by one, those faces began to take on names and became familiar to each of them. Are you okay, dear? They were all there: The O'Connors, The Logans, Ms. Johnson; they all were there.

"What are you doing here?" asked Debbie. Devon tried to ignore Clancy's inquiries directed at him: "What's going on here?" He asked.

"Let's get her inside," said Mrs. Myrtle, who was by now taking charge of the situation.

"I'm alright," said Debbie, "I'm alright; why are all these people here?" She was a bit self-conscious; her place was in no shape to be entertaining strangers, she thought, and she herself was no better off in those regards.

"Don't worry, honey, everything is going to be okay," her mother reassured her. Debbie walked up the front doorsteps while being supported by Clancy and Devon on either side of her. Upon entering the living room, she quickly noticed the difference. The place was in immaculate condition, with fresh paint on the walls, a brand-new kitchen counter, and cabinets. New stove and refrigerator, and paintings hanging on the wall, including her favorite family portraits. She dismissed the "helpers" who were helping to hold her back rather than bearing her up, as she walked around surveying the house. It looked nothing like she had seen it before, but she was more than pleased with what she saw. Her chief point of interest, though, was the studio space across the hall; she pointed her nose in that direction, her mother in tow. It was breathtaking, all the adherence to details in the outlines and texture right on down to the very clock on the wall left no doubt in her mind that this was all her mother's doing.

"Whose idea was this?" she asked as she mounted the stairs towards the second floor, where the three bedrooms lay nestled on either side of a short, carpeted passageway with the bathroom wedged beside one of those bedrooms to the backside of the house.

It all looks like something out of one of those "Modern Homes" magazines. But the bathroom was what she really went upstairs to see, and it didn't disappoint one bit. It was breathtakingly beautiful; a whirlpool bathtub beside a neck-high frosted glass, shower chamber, and marble stone tiles. The gold and white faucet, toilet, and basin greatly enhanced the outcome.

"Thanks, Mom," she said, as she fell on her mother's neck and hugged her.

"It's not my doing, dear, well, not just me, it was a team effort. But don't be concerned with that now, just enjoy it with your husband and your family, which, as I can see, is growing," said Mrs. Myrtle. While patting her on the tummy and rounding it out into a ball. No, mom, not at all... "Let's go join the others," she said. They descended the stairs. There were many more people there than there were just a short while ago, and folks were still coming in, bearing pots and pans, bags and packages in sizes both great and small.

Meanwhile, the air was flowing heavily with the smell of savory food and mouthwatering delights. Just then, Debbie felt the hunger pangs and recalled that she (as well as her husband) had not eaten much since the morning. It was as if someone had read her thoughts because Ms. Johnson asked straight away if she had eaten, and if she wanted to have something to eat now.

"Yes, please," she said, "where's Clancy? Did he have something to eat?" Coming right up, dear, Ms. Johnson replied. "Something for both of you and your cousin, too, I don't think he has eaten anything yet either."

Debbie followed her mother-in-law back into the kitchen. There was food everywhere, and a big pot was over the fire on the stove, boiling, cooking up something.

"We have a special breakfast made just for you guys," Ms. Johnson informed her. "But you may have other food if you prefer; there is food everywhere, as you can see, you choose."

"Where is Clancy?" Debbie asked again.

"Oh, he'll be back shortly," said Ms. Johnson, "he went down the road with Devon." Debbie went through the rear door that leads into the backyard, where a rowdy bunch (mostly men) was gathered around a domino game. Among them was Mr. Brown of Brown's & Son's renovations.

"Mr. Brown, how are you?" Said Debbie as she walked over to greet him with a hug. Debbie would have managed to develop some sort of rapport with Mr. Brown over the period while he was doing the renovation at the family home on Mount Rosser. Now, she was getting the strange feeling that he had something to do with the work done in her own house. It was the typical excellent finish that she'd come to associate with him.

"It's so nice to see you," said Debbie. "The pleasure is mine," said Mr. Brown.

"Debbie?" Mrs. Myrtle called out to her from the kitchen window. "Your husband is looking for you? Come on in and get something to eat." She excused herself and went back inside. Clancy showed her to the table where he had placed the plates containing steamed fish, dumplings, yellow yams, and boiled green bananas.

"Coffee, chocolate, or tea?" he asked as she sat down at the table. "Hot Chocolate, please," she said, "and a large one too." The rest of the day was electric; everybody who was anybody (so to speak) was there, and more. But how did they all get there? Debbie would have noticed that only about four or five vehicles were parked out front, and as the day was beginning to fade into the night, she couldn't help but wonder, How in the world are they going to get so many people cleared out of the house tonight? Or did they have other "secret" plans? She beckoned to her mother, who came walking towards them, still sitting there at the table. She whispered into her mother's ear; How did all these people get here and... "...And how are we going to get them out of here?" her mother finished the question for her. "Not to worry, dear, we've got this all covered, everything is under control," she said as she turned around and walked away.

**H**ome and Good.

Mrs. Myrtle was busily making the rounds between the various groups wherever they were gathered. From the kitchen to the living room, and out into the backyard, she was busily getting them to wind up the activities and to get ready to move.

"Thank you all for coming," she said after she had managed to get their attention, "and for helping to make this evening the success it has been, but all good things must come to an end, as they say. Plus, you all know very well that this house must be consummated tonight?" Bap, bap, bap, came the poundings on the tables, and the laughter. She continued to speak when the laughter subsided; Mr. and Mrs. O'Connor want to thank all of you for your kind gestures and support. As a matter of fact, why not hear it from the newlyweds themselves? Ladies and gentlemen, The O'Connors? The younger O'Connors, that is, seeing we also have the senior O'Connors here. They hesitated for a while, both trying to pass the task off to each other since neither one had planned on doing anything like that. But then, Clancy got up and represented his family like the "real big man he was."

"On behalf of my wife Debbie and..." There they were again with those cheers, and...

Clancy continued after they managed to tone it down somewhat; on behalf of my wife Debbie and myself, I take this opportunity to thank each and every one of you for your love, kindness, and support. We greatly appreciate it all and want to thank you from the bottom of our hearts.

At the risk of omitting someone and then having to face their wrath later, I will stay away from the name-calling; however, we want to say a big thank you to our parents on either side. To the extended family as well, to the cooks who prepared all that tasty food and treats. Thanks to Mr. Brown of Brown's renovations. Special thanks also go out to my armor bearer, right-hand man, best friend, and chauffeur. By the way, how are you planning on getting home from here? "You know you are not taking my car, right?" he said to Devon, who was laughing his face off. Thanks again, my friends, and may you all be blessed in like manner as you have blessed others, even us here today. Thank you very much.

"The bus is ready for boarding," Mrs. Myrtle said when she took to the floor again after Clancy was done.

"The bus, what bus?" Debbie inquired while leaning sideways to look out the door. There it was, a coach bus was parked in front of the house, and some of the people were already on, or getting on.

"You knew about this?" She asked her husband, seeing that he did not appear the least bit surprised by this one.

"I found out about it a short while ago," he replied. Devon had just told him that he was going back on the bus, which was in response to Clancy's query, again, as to how he was getting back home. Just then, Debbie recollected that she had seen that bus parked on the corner about two or three blocks down while they were on their way in. But she had no clue then (and no reason to know) that it had anything to do with them.

"You all are so sneaky," she said, "How could anyone hide a bus?"

"We did, didn't we?" The answer came from voices; she couldn't tell whose they were in particular, due to the laughter that followed. The party atmosphere seemed to be continuing on the tour bus too, but all that those people on that bus were leaving behind was Clancy and Debbie, and, and, well...

Both of them stood there on the front doorstep looking on and waving at the loaded tour bus as it pulled away from the gate and off into the lonely night. Lit dimly by streetlights and a low-hanging moon. Clancy leaned up against the side rail, the same one over which he had almost fallen earlier that day. Resting the round of his bottom atop the rail, he pulled Debbie in closer to himself, and after placing both arms like a ring around her, holding finger-to-finger, just below her belly button. Slightly magnifying the round of her growing stomach, in so doing. "I think we are blessed, you know," he said, as he leaned in and kissed her neck. Debbie angled her head up for more, and with Clancy's long arms about her like a wool-a-hoop, she turned herself around to face her man squarely. Reaching up with the right hand, she pulled his head down to her own reach, then they kissed long and hard, like this.

"Shiu! Boy, it sure is hot out here," she said, "did you check on the air conditioning system to see if it's working properly?"

"It had better be," he replied, as he followed her inside. "It's much cooler in here? Everything works better on the inside, right?" he said, as he turned around and closed the door behind them, and walked side by side toward...

The end.

Just a couple more poems before we close the door. This one is called **Merry Christmas**.

Merry Christmas, my dear, friend list

What a fabulous year it has been since we began the practice.

Once we got started underneath the orchids, we haven't been able to miss a single beat. Or did...

Merry Christmas, my dear friend list, don't forget to remember this.

I won't be able to exchange gifts, as regular as the norm was, because...

It's that time of year again, when old acquaintances and annoying family friends come dropping in on our comfort zone.

Like, this annoying Martin, remember him? Yes, and grumpy old Huntley, always pocketing something to hustle. Only...

Yeah, that's our uncles for you. They're coming over again this week, and there's nothing I can do to stump it.

"They're family," I'm told, hungrily and hissed, "and we don't get to choose ours," table fist.

Which always serves to get me bursting through the door, first thing, and hastening towards the first exit, I'm more than certain.

But there's one bright spot to look at, and take comfort in knowing more, that.

This Christmas break will soon be o'er, then we'll get back to our doing as before

With such familial burdens placed on me to handle, Leigh

None of this will stop or steer me clear of saying to you this year;

Merry Christmas, my dear friend list, and a very happy New Year, too, the following week. Thank you, so to speak.

Here for you is another poem of the times called:
Prelude.
Fling-flung emotions sprang. Holding on to Diablo's careless hand. Like the sad refrain of an ancient song, about Dan, and a man and a van?

Coated sugar cubes as the errands went. Hellenor's exhausted vacation is spent. Sitting in limbo, gripping wistful lament. Hastily made decisions mask in repent...

Sweet revenge is a mother's seed. Hovering north of the tender reeds. Heavy eyelids await gluttonous sleep. Morn's piercing notes to jerk the feet

Like cords hung loose on fizzled ends. Too far removed from making amends. Blissful lovers have long gone and spent. Lifeline extended, Western Union, send.

Fling-flung emotions sprang. Diablo's cold crooked fingers still, still holding strong, Oct. 2016.

## Black History Is Not My Story

A poem for Black History Month.

Freedom, is it free? So, tell me, who is going to teach our children our history, and I mean, the real history? Since our history, sure as hell, did not begin with slavery. About justice and morality, what's now being asked of you and me? More of the same? No. Such a shame.

Many of our great people would have suffered and died fighting to be free, to pass on the knowledge to somebody. Now, tell me, don't we have continuing inequality today? Look at it this way, you'll see. It's being maintained by governmental systems and international treaties.

Don't believe me? Well, go learn the actual history of our African sovereignty. You're likely to encounter things like these:

The whole period of the last five hundred years of dominance of the European over the rest of the world's population has been unjust.

Many people would have suffered and died, fighting for liberty on this side, what little of it there may be. We've paid a heavy price to be free, yet hear me clearly, can you still see? Well, I'm sure you'll agree with me; freedom is certainly not free.

Five hundred years is a very long time for any people to be brutalized and dehumanized. For having to go through hell on Earth, what's the prize? Heaven, when we die? Crush that lie. Now what, five hundred more to close our eyes? No, my guys, no more.

From slavery to colonization, from the plantation to neo-colonialization. Without any form of restitution; for labor stolen, a people (savagely) broken.

After the plantation, then comes neo-colonialism. Yes, it's with us today in the form of the IMF, the World Bank, the World Trade Organization, and the United Nations. So, tell me:

Where is the black man's vibrant and progressive country? Where is the power of his economy? Where are the Garveys, Martin Luthers, Malcolm Exes, Patrick Namumba, and Kwame Nkrumah?

Without them, who will commit to reconstruction, who is going to redeem the African civilization?

Africa is not a wasteland, as some might have had the notion. She has been giving to the world from day one, in the form of the first human, and the first Civilization.

So black man, know who you are, or someone else will define and tell you who you are. Know thy God also, while you're at it. Because while many profess religious values and morality. Every day, and all around me, I see them practicing immorality (routinely).

So, black man, tell me, what is your plan? Are you satisfied with just being accepted by the other man? He who is, actually, your mortal enemy, or will you rise, stand up, and pursue your freedom and dignity?

The aged person must now teach the younger ones, in the homes, in communities, and in your institutions. Because the battles of the future are going to be the battles of the mind, for the mind; it's all about knowledge and science now.

It's your job, therefore, to perfect yourself, black man. That is the whole purpose of your life, from now on. That struggle on a day-to-day basis to improve yourself. So, be proud, black man, press on forward, you mighty man, you are a black man, yes, you are an African.

Adopted from a Garvey speech at a Black History Month event some time ago, and cast in this block of poetic cement, I'd like you to know. And now, this poet has spoken, over to you to like, share, and comment. We would certainly appreciate it if you were to subscribe and follow us somewhere, too. Thank you.

Note: Just a note to say "thank you" for choosing to read my book and for sticking with the story thus far. You must have liked it a lot. At this point, I want to ask you, my reader, to take a minute to post a review on the Sales pages at Amazon and/or, any other such sales pages such as: Barnes and Noble, and Kobo. This small gesture is so very much appreciated. So, go ahead, and show the vine some love. And don't keep it to yourself, be sure to share this with your list of friends. Thank you.

E Lloyd Kelly is WritingElk, an Author, poet, and songwriter, among other things. Born in Jamaica West Indies, to Raglan and Alma Kelly. Now resides in Montreal, Quebec.

If you haven't yet done so, be sure to read the "Real Inky Trail" book series.

Book 1 is a story called "New Hiking Trail, Cast Shadow on the Tattooed."

Book 2 is, "Twisted Tales from the Big Fail."

Book 3 is, "The Sword, the Word, and the Writings. All are available wherever books are sold. If you can't find it, ask for it, they will get it for you. Thank You.